Regulation
and the Accounting Profession

EDITED BY

John W. Buckley

J. Fred Weston

Lifetime Learning Publications
Belmont, California

A division of Wadsworth, Inc.

Printed in the United States of America

1 2 3 4 5 6 7 8 9 10—84 83 82 81 80

Library of Congress Cataloging in Publication Data

Main entry under title:

Regulation and the accounting profession.

   A compendium of papers presented at a conference held at UCLA.
   Bibliography: p.
   1. Accounting—United States—Congresses.
2. Accounting—Law and legislation—United States—
Congresses. I. Buckley, John W. II. Weston, John
Frederick.
HF5616.U5R43   657'.0973   79-28661
ISBN 0-534-97983-1

THE UCLA EXTENSION CONFERENCE SERIES:
CRITICAL ISSUES IN MANAGEMENT

With the acceleration of change in our national and international socio-economic conditions, critical questions arise relating to many business elements of our society. Broad and demanding questions such as degree and direction of government control of private enterprise, the role of the corporate boards of directors, the role and responsibilities of public corporations in social and ethical matters, and other issues need to be examined in a forum where our nation's outstanding scholars and practitioners can present their ideas and engage in critical intellectual discourse.

UCLA Extension is providing a forum for such presentations. "Regulation and the Accounting Profession" was the first of this series. As additional topics are brought into focus and presented, the results of such forums will also be made available to the public.

> Warren J. Pelton
> Director, Continuing Education in
>   Management, Labor and Business
> UCLA Extension

Contents

Foreword

Recent advances in accounting research and developments in related fields, such as finance, economics, and the behavioral sciences, have greatly increased the significance of the role of accounting in business operations as well as in the economy generally. These intellectual advances have been accompanied by a real revolution in the technologies of data processing and empirical analyses. At the same time, the role of accounting as an industry and as a profession is being reassessed by individual scholars as well as by governmental bodies.

As accounting has grown in importance, it has become the object of increasing scrutiny. Questions have been raised about the relevance of the information accountants provide to investors and other users of its products, about the quality and integrity of the audit function, especially the compatability of auditing and consulting services with professional independence, and about many other aspects of technical and professional service. A central issue of concern is currently the *structure* of the accounting industry, that is, the degree of competition that exists in the industry, whether its conduct promotes or opposes free market forces, and whether the industry's performance results in extraordinary returns.

This publication is a compendium of papers which were presented at a recent conference held at UCLA on the subject of *Regulation and the Accounting Profession*. An eminent group of accounting theorists, economists, lawyers, accounting practitioners, and government regulators were assembled to examine these questions as well as the positions taken regarding the *structure* of the accounting profession.

The accounting profession has experienced mounting regulatory pressures in recent years. These pressures have taken several forms, including congressional investigations and hearings, a more activist stance by the Securities and Exchange Commission, reorganization of the American Institute of Certified Public Accountants (AICPA) to include an SEC Practice Section and a Public Oversight Board, and many other actions.

This book details and examines these developments. More important, the reader may find answers to questions like these: (1) What are the underlying causes for increased regulatory pressure? (2) What theories and assumptions guide the behavior of the regulators? (3) Do empirical findings support these theories and assumptions? (4) What is the likely course of development in the regulation of the accounting profession? (5) Are there feasible and desirable alternatives to the current course of action?

If you find these questions challenging and germane, then I think you will enjoy reading this collection of essays. In sum, they constitute a significant contribution to an area of accounting literature that has not received much formal attention. I know that this publication will broaden our understanding of some very difficult concepts and issues, encourage more scholarship on this important topic, and provide a basis for enlightened discussions of the role of the accounting profession in contemporary American society.

J. Clayburn La Force, Jr.,
Dean, Graduate School of Management
University of California, Los Angeles

Preface

The public accounting profession in the United States has experienced phenomenal growth over the past four decades. The industry today is characterized by a small number of large firms (the so-called "Big Eight") which audit and perform other services for large organizations, public and private; and a large number of small firms which provide services to correspondingly small firms. Because the audit as such is not required for private firms, much of the work done by small accounting firms consists of non-audit services: bookkeeping, preparation of financial statements, tax, and business advisory services. By contrast, the typical large accounting firm derives a majority of its revenue from auditing. In addition, it also provides its clients with tax and business advisory services.

If we focus on the audits of large, publicly held companies, it is impossible to avoid the conclusion that the industry is concentrated. The Big Eight firms audit more than 90 percent of the companies whose securities are registered on the New York Stock Exchange, and 73 percent on the American Stock Exchange. Indeed, this was the conclusion drawn by the *Staff Study* (1977) of the U.S. Senate Committee on Government Operations. The concentration ratio is one of the "structural" conditions which typically has prompted federal legislative or regulatory intervention. Briefly, these conditions are:

1. A concentration ratio among the top four firms in excess of 50 percent
2. An absence of effective price competition
3. No significant entry within the past five years
4. An above-average return (net income in relation to net worth); that is, above 15 percent per annum in five of the last seven years

These conditions are pertinent to the so-called *structural theory* of industrial organization. Simply stated, this theory posits that industries with high seller concentrations (that is, "oligopolies" or "monopolies") are prone to charge higher prices and earn greater profits than industries with low concentrations. It is called "structural theory" because, based upon certain structural facts and relationships (such as concentration ratios), inferences can be drawn to practices which may exhibit allocative inefficiency in the form of restricted output and excessive profits.

It is fair to say that the structural theory of industrial organization has provided the principal rationale for federal legislative and regulatory intervention into private sector operations, even though its assumptions have been severely challenged by the results of empirical research (demonstration, for example, that concentrated industries do not earn abnormally high returns). And certainly the structural theory was invoked in the *Staff Study* and other congressional deliberations concerning the regulation of the accounting profession.

Even if the structural theory is defective or is misapplied to the accounting profession, the regulatory initiative confronting the profession is not based solely on economic grounds—on allocative efficiency. Mixed in with the economic arguments are a variety of *equity* and *public interest* arguments. The latter have always provided the justification for public intervention in private markets on absolute terms, that is, without regard to allocative efficiency. Societies are willing to tolerate economic inefficiencies in order to pursue certain nonmarket objectives. This situation prevails in accounting. Thus, many small firms complain about the dominance of the large firms in managing institutional affairs. They also decry the displacement of their clients by large firms whenever the former decide to go public or gain greater respectability in financial circles by having one of the major accounting firms audit and attest to their financial statements. The issue at stake in the struggle between small and large firms is not efficiency but equity.

These and a host of other issues are discussed at length in the chapters in this volume. Taken as a whole, these essays represent the most complete discussion available today, from a variety of different viewpoints, of the regulatory environment in accounting.

This volume should appeal to a number of audiences. Certainly certified public accountants who have been surprised and alarmed by the fast-moving events in Washington should find this book informative in explaining the reasons for the new regulatory onslaught, and it provides a script for the probable unfolding developments in the next few years. Academics, particularly those who specialize in accounting, law, and industrial organization, will find a wealth of material in this volume, as well as many unanswered questions, providing them with a fertile ground for further research. Practicing lawyers, particularly those who specialize in government relations or antitrust, will find this volume helpful because it provides an excellent case study of the regulatory forces at work against one of the major professions in the United States. Those who regulate will find this volume of interest because it attempts to provide a balanced and objective discussion of the issues. Students preparing for careers as accountants, lawyers, political scientists, or scholars will find that this book opens up new areas of startling and profound interest. And, finally, the American public generally is developing new and more conservative attitudes toward government regulation. This book will provide many Americans with an indepth analysis of the regulatory trauma that now afflicts one of the leading professions.

Acknowledgments

As editors of this volume, and as cochairmen of the Conference on Regulation and the Accounting Profession, we wish to pay special tribute to several people who contributed to the success of the conference and/or the publication of this volume.

Phil Frandson, Warren Pelton, and Tom Badger of UCLA Extension funded the conference, and participated actively in each step of the process leading to the publication of this volume. Without their guidance and financial assistance, these important issues would not be brought to public light.

Assistance was also provided through the Arthur Young & Co. Professorship at UCLA and the Research Program in Competition and Business Policy. We also gratefully acknowledge the cosponsorship of the Graduate School of Management, UCLA.

Patt Bennett was enormously helpful and efficient in handling the administrative arrangements for the conference. David McNary assisted in initial editing of the papers and preparing the volume for publication.

We are indebted to these and many other persons who contributed to the success of the project.

UCLA   J. W. Buckley
                                                      J. Fred Weston

I

Theories of Regulation

House Resolution 13175 seeks to formalize the federal regulation of public accounting through the establishment of uniform operating principles. The bill's author, former Congressman John Moss of California, believed its passage would make the accounting profession more competitive and provide more protection for investors.

The structural theory of firm and industry behavior helps provide justification for such a belief. This theory asserts that collusion by a firm can be established through such measures as high concentration ratios, high rates of return, and the existence of barriers to entry. The Big Eight firms of the accounting profession represent what Granfield terms an "ideal candidate" for an attack based on structural theory, even though the firms have responded in depth to allegations of anticompetitive behavior.

In Chapter 1, Buckley and O'Sullivan examine the conduct and performance of the Big Eight specifically and the profession in general. They find little indication of reduced competition, arguing that the capability of the Big Eight to provide specialized services is what makes them attractive to clients. Government criticism of high profit margins, poor standards, and lack of independence in the profession is judged as "largely unfounded, or at least unproven." In Chapter 2, Granfield finds that the evidence of collusion itself is generally superficial. Collusive agreements within any industry, he contends, would be highly difficult to sustain.

A theme that emerges from Buckley and O'Sullivan is that regulatory behavior is characterized by an emphasis on making decisions the right way rather than making the right decisions; in other words, form prevails over content. And SEC involvement in regulation has demonstrated weaknesses, they add. Its involvement in accounting issues is ancillary to its primary objectives. Granfield attacks structural theory because in six tests it fails to produce results confirming the conditions of tacit collusion, nor does it add to societal welfare because of the increase in costs its application would create.

For Buckley and O'Sullivan, the issue is efficiency versus equity and, in a larger sense, freedom versus fairness. Granfield, however, concludes that even though Congress is concentrating on the wrong set of problems, the profession must reduce its vulnerability by removing the appearances of cartel behavior and concentrating on investor welfare.

1

Regulation and Public Accounting: What Are the Issues?

John W. Buckley

Arthur Young Professor of Accounting
Graduate School of Management
University of California, Los Angeles

Peter O'Sullivan

Doctoral Student in Accounting
Graduate School of Management
University of California, Los Angeles

Because of the unusual length of this first chapter, it is divided into four parts. A brief description of the content of each part follows.

Part I – Background: Laying Out the Issues

This section describes the "new regulatory initiative" confronting the accounting profession in the United States and distinguishes this initiative from the traditional patterns of regulation in the past.

Included in this section is a summary of the issues (complaints) underlying the new regulatory thrust and the profession's responses to those complaints. Those pressing the charges against the accounting profession feel that the reforms to date are inadequate, and the controversy continues.

Part II – Types of Regulatory Initiatives

Four major types of regulatory initiatives are identified in this section: (1) equilibrium, (2) capture, (3) public interest, and (4) societarian. These initiatives are differentiated in terms of diffused versus concentrated costs and benefits.

The authors argue that historically "capture theory" has defined the essential relationship between government and the accounting profession, but that the recent onslaught has all of the characteristics of a "public interest" initiative.

Each type of regulation has a particular sociology, which is detailed in this chapter. A knowledge of how these initiatives work will improve the reader's understanding of the factors that make the current regulatory situation in accounting, and its prospects, so markedly different from conditions in the past.

Part III — The Structural Theory of Antitrust Applied to the Accounting Profession

The current regulatory initiative in accounting employs the so-called "structural theory" of antitrust in reaching the conclusion that the accounting profession is oligopolistic; that is, the industry is dominated by a few large firms, lack of competition, barriers to entry, market concentration, and excessive profits. The structural theory implies a chain of causality flowing from an industry's structure, through its conduct, to its performance.

Applied to the accounting profession, the structural theory supports certain conclusions regarding such matters as concentration, product differentiation, barriers to entry, growth rate of demand, pricing practices, and so forth. The authors have closely examined these conclusions, and based upon the facts and data they have assembled, it becomes clear that the major accusations made during the congressional inquiries are largely unfounded or at least unproven. In a subsequent chapter by Professor Granfield, the validity of the structural theory itself is challenged.

Part IV — Regulatory Effectiveness

Where problems arise in industries that are subject to government regulation, the culprit is invariably perceived to be some market (industry) failure. But an equally plausible culprit might be regulatory failure.

Several types of common regulatory failure are described in this fourth section, including: (1) the "zero-cost" phenomenon, (2) regulatory lag or nonfeasance, (3) the "regulatory trap", and (4) the "tar-baby effect." Examining these regulatory failures in the context of the accounting profession, the authors conclude that not all of the profession's difficulties can be attributed to market failures, but that the regulatory agencies involved, particularly the SEC, have contributed to the problems and therefore their reformation must be part of the solution.

Part I — Background: Laying Out the Issues

The environment of public accounting is generally perceived to be growing increasingly turbulent and hostile. Legislatures, courts, and administrative agencies are actively criticizing the process of accounting policy formulation and the structure of public accounting practice. Their criticisms have been accompanied by proposals for regulatory interventions to impose new liabilities and responsibilities in some areas and new limitations and restrictions in others. In such an environment, it is appropriate to consider the nature of regulation in accounting and the consequences that are likely to attend any increased regulation. Several of the chapters in this volume make educated guesses about what those consequences will be. Chapter 1 intends to lay a foundation for this discussion by focusing on the phenomenon of the new regulatory initiative in accounting and the issues that underlie it.

We refer to the "new regulatory initiative" to distinguish what is happening now from what has existed in accounting for at least eighty-three years—that is, since 1896, when New York State first required the certification of those engaged in the public practice of accounting.[1] A significant impetus in the regulation of public accountants occurred in 1933 and 1934 with the passage of the Securities Act and the Exchange Act, respectively, and the creation of the Securities and Exchange Commission (SEC). The purpose of these acts was first, to protect those who rely upon the financial statements of public companies to make investment decisions and second, to maintain fair and orderly trading. The acts have been characterized as a corporate "Freedom of Information Act" for investors (U.S. Congress, 1976: 18).

Specifically, the Securities Act of 1933 charged the SEC with the responsibility of prescribing "accounting standards, principles and practices" as well as determining the form and content of registration statements and other filings. The act further required that financial statements and other documents filed with the Commission in connection with a public offering be certified by an independent "certified" or "public" accountant. Thus, a regulatory link was forged between the SEC and public accountants which makes this profession structurally different from many others.

Accountants are accustomed to *that* type of regulation. Ironically, public accountants who are now opposed to increased government regulation have actively sought it in the past. For example, they lobbied intensively to secure state regulatory legislation at the turn of the century (Carey, 1969: 44), including certification based upon an education and experience requirement, and passage of the uniform CPA examination. More recently, they have lobbied on behalf of continuing education legislation, fifth-year education requirement, accreditation of accounting programs, and many other issues.

Like the other professions, accountants have enjoyed and prospered under this type of regulation. What is causing consternation today is regulation of quite a different sort—that threatens to subtract rather than add to the profession's esteem, to its ability to manage its own affairs, and perhaps even to its income-generating capacity. Within the past several years, the accounting profession has been buffeted with criticism, congressional investigations and hearings, demands for reform, proposed corrective legislation, and so forth. These concerns and activities *in toto* are portents of increased regulation in public accounting.

Perhaps the attack on accounting is integral to an increased broader concern with professions generally. As Barber points out (1978: 599):

> Everywhere in the United States the Professions have reached new heights of social power and prestige. Everywhere, because of the power of their special knowledge, they are of increasing consequence in the lives of individuals and in the affairs of groups, the polity and society as a whole. Yet everywhere they are also in trouble, criticized for their selfishness, their public irresponsibility, their lack of effective self-control, and for their resistance to requests for more lay participation in the vital decisions professionals make affecting laymen.

Undoubtedly, the concern is widespread and not limited simply to the accounting profession. In the final analysis, however, the cases are processed independently. Thus, our immediate attention must be focused on the changing nature of the regulation as it affects public accounting.

The Complaints

We will not deal extensively with the many claims and counterclaims which have surfaced during the course of investigations and hearings or have appeared in speeches and publications. That material is part of the public record. A few of the more significant complaints, however, should be noted.

A subcommittee of the House of Representatives (U.S. Congress, 1976: 31) observed that:

> The results of the Commission's 1938 decision, by a 3 to 2 vote, to rely primarily on the private accounting profession to establish accounting principles has been disappointing at best.
> In 1940, the Committee on Accounting Procedure (CAP) was established by the AICPA, then known as the American Institute of Accountants. The CAP dealt almost exclusively with the articulation of existing accounting practices and pragmatic solutions to specific accounting problems. Little effort was devoted to the development of a rational conceptual structure. The AICPA finally reacted to the CAP's failure by creating the Accounting Principles Board (APB) in 1959. The APB folded in the early 1970's, after destroying its credibility as an organization capable of resolving financial reporting controversies. Its failure to set down hard and fast rules about merger accounting until October 1970, after billions of dollars had been ac-

counted for by inadequate and often misleading methods, brought condemnation from public investors, financial analysts, academicians, accountants, and the Congress. . . .

In the wake of the APB's disintegration, the AICPA created the Financial Accounting Standards Board (FASB). Instead of reacting to the dismal record of the FASB's predecessor boards by reversing its 1938 decision, the SEC continued to recognize the standards, principles, and practices promulgated by the private sector through the FASB. . . . The FASB has accomplished virtually nothing toward resolving fundamental accounting problems plaguing the profession. These include the plethora of optional "generally accepted" accounting principles [GAAP's], the ambiguities inherent in many of those principles, and the manifestations of private accountants' lack of independence with respect to their corporate clients. Considering the FASB's record, the SEC's continued reliance on the private accounting profession is questionable.

In March, 1977, the staff of a subcommittee of the Committee on Government (U.S. Senate, 1977) issued its capacious report (1760 pages; hereafter called the *Staff Study*), which laid down several serious charges. According to this report, the accounting profession is dominated by the "Big Eight" firms.[2] These firms audit 85 percent of the accounts of companies listed on the New York Stock Exchange. They determine policy in accounting through their control of committees, offices, and staff. Their claim to independence is repudiated by their close identification with their client's interests, including lobbying on their behalf for favorable legislation. The Big Eight advocate and practice "creative accounting," standards which are so flexible that profits can be called losses or vice versa to suit the client's needs.

Actions were proposed to correct these alleged deficiencies, including: (1) strong oversight of accounting practices by Congress; (2) direct establishment of accounting standards by government or a special regulatory commission created for that purpose; and (3) participation by all segments of the public in these tasks.

Following the Committee's hearings on the report, the senators finally abstained from recommending any legislation toward these ends at that time, but instead responded to proposals from the profession's leaders that would give it an opportunity to set its own house in order.[3] The SEC was given the task of monitoring the profession's efforts and reporting annually to Congress on the effectiveness of the self-reform efforts.[4]

The Profession's Efforts at Self-Regulation

Again, we will not detail the efforts which the profession has made, either on its own initiative or in response to the prodding of Congress and the SEC to reform its organizational structure, standards, or practices.

These actions are summarized in hearings before the Moss Committee (U.S. Congress, 1978: 19–64) in the form of a progress report by the American Institute of Certified Public Accountants (AICPA). The report refers to some of the actions taken by the AICPA in response to "rising public needs and expectations." They include:

1. The *Study on the Establishment of Accounting Principles* (AICPA, 1972), which led to the creation of the Financial Accounting Standards Board (FASB) in 1972
2. The *Study on the Objectives of Financial Reporting* in 1973, which laid the foundation for substantive progress toward the development of a conceptual framework (FASB, December 2, 1976)
3. The study on the responsibilities of auditors conducted by a commission appointed in 1974
4. Adoption by the Institute in May, 1976 of a program for periodic quality control reviews of CPA firms[5]
5. Development and implementation of more effective disciplinary procedures through the integration of the ethics committees, the trial boards of state CPA societies, and the Institute
6. Adoption in 1971 of a policy supporting mandatory professional education for all CPAs in public practice as a requirement for retention of rights to practice
7. Organization of an SEC Practice Section of the AICPA Division for CPA firms on September 17, 1977
8. The meetings of nine AICPA senior committees and the governing council were made open to the public (held in the "sunshine") starting January 1, 1978
9. Beginning October 1, 1977, the reduction of representation of the eight largest firms to five or less on each senior AICPA committee (all such committees have fifteen or more members, and their decisions require either a majority or two-thirds vote)
10. Establishment of a Public Oversight Board for the SEC Practice Section of the AICPA Division of CPA firms on September 17, 1977

Recently, the Institute membership has voted to remove the restrictions on advertising[6] and the solicitation of CPAs in the employ of other firms.

In addition to actions already taken, the Institute reports progress on a number of other critical issues (U.S. Congress, 1978: 40–46), such as:

1. *Audit committees.* The New York Stock Exchange amended its "listing agreement" on July 1, 1978 to require that all listed companies have audit committees made up of outside directors. Chairman Williams of the SEC has suggested that CPA firms require audit committees as a precondition to the auditor's issuance of an unqualified opinion. Although many in

the profession believe that the SEC should impose this requirement itself, the Institute has nevertheless appointed a special committee to study the issue.

2. *Change of auditors.* The Institute has supported three SEC initiatives in this area: (a) that Form 8-K should include information concerning the reasons for a change of auditors, (b) that Form 8-K disclosures be included in the annual report, and (c) that a change of auditor must be approved by board or audit committee action.[7]

3. *Management consulting services.* The SEC Practice Section has adopted rules which prohibit a member firm from engaging in certain types of consulting services (e.g., psychological testing, public opinion polls, mergers, and acquisitions for a finder's fee), or any services which would create a loss of independence or are predominantly commercial in character. In addition, member firms are required to report annually to the board or audit committee the total fees received from the client for consulting services and the types of services rendered. The SEC has gone one step further in proposing a rule that would require annual proxy statement disclosure on the amount of fees paid the CPA firm for consulting services and the nature of such services.[8]

4. *Internal control.* In light of the responsibilities set forth in Section 102 of the Foreign Corrupt Practices Act of 1977 and SEC's proposed Rule 136-4, the Institute has appointed a special committee to define criteria for the evaluation of internal control systems. Also, the Auditing Standards Executive Committee (AudSec) has adopted a rule requiring that auditors report on internal control deficiencies to the board or audit committee, and the Institute has endorsed the concept that auditors should review and report publicly on SEC clients' internal control systems. AudSec has been asked to develop standards for such engagements.

5. *Detection of fraud.* Auditing Standards Nos. 16 and 17 define more clearly the auditor's responsibility for detecting errors and irregularities affecting financial statements as well as illegal acts by clients.[9]

6. *Corporate conduct.* Following recent disclosures of illegal and questionable conduct by American companies at home and abroad, the Institute has urged managements to adopt corporate codes of conduct. AudSec has been directed to develop standards to be followed by auditors who will be engaged (separately) to review and report on compliance with these codes of conduct.

7. *Uncertainties.* An Institute committee which includes representatives of the Financial Executives Institute and the American Bar Association is

grappling with the issue of appropriate footnote disclosure, which would deal with the many uncertainties that affect a business enterprise or impair the usefulness of its financial statements.

8. *Preferability.* Since September, 1975, the SEC has required that whenever a registrant makes a change in an accounting method, that action should be accompanied by a letter from the independent auditor stating that the new method is "preferable" to the old one. The Institute has asked AudSec to determine the feasibility of incorporating preferability in the information provided in published financial statements.

These and other efforts at reform are viewed by the profession as evidence of its ability to accept criticism and respond with affirmative actions. The Institute's report observes (U.S. Congress, 1978: 37) that:

> Perhaps never before has a profession in so short a time adopted so ambitious a program to improve its performance, police itself, report on its conduct to the public and submit itself to public scrutiny.

Continuing Regulatory Pressures

Despite these efforts at improving the situation through self-regulation, the pressures continue. As Dopuch (1978: 1) observes:[10]

> ... it does not appear that the extent of regulation of accounting is decreasing; rather there exist warnings that the opposite is occurring.

What are some of these warnings? In Congress, the House Subcommittee on Oversight and Investigations is continuing its surveillance of the profession. Congressman Moss has drafted legislation to create a self-regulatory organization, patterned after the National Association of Securities Dealers,[11] that would function under direct SEC oversight. All auditors who certify financial statements filed with the SEC would be required to join the organization.

The Senate Committee on Government Operations, chaired by Senator Eagleton, and the Subcommittee on Reports, Accounting, and Management, chaired by Senator Percy, have expressed their interest in continuing surveillance of the profession.

The SEC with its activist chairman has supplied initiatives in many areas, including: (1) disclosure of consulting services and fees in annual proxy statements, (2) change of auditor disclosure in Form 8-K and financial statements, (3) audit and disclosure of internal control deficiencies and corporate misconduct, (4) existence of "independent" audit committees as precondition for rendering an unqualified audit opinion, (5) more public participation in the management of the profession, and (6) autonomy for the Public Oversight Board.

In the area of accounting principles, the SEC has shown a greater willingness to reject standards promulgated by FASB, such as proposed standards on "inflation" and "oil and gas" accounting, and has issued its own rules instead.[12] There has also been increased activity in the Enforcement Division. Specifically, the SEC has accepted the responsibility for monitoring the profession's efforts at self-regulation and reporting its findings to Congress on an annual basis.[13]

The Federal Trade Commission has increased its scrutiny of competitive practices in public accounting and is currently conducting a comprehensive study of the structure of the state boards of accountancy and the regulations they promulgate.[14] The inquiry seeks to determine whether practices such as educational and experience requirements, the continuing education requirement, and others raise excessive barriers to entry and restrict competition in the industry. The FTC plans to issue its report later this year, which undoubtedly will be accompanied by attempts to correct the deficiencies which the study may uncover.

And the criticism continues from other quarters—the client community, academia, "small" accounting firms, social advocates, and elected officials.

John C. Burton, for example, cites six reasons "why the AICPA (self-regulatory) program is not likely to achieve its objectives or meet the public need" (U.S. Congress, 1978: 324–325). These reasons are, briefly:

1. That the AICPA does not have the legal authority to achieve effective surveillance and discipline over the profession, i.e., it is a voluntary association.
2. AICPA sanctions would take the force of law and therefore require the SEC to conduct its own investigation and cite the firm under Rule 2(e) or other formal proceeding.
3. The problems of public perception continues. The "peer review" program is likely to be seen as a process of "mutual back scratching," and the Public Oversight Board would not be perceived as an "effective substitute for statutory regulation."
4. The AICPA program does not deal with the enormous legal costs, delay, and legal obstruction which face plaintiffs in cases where they seek to recover damages from accountants. It is essential to have a process which will provide prompt "administrative" determination of professional culpability in cases where investors sustain losses which can be attributed to deficient financial reporting.
5. The AICPA program does not provide for participation by those without self-interest, in determining auditing or peer review stan-

dards, neither are those standards reviewed by a governmental body. Therefore, there are no checks or balances.

6. The AICPA program will have no effect on the potential liability of CPA firms, whereas liability could be limited under some system of statutory regulation. Unlimited liability deters innovation in auditing, raises the cost of auditing, and reduces competition in the industry.

Burton concludes with the recommendation that legislation be enacted to create a formal "self-regulatory" system similar to National Association of Security Dealers (NASD). Burton's suggested name for the accounting regulatory organization is the National Association of Registered Accounting Firms (NARAF).[15]

Eli Mason[16] testified at the Moss Committee hearings as a member of a small CPA firm, as follows (U.S. Congress, 1978: 172–186):

1. The proliferation of authorities, standards and rules has created an accounting structure that is obsolete, inefficient and redundant. The situation is aggravated by the existence of fifty-four state boards of accountancy with different powers, terms of office, and all promulgating different rules and standards. Accordingly, he calls for a Federal registry of accountants, a national CPA certificate, and a proviso that "no state or agency may interfere with a registered accountant who is engaged in the conduct of an audit pursuant to the securities laws of the United States." Accounting, he observes, is not a "provincial occupation." "Public accounting is a national, if not international, profession. The present system of restricted work barriers, reciprocal certificates, and other impediments work to the detriment of the public."

2. He refers to the problem of displacement, noting that when the clients of a "good local accounting" firm go public they are consistently displaced by one of the Big Eight firms. He notes further that Big Eight firms lose their clients to other Big Eight firms. When "second-tier" firms lose clients, however, they invariably go to a Big Eight firm.

In summarizing his position, Mason concludes (U.S. Congress, 1978: 174) that "if we smaller and medium-sized practitioners have to make a choice, we will make a choice that we take the future prospect of regulation by the SEC, which has always been fair and even-handed, to the record of the profession and the AICPA which has not been fair."

Kaiser, on behalf of Harris, Kerr, Forster & Co.,[17] is strongly opposed to the restructuring of the AICPA, asserting that such a move would intensify current excessive concentration in accounting by the "so-called big eight," and "is tantamount to giving the inmates control of the asylum" (U.S. Congress, 1978: 204).

Joseph Alan of Alan & Company (Detroit) has made these observations (U.S. Congress, 1978: 226–238):

1. The major accounting firms set excessive rates of growth and excessive profitability standards. If they wish to grow at 20 percent a year, when the "national economy" is growing at 4 percent, the growth is out of the hides of the small practitioners.

2. Major accounting firms put on "centrally-prepared and canned seminars" which present large firms as experts in various areas such as executive compensation; whereas the ethical standards preclude small firms from billing themselves as specialists.

3. Large firms compete unfairly. They cut fees beyond the point where a small firm can compete effectively. When a large firm decides that they don't have enough business in a given market area, "they go out and get it, and they get it at somebody else's expense. They don't get it based on capability, they don't get it based on superior technical knowledge. They get it based on price."

4. The "relationship of the academic community is important to the small firm. We have a very difficult time competing for the top graduates." The situation is aggravated by the close affinity between accounting professors and the major firms. He argues that "fees are paid on a regular basis to accounting professors to do research projects. They are paid for developing staff training materials. They are paid for conducting staff training seminars. Many of them have even summer employment with the large accounting firms. Can you imagine the position that puts us in when we go to the universities and colleges and attempt to compete for students?"

5. The committee system of the AICPA is "relatively closed" to small-firm members.

And so the controversy continues. While many leaders in the profession have expressed the hope (or conviction) that the "worst is behind us," some of the critical questions which gave rise to the congressional inquiries remain open.

Meanwhile, the inquiry itself appears to be developing along more formal lines, so that issues that were sociological in origin are now being processed via economic models and theories of law.

Part II — Types of Regulatory Initiatives

We have already recognized that different types of regulatory initiatives exist, and indeed this subject is discussed extensively in the literatures in economics and political science. A useful framework for studying the "old" and "new" accounting regulation is provided by Wilson (1974). Analyzing regulation from a political science perspective, he explains regulatory processes in terms of the relative distribution of costs and benefits, as depicted in Table 1-1.

Each of these four models has a distinct socionomy. Type 1 can be labeled the "equilibrium theory" of regulation. It is designed to balance or to adjudicate between powerful competing interests. A classic example of Type 1 theory is the legislation and regulatory effort that mediates between the interests of labor and management.

The sociology of this type of regulation has the following familiar characteristics:

1. Politicians are reluctant to become involved because they risk losing one powerful constituency or the other.
2. The legislation is generally in the nature of a "charter" (e.g., the Taft-Hartley Act), which defines the competing rights and obligations of each party and articulates the rules by which disagreements will be resolved.
3. Neither party will be able to dominate permanently the administrative arrangements created to implement the charter.
4. There will be continuing efforts to renegotiate or amend the charter.
5. The visibility of the issues will be high because of the conflict generated as each party solicits allies and seeks to influence public opinion.

The accounting profession does not face this type of regulatory initiative unless or until its labor force becomes unionized; hence Type 1 is only of passing interest in terms of our discussion.

Type 2 initiatives (concentrated benefits/diffused costs) have, according to Wilson (1974: 142), the following distinctive characteristics:

1. There will be elimination or reduction of price competition within the affected industry.

Table 1.1

COSTS AND BENEFITS OF REGULATION

		Benefits	
		Concentrated	*Diffused*
	Concentrated	1	3
Costs	*Diffused*	2	4

Source: Wilson (1974).

2. Entry to the industry will be restricted or at least made more expensive.
3. The organized beneficiary will strongly influence the regulatory agency that administers the policy.
4. The industry and its agency will strive to maintain a position of low visibility to avoid stimulating the formation of organized resistance.
5. Should the regulation become controversial, it will be defended by attempting to show that eliminating competition is justified on the grounds of ensuring public safety, ending fraud, or promoting amenity.

The "capture" regulatory process generally results in concentrated benefits and diffused costs—that is, "when the benefit is entirely concentrated on a single group but the cost is diffused, an organization will quickly form to propose a regulatory arrangement to institutionalize the benefit" (Wilson, 1974: 141). For example, the Florida Milk Commission was created in 1939 to eliminate "overproduction" and "predatory" price cutting. The benefits to the producers were great, and the cost to the average consumer was relatively small. Wilson (1974: 142) observes that over seventy-five occupations in the United States require licenses to practice, including "the Oklahoma State Dry Cleaning Board which is charged with many duties, including the prevention of fires, but over the years has been chiefly concerned with eliminating price competition."

A number of theories have been proposed to explain the "capture" process. Radical capture theories are based on the syllogism: Big business controls the institutions of our society; regulatory agencies are among these institutions; therefore, big business controls the regulatory agencies. For example, the origin of the Interstate Commerce Commission is explained as the use of government power by the railroads to establish the stable cartel that they were unable to establish by collusion (MacAvoy, 1965). This theory does not explain why much regulation is sponsored by liberal groups and opposed by industry, nor why the prime beneficiaries are frequently small business and labor.

Others explain capture as a matter of goal deflection and conflict resolution. This approach says that a regulatory agency is typically established with a strong commitment to the public interest, under the spotlight of attention from consumers, environmentalists, labor, Congress, and other groups. Over the life of the agency, however, the crisis which gave rise to its establishment recedes, the attention of Congress and others shifts to newer issues, the agency deals more and more exclusively with the regulated industry, and exiting agency personnel find attractive employment in industry. Eventually, the industry's position comes to seem more and more reasonable to the agency. Capture is complete when a congruence of goals occurs: Both regulator and regulated have an interest in blocking competition from without and establishing market structures which ensure acceptable profits for all firms within the industry.

George J. Stigler (1971) proposed a type of capture theory in his application of economic analysis to the phenomenon of regulation. According to Stigler, regulation exists because some members of society have incentive systems which cause them to demand it and others have incentive systems which cause them to supply it. The incentives operating in any particular context can be analyzed to predict what equilibrium level of regulation will result and what form it will assume. The state's basic resource is its power to coerce. The benefits an industry could seek from the state include its use of that power to pay the industry direct subsidies, to restrict new competitors, and to fix prices. The state will supply its power in exchange for votes and contributions. Stigler (1971: 3) concludes that ". . . as a rule, regulation is acquired by the industry and is designed and operated primarily for its benefit." The Interstate Commerce Commission and trucking, railroads, and barge lines; the Civil Aeronautics Board and the trunk airlines; and the Federal Communications Commission and the telephone and other "record carriers" (e.g., Western Union) are frequently cited as agencies which were created for the benefit of (and subsequently have been "captured" by) the industries they were ostensibly designed to regulate.

The historical regulation of public accounting (and other professions) is consistent with the "capture" theory. For example, the SEC has been described as a captive of the accounting interests (U.S. Senate, 1977: 173–174):

> The summary of accounting authority and responsibility prepared by the SEC describes the close relationship that has developed between the SEC and the AICPA, which is controlled by the "Big Eight" and other large national accounting firms. It also illustrates the role reversal which the SEC has deliberately permitted to occur in failing to exercise its congressional mandate. Instead of sharing compliance responsibilities with independent auditors following standards established by the SEC to protect the public, the SEC has acquiesced in permitting the AICPA to establish auditing and accounting standards directly on behalf of the accounting profession.

The accounting profession has also "captured" the state boards of accountancies, while the Big Eight firms have been accused of "capturing" the AICPA (which can be viewed as a voluntary regulatory agency), and the FASB.

Although past regulation in accounting was of the Type 2 variety, it has come full circle. Regulatory pressure on public accounting now comes from the opposite direction.

Much of current thinking on regulating the accounting profession is contained in the last sentence of the summary of the *Staff Study* (U.S. Senate, 1977: 2): "Accounting issues are too important to be left to accountants alone." To the Metcalf Subcommittee staff, this statement provided a compelling rationale for extensive regulatory intervention in accounting policy and practice. The framework of the statement is adaptable to virtually any regulatory expediency. For example, in a commencement address at the University of Michigan, then Secretary Joseph Califano of the Department of Health, Education and Welfare, proclaimed that ". . . science has become too important to be left to scientists."[18]

Both statements are derived from an observation attributed to the French statesman, Charles Maurice de Talleyrand (1754–1838), that

> War is much too serious a thing to be left to military men.[19]

This kind of thinking, in the realm of public accounting, signals a different type of regulatory initiative, known in the literature as the "public interest theory of regulation," or Type 3 in the preceding framework (Bonbright, 1961; Davis, 1970; and Friendly, 1962). This theory holds that regulation is supplied in response to public demands to correct inefficient or inequitable market practices.[20] Two assumptions underlie this theory: (1) that markets are fragile and tend to operate inefficiently (or inequitably), and (2) that the government regulation is virtually costly. With these assumptions, Posner (1974: 336) observes:

> . . . it was easy to argue that the principle government interventions in the economy—trade union protection, public utility and common carrier regulation, public power and reclamation programs, farm subsidies, occupational licensure, the minimum wage, even tariffs—were simply responses of government to public demands for the rectification of palpable and remedial inefficiencies and inequities in the operation of the free market. Behind each scheme of regulation could be discerned a market imperfection, the existence of which supplied a complete justification for some regulation assumed to operate effectively and without cost.

Exemplifying this last assumption are these excerpts from an SEC report (1963: 268, 400) on injury to investors caused by the actions of incompetent security dealers:

> There is no evidence that these practices are typical . . . but regardless of their frequency they represent problems too important to be ignored . . .
> The mere fact that there have been any losses at all is sufficient reason to consider whether there are further adjustments that should be made for the protection of investors.

The report assumes that no matter how trivial or infrequent present failures are, regulatory intervention is justified.

More recently, in issuing *Accounting Series Release* No. 190, which required certain large companies to report replacement cost data for inventories and fixed assets, the SEC dismissed the cost of providing this information as inconsequential in relation to the assumed benefits to be derived.

"Public interest" regulation has a result opposite to that described earlier—that is, it produces diffused benefits and concentrated costs. According to Wilson (1974: 143–144), this means that "(politically) a small group, faced with the immediate prospect of increased burdens, is unable to defeat a proposal brought on behalf of large numbers of (inevitably unorganized) persons, each of whom may benefit, if at all, only in the future." Wilson (1974: 165) attributes the fact that there is a large political market for programs with diffused benefits to

> a shift in the national mood, the increasingly critical posture of the mass media, the appeal that consumer and ecological issues have for presidential hopefuls, the changing attitudes of the business elite itself.

Further (Wilson, 1974: 166):

> The creation, reaffirmation and institutionalization of symbols is a vitally important and easily neglected casual factor in politics. Adopting policies that provide largely symbolic gratifications for demands may achieve little of substance in the immediate case but constitute nonetheless a positive reinforcement for the demands themselves and the legitimation of a governmental role in dealing with these demands. The decisive stage in the ebb and flow of social conflict is control over the public agenda: what government may or may not do is chiefly determined by what people have come to believe is properly a "private" or a "public matter."

"Public interest" regulatory initiatives have certain distinctive features, as Wilson (1974: 146) notes:

1. Issues of this type must arouse the public. Publicity is the key. Exposés of wrongdoing fuel the passions.
2. Legislators eagerly take up the cause—they are anxious to be identified with public interest causes, such as "law and order," "health and safety," "protecting the investor," and so forth.
3. Proposals tend to be strong and unequivocal, as yielding to interest groups will be viewed as wavering in resolve or (worse) outright capitulation.
4. The solutions will be less substantive than procedural (e.g., the Moss proposal to create a self-regulatory organization patterned after the National Association of Security Dealers). The solutions

will reemphasize that the focus of social control is the U.S. Congress.

5. The solution will be shaped more by the political process itself than in terms of the intrinsic problems which gave rise to the initiative.
6. The issues are evasive and inexhaustive. Resolving one set of problems only seems to give rise to another set. Because no system is perfect, new or additional faults can always be found. Attempts at self-improvement tend to be viewed as self-serving and/or cosmetic.
7. The victim will chafe under the legislation and delay and frustrate its implementation, while pretending to support it.
8. If vigilance weakens, the affected party will seek to have the law amended or at least not enforced. So either vigilance groups will form (e.g., "Americans for Clean Air") *or* the vigilance will be vested in a new regulatory agency (which the party will then try to capture).

The public interest theory is sometimes called the "market failure" theory because the need for regulation is triggered by failures in the performance of the free market. Some of the proposed classes of market failure are: natural monopolies, externalities, public goods, and asymmetrical information.

The Pure Food and Drug Act of 1906, the Meat Inspection Act of 1906, and the Food, Drug and Cosmetic Act of 1935 are early public interest laws. The number of such laws has increased dramatically in recent years. Congress passed twenty "consumer" bills between 1962 and 1970—bills aimed against postal fraud, flammable fabrics, unwholesome meat and poultry, radiation, automobile and highway dangers, unsafe toys, exploitative credit practices, deceptive package labeling, and inadequate testing of drugs. In the area of ecology, there was the Water Quality Act of 1965, Motor Vehicle Air Pollution Control Act of 1965, Clean Water Restoration Act of 1966, Air Quality Act of 1967, National Environmental Policy Act of 1969, Water Quality Improvement Act of 1970, and so forth.

Many of these initiatives followed major scandals—sulfanilamide, thalidomide, Nader's attack on General Motors, and so on.

It is hard to ignore in context the failures and scandals in public accounting—Equity Funding, Penn Central, Westgage, *ad nauseam;* or the diatribes of Abraham Briloff[21] and other critics. To these scandals and calamities can be added the cries for redress by small accounting firms who feel tyrannized, abused, and displaced by the large firms. Certainly, all the sociological and political concerns needed to fuel the fires of regulatory zeal and reform have been present in the recent history of the profession.

Type 4 policies (diffused benefits/diffused costs) will be not discussed at length here. They are generally based on some broad perception of social need, supported by appeal to humanistic principles, the Constitution, or other moral authority. An apt title for this type of regulatory initiative is "societarian," in that society as a whole bears both benefit and cost. The legislation is typically vague about who will benefit (so as to induce the support of as many hopefuls as possible) and who will pay the cost (so as not to arouse opposition). The vagueness of the legislation requires the administrative agencies to issue regulations specifying the *real* costs and benefits. Any criticism will then lodge with the agency for "misinterpreting the will of Congress." "Tax reform", socialized medicine, social security, and so forth, typify this type of regulatory initiative.

Returning to Type 3 regulation, the public accounting profession faces the onslaught of a public interest initiative. It must, therefore, understand the nature and workings of this force to be reckoned with.

It is the nature of government workings, however, that problems of sociological origin are translated into the more formal language of economics and still later into the oblique and obfuscative language of politics and law.

Part III – The Structural Theory of Antitrust Applied to the Accounting Profession

An economic model commonly known as the "structural theory of antitrust" has been applied in the analysis of the accounting profession. This model, which underlies much of the recent discussion of regulation and accounting, deserves to be explored, a little more fully.

Congressional critics of public accounting have claimed that the big firms exercise monopolistic or oligopolistic power, which enables them to engage in anticompetitive practices with undesirable impacts on corporations, investors, and the public. For example, Congressman Moss ("Accounting Profession," 1978: 33) has charged that:

> The accounting profession is essentially an oligopoly with the largest firms exercising too much control over the rest.

Similarly, the *Staff Study* (U.S. Senate, 1977: 43) asserted:

> The traditional problems associated with lack of competition and excessive market concentration may be evident in the supply of auditing, accounting, and other services by the "Big Eight" firms to major corporations.

Table 1-2

ELEMENTS OF INDUSTRIAL ORGANIZATION

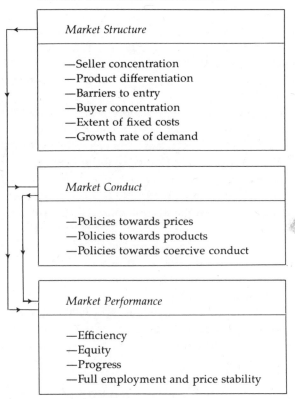

Market Structure

—Seller concentration
—Product differentiation
—Barriers to entry
—Buyer concentration
—Extent of fixed costs
—Growth rate of demand

Market Conduct

—Policies towards prices
—Policies towards products
—Policies towards coercive conduct

Market Performance

—Efficiency
—Equity
—Progress
—Full employment and price stability

Source: Derived from Caves (1977: 14, 15, 17, 51, 66).

Such criticisms imply causality from an industry's structure through its conduct to its performance. Table 1-2 shows one representation of these elements of industrial organization.

The concepts of structure, conduct and performance can be defined as follows (Caves, 1977: 14):

Structure: Those relatively stable features of the environment that influence the rivalry among buyers and sellers.

Conduct: The policies that participants adopt towards the market regarding price, product characteristics and other terms that influence market transactions.

Performance: A normative appraisal of the social quality of the allocation of resources that results from a market's conduct.

We will now turn to the elements most relevant to public accounting.

The Structure and Conduct of Public Accounting

Concentration

The *Staff Study* was strongly and repeatedly critical of the concentration of power it claimed to find in public accounting. The *Study* describes the market share held by the largest firms as "excessive" (1977: 23), "extremely high" (1977: 43), "extraordinary" (1977: 45), "truly extraordinary" (1977: 42) and "phenomenal" (1977: 42).

Concentration measures are operationalizations, in continuous forms, of the discrete categories of economic theory—"perfect competition," "oligopoly," "monopoly." Concentration is typically measured by computing the ratio of total revenue or employees of the N largest firms divided by total revenue or employees in the entire industry (Caves, 1977: 8). Most of the *Staff Study*'s analysis, it should be noted, is based on unusual measures of concentration whose validity is problematical. This matter will be discussed further.

Table 1-3 summarizes concentration data for eight firms in the manufacturing industry, based on four-digit SIC codes. The table shows that in thirty-six industries the largest eight firms account for over 90 percent of total industry revenue.

Table 1-4 shows concentration ratios for a broader range of industries based on three-digit SIC codes. Table 1-5 shows concentration ratios for selected service industries based on the most recent census information. Accounting, auditing, and bookkeeping services (SIC code 893) were not included in the 1972 census of service industries. Traditionally, not a great deal of operating information has been available on public accounting, although there is a trend towards greater voluntary disclosure and a growing number of published studies of the organization of the industry. Table 1-6 shows some measures of concentration based on numbers of personnel. These figures reveal relatively modest concentration. It is interesting to note that a 1975 study of the twenty largest firms (in terms of AICPA members) found that none of the Big Eight was among the six fastest-growing firms (Reece and Kinkade, 1975: 21).

Most studies of concentration in accounting, including the *Staff Study*, employ restricted definitions of the industry and measure auditor size in terms of client size. Depending upon the restrictions imposed, arbitrarily high concentration ratios can be produced (see the *Staff Study*, 1977: 40–42). Even if these restricted measures can be validly compared with conventional concentration measures in other industries, however, they are not "extraordinarily" high. Further, as Table 1-7 shows, the distribution of CPAs across firms of various sizes has remained relatively stable since 1970. In that year, 38.6 percent of practicing CPAs were associated with the twenty-five largest firms, as compared with 38.2 percent in 1976. The proportion of

Table 1-3

CONCENTRATION IN MANUFACTURING, 1972

Eight-Firm Concentration Ratio (%)	Number of Industries	Cumulative Value of Shipments as % of All Manufacturing Shipments
90–100	36	10.6
80– 89	33	17.5
70– 79	51	26.8
60– 69	52	37.2

Source: Biegler (1977: E9).

Table 1-4

CONCENTRATION RATIOS IN SELECTED INDUSTRIES

	Percentage of Industry Revenue		
	Largest Company	Largest Eight	Largest Fifteen
1. Glass products	29	91	99
2. Aerospace and aircraft	18	84	96
3. Motor vehicles and equipment	36	87	94
4. Air transportation	17	81	94
5. Office equipment and computers	38	88	93
6. Farm, construction, mining, and materials handling machinery	25	77	91
7. Petroleum refining	22	72	88
8. Drugs	15	64	88
9. Grocery and miscellaneous food stores	16	68	88
10. Lumber and wood products	19	75	87
11. Electrical equipment	41	77	86
12. Meat products	17	68	84
13. Chemicals, plastics, and synthetics	15	65	82
14. Nonferrous metals and mining	24	64	81
15. Textile mill products	17	58	76
16. Iron and steel	19	65	75
17. Publishing	11	54	73
18. Banking	9	41	54
Average	22	71	85

Source: Hanson (1977: 91).

Table 1-5

CONCENTRATION RATIOS IN SELECTED SERVICE INDUSTRIES

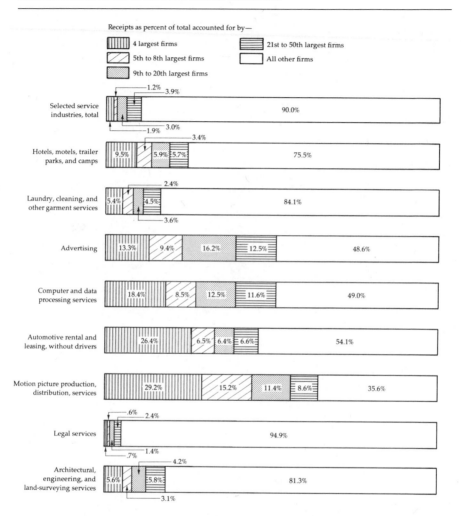

sole practitioners (20.3 percent in 1970 and 21.5 percent in 1976) has also been constant.

Besides citing concentration across all client industries, considerable criticism has been leveled at concentration within industries. The *Staff Study* examined concentration in the ten top companies in six industries. Tables 1-8, 1-9, and 1-10 show intraindustry concentration ratios for a larger number of industries and for more firms in each industry (where practicable). Predictably, the more complete figures reveal less dramatic concentration.

Table 1-6

CONCENTRATION RATIOS IN PUBLIC ACCOUNTING

	Number of Employees[a] (%)	Number of CPAs in Public Accounting[b] (%)	Number of CPAs in Firms Auditing Public Companies[c] (%)
Largest firm	4	5	9
Largest four firms	13	16	—
Largest eight firms	22	28	54

Sources: [a]*Staff Study* (1977: 30) and U.S. Dept. of Commerce (1978: 87).
　　　　[b]Reece and Kinkade (1975: 31).
　　　　[c]Hanson (1977: 88).

Table 1-7

PERCENTAGE DISTRIBUTION OF AICPA MEMBERSHIP IN PUBLIC ACCOUNTING

Firm Size	1970[a] (%)	1976[b] (%)
Largest twenty-five firms	38.6	38.2
Ten or more members (excluding above)	7.5	10.7
Two to nine members	33.6	29.6
One member	20.3	21.5
AICPA members in public accounting	100.0	100.0

Sources: [a]Buckley and Buckley (1974: 28).
　　　　[b]*Staff Study* (1977: 85).

The *Staff Study* did not make an international comparison on concentration. Table 1-11 shows various concentration measures for New Zealand, Australia, the United Kingdom, Canada, and the United States.[22]

To deny that extraordinary concentration exists in public accounting is not to deny that large firms are present in the industry. It is reasonable to hypothesize that environmental and market factors contributed to this situation and to seek to discover what those factors are.

First, financial statement user groups have pressured to have corporations audited by nationally known firms. For example, as long ago as 1914, a business journal (quoted in Carey, 1969: 792) reported:

Table 1-8

PERCENTAGE OF COMPANIES AUDITED—NUMBER OF COMPANIES AS THE CRITERION: 1973[a]

		AA	AY	CL	EE	HS	PMM	PW	TR	O	N.a.	Total Number of Companies
1.	Aerospace	13	20	7	20	7	7	7	13	7	0	15
2.	Air transport	19	6	6	19	19	19	6	0	6	0	16
3.	Amusements	25	17	0	8	8	25	17	0	0	0	12
4.	Auto parts	5	10	0	33	14	24	10	5	0	0	21
5.	Autos	17	0	17	17	17	0	0	33	0	0	6
6.	Building	30	5	15	10	10	5	10	10	5	0	40
7.	Chemicals	11	9	9	2	20	20	18	2	7	0	44
8.	Containers	7	7	7	0	20	0	47	7	7	0	15
9.	Drugs	17	4	8	13	4	17	25	0	13	0	24
10.	Electronics	16	11	11	16	3	11	14	8	11	0	37
11.	Home furnishings	0	0	50	0	0	50	0	0	0	0	2
12.	Leather and shoes	25	0	0	25	0	50	0	0	0	0	4
13.	Liquor	17	17	0	0	0	0	67	0	0	0	6
14.	Machinery	28	0	8	15	8	13	18	5	5	0	39
15.	Metals—aluminum, copper, fabricating	13	7	40	7	7	13	13	0	0	0	15
16.	Metals—lead, zinc, gold	0	0	17	0	33	17	17	0	17	0	6
17.	Office equipment	9	0	18	0	9	18	45	0	0	0	11
18.	Oil	20	17	10	13	3	13	17	7	0	0	30
19.	Paper	17	0	8	0	25	8	25	8	8	0	12
20.	Communications	8	15	8	15	15	23	8	0	8	0	13
21.	Railroad equipment	20	20	0	20	0	0	40	0	0	0	5
22.	Railroads	0	0	0	0	28	17	33	0	0	22	18
23.	Retail trade—I	11	5	11	7	7	29	7	14	7	4	28
24.	Retail trade—II	20	0	5	10	5	15	15	25	5	0	20
25.	Rubber fabricating	0	0	17	33	17	0	33	0	0	0	6
26.	Soft drink and candy	25	25	0	50	0	0	0	0	0	0	4
27.	Steel	23	0	14	14	5	9	32	5	0	0	22
28.	Telephone	25	25	25	0	0	0	25	0	0	0	4
29.	Textiles—apparel	0	28	0	8	28	13	8	4	25	0	24
30.	Tobacco	0	17	33	17	33	0	0	0	0	0	6
31.	Utilities—electric	22	0	17	0	31	3	22	0	6	0	36
32.	Utilities—gas	50	0	0	0	10	20	10	0	10	0	10
33.	Trucking	18	0	0	18	18	9	0	18	18	0	11
34.	Food	12	9	5	8	6	15	25	8	8	5	65

[a]Some minor errors appear due to rounding.

Source: Schiff and Fried (1976: 121). Abbreviations represent, as follows:

AA	Arthur Andersen & Co.	PMM	Peat, Marwick, Mitchell & Co.
AY	Arthur Young & Co.	PW	Price Waterhouse and Co.
CL	Coopers & Lybrand	TR	Touche, Ross and Co.
EE	Ernst and Ernst	O	Other
HS	Haskins and Sells	N.a.	Not available

Table 1-9

PERCENTAGE OF COMPANIES AUDITED—SALES VOLUME AS THE CRITERION: 1973[a]

	AA	AY	CL	EE	HS	PMM	PW	TR	O	N.a.	Total Number of Companies
1. Aerospace	14	15	1	22	14	1	10	17	5	0	15
2. Air transport	28	12	12	7	21	9	10	0	1	0	16
3. Amusements	12	13	0	4	22	11	38	0	0	0	12
4. Auto parts	2	5	0	36	25	20	10	3	0	0	21
5. Autos	1	0	31	2	48	0	0	18	0	0	6
6. Building	41	6	16	9	7	4	7	7	3	0	40
7. Chemicals	14	5	5	1	26	14	16	10	9	0	44
8. Containers	6	16	19	0	30	0	22	5	2	0	15
9. Drugs	20	2	11	9	3	15	26	0	14	0	24
10. Electronics	21	20	4	7	0	26	12	5	4	0	37
11. Home furnishings	0	0	44	0	0	56	0	0	0	0	2
12. Leather and shoes	15	0	0	24	0	62	0	0	0	0	4
13. Liquor	15	19	0	0	0	0	66	0	0	0	6
14. Machinery	20	0	4	17	10	14	28	2	4	0	39
15. Metals—aluminum, copper, fabricating	6	3	47	11	10	6	18	0	0	0	15
16. Metals—lead, zinc, gold	0	0	32	0	36	16	9	0	8	0	6
17. Office equipment	4	0	10	0	10	16	60	0	0	0	11
18. Oil	17	19	8	5	1	3	47	1	0	0	30
19. Paper	25	0	12	0	27	3	18	11	3	0	12
20. Communications	5	16	21	14	10	21	3	0	9	0	13
21. Railroad equipment	14	38	0	16	0	0	31	0	0	0	5
22. Railroads	0	0	0	0	42	11	26	0	0	21	18
23. Retail trade—I	6	1	13	3	17	0	7	12	6	4	28
24. Retail trade—II	14	0	2	6	5	16	18	37	2	0	20
25. Rubber fabricating	0	0	24	16	16	0	45	0	0	0	6
26. Soft drink and candy	10	37	0	53	0	0	0	0	0	0	4
27. Steel	7	0	3	16	9	4	58	2	0	0	22
28. Telephone	2	3	93	0	0	0	2	0	0	0	4
29. Textiles—apparel	0	14	0	6	17	28	6	2	26	0	24
30. Tobacco	0	7	47	31	15	0	0	0	0	0	6
31. Utilities—electric	26	0	14	0	27	2	22	0	9	0	36
32. Utilities—gas	49	0	0	0	11	18	9	0	13	0	10
33. Trucking	27	0	0	18	15	4	0	28	9	0	11
34. Food	15	10	3	4	5	13	29	10	6	3	65

[a]Some minor errors appear due to rounding.
Source: Schiff and Fried (1976: 122). Abbreviations represent, as follows:

AA	Arthur Andersen & Co.	PMM	Peat, Marwick, Mitchell & Co.
AY	Arthur Young & Co.	PW	Price Waterhouse and Co.
CL	Coopers & Lybrand	TR	Touche, Ross and Co.
EE	Ernst and Ernst	O	Other
HS	Haskins and Sells	N.a.	Not available

Table 1-10

FORTUNE 1300 COMPANIES BY AUDITOR AND INDUSTRY, 1971

SIC	Industry	Number of Companies	Market Share[a] of Clients in Each Industry								Largest Other	Remaining Others
			AA	AY	CL	EE	HS	PMM	PW	TR		
24, 26	Forest products	55	25.5	1.8	9.1	10.9	10.9	5.5	25.5	3.6	SDL 3.6	3.6
25	Furniture, fixtures	8	12.5	0.0	12.5	25.0	0.0	0.0	0.0	0.0	SS 37.5	12.5
32	Stone, clay, glass	40	22.5	7.5	15.0	15.0	12.5	2.5	15.0	5.0		5.0
33	Primary metals	62	9.7	3.2	21.0	16.1	6.5	9.7	25.8	3.2		4.8
34	Fabricated metals	45	17.8	2.2	11.1	24.4	15.6	8.9	11.1	4.4		4.4
35	Machinery	88	19.3	5.7	9.1	15.9	6.8	13.6	15.9	5.7		7.8
36	Electrical equipment	80	12.5	12.5	8.8	15.0	5.0	12.5	15.0	7.5	AG 5.0	6.3
37	Transportation equipment	68	17.6	11.7	8.8	16.2	5.9	10.3	10.3	10.3	AG 2.9	5.8
38	Precision instruments	36	19.4	8.3	8.3	8.3	8.3	11.1	25.0	2.7		8.3
19, 39	Conglomerates, miscellaneous	74	21.6	6.7	5.4	13.5	17.6	10.8	14.9	8.1		1.4
	Subtotal Durables	556	18.0	6.8	10.4	15.3	9.4	9.9	16.9	5.9	AG 1.4	5.9
20	Food	126	11.1	10.3	10.3	10.3	7.1	11.9	20.6	7.1	ML 2.4	8.7
21	Tobacco	6	0.0	0.0	50.0	33.3	16.7	0.0	0.0	0.0		0.0
22	Textiles	37	8.1	13.5	8.1	10.8	10.8	18.9	0.0	2.7	SDL 13.5	13.5
23	Apparel	32	3.1	0.0	3.1	9.4	9.4	15.6	9.4	9.4	CR 12.5	28.2
27	Printing/publishing	33	9.1	15.2	9.1	18.2	12.1	15.2	9.1	3.0		9.0
28	Chemicals	86	5.8	7.0	15.1	9.3	9.3	20.9	20.9	1.1	ML 3.5	7.0
29	Petroleum	29	10.3	10.3	17.2	17.2	6.9	13.8	20.7	0.0		3.4
30	Rubber	15	6.7	13.3	6.7	40.0	6.7	13.3	6.7	0.0		6.7
31	Leather	5	20.0	0.0	0.0	20.0	0.0	20.0	0.0	20.0		20.0
	Subtotal Nondurables	369	8.4	9.2	11.4	13.0	8.7	15.4	15.4	4.3	SDL 3.0	11.2

Code	Industry	n											
	Subtotal Manufacturing	925	14.2	7.8	10.8	14.4	9.1	12.1	16.3	5.3	SDL	1.6	8.5
10–14	Mining, drilling	17	41.2	0.0	5.9	17.6	0.0	17.6	11.8	5.9			0.0
50	Wholesale trade	19	15.8	5.3	5.3	5.3	10.5	5.3	5.3	5.3			42.2
60–69	Miscellaneous financial	7	0.0	14.3	0.0	0.0	14.3	28.6	14.3	0.0			28.6
15–16, 72–73, 78, 89, 48	Business services	26	30.8	7.7	7.7	0.0	11.5	19.2	11.5	3.8			7.6
01, 40, 49	Other miscellaneous	6	0.0	0.0	16.7	0.0	16.7	0.0	33.3	16.7			16.7
	Subtotal Nonmanufacturing	75	24.0	5.3	6.7	5.3	9.3	14.7	12.0	5.3			17.3
	Subtotal Fortunes Industrials	1000	14.9	7.6	10.5	13.7	9.1	12.3	16.0	5.3	SDL	1.5	9.1
	Retailers	50	12.0	0.0	14.0	8.0	6.0	20.0	12.0	20.0	LKHH	4.0	4.0
	Transportations	50	12.0	4.0	4.0	12.0	20.0	20.0	22.0	2.0		4.0	4.0
	Utilities	50	28.0	2.0	14.0	0.0	24.0	6.0	20.0	0.0	NN	4.0	2.0
	Commercial banks	50	10.0	2.0	4.0	22.0	8.0	24.0	14.0	4.0			12.0
	Divers financials	50	4.0	10.0	8.0	20.0	14.0	18.0	6.0	8.0	JFro	4.0	8.0
	Life insurance companies	50	4.0	2.0	12.0	16.0	6.0	8.0	8.0	2.0			42.0
	Subtotal Nonindustrials	300	11.7	3.3	9.3	13.0	13.0	16.0	13.7	6.0	JFro	1.0	13.0
	Total 1300 Companies from Fortune Directory	1300	14.2	6.6	10.2	13.5	10.0	13.2	15.5	5.5	SDL	1.2	10.2

[a]Market share = (number of clients in each industry)/(total number of companies in the same industry) times 100%.
Source: Reece and Kinkade (1975: 17, 18).

Table 1-11

CONCENTRATION MEASURES IN PUBLIC ACCOUNTING: AN INTERNATIONAL COMPARISON

Country and Year Index	New Zealand			Australia	U.K.	Canada	U.S.	
	1968	1973	1976	1972	1975	1968	1964	1971
Four-firm concentration ratio	40	51	59	50	56	72	72	72
Eight-firm concentration ratio	63	83	86	77	83	92	96	97
Gini coefficient	.74	.72	.77	.73	.76	.80	.80	.84
Eight-firm Herfindahl Index	.05	.09	.11	.08	.11	.15	.15	.15
All-firm Herfindahl Index	.06	.09	.11	.09	.17	.16	.15	.15
Numbers-equivalent eight firms	20	11.1	9.1	12.5	9.1	6.7	6.7	6.7
Numbers-equivalent all firms	17	11.1	9.1	9.1	5.9	6.3	6.7	6.7

Source: Stanton and Gilling, 1977: 9.

Statements put out by mercantile concerns desiring credit are frequently accompanied by accountants' certificates, and banks which buy commercial paper look with disfavor upon certificates issued by accountants unknown to them.

A more recent instance is vividly described by Eli Mason, managing partner of Mason & Co., in testimony before the Moss Subcommittee:

In the early 1960's, our accounting firm conducted an audit for the registration of a company that was going public. The reason that we were called to perform this audit was interesting. The treasurer of the company was a CPA. His brother was president and therefore he was not independent. He knew of my firm and asked if we would conduct the audit. We did. We filed the prerequisite forms and the audit report with the SEC.

The company went public. We conducted the audit for approximately 6 years with complete satisfaction to the client and to all parties concerned.

I received a telephone call one day from the treasurer of the company and he said, "Mr. Mason, I have some bad news for you." I said, "What is it?"

He said, "The company is going into the underwriting community for several millions of dollars of additional capital and the underwriter is requesting a "Big 8" firm. I told him that you had been the auditor for approximately 6 years and that we were pleased with the services." I said, "You have no problem. I will visit with the underwriter and tell him of our background and services and I am sure I will convince him that we can continue to perform the audit."

My partners and I visited the office of the underwriting firm and, sir, I could no more move them than I could move the U.S. Capitol Building. They said, "We want a 'Big 8' firm."

I said to them "Any 'Big 8' firm?" and they said, "Any 'Big 8' firm."

The underwriter said to me in a very kindly way, "This is no reflection on you." If I were looking for an auditor for my church, I would select you rather than a 'Big 8' firm." My response was, "I don't want to audit your church. I want to continue to audit this company."

I then telephoned the chief accountant of the SEC, Mr. Andrew Barr, who is in this room today. I telephoned the President of the American Institute of Certified Public Accountants, Mr. Louis M. Kessler. I telephoned the Chairman of the AICPA Committee on Displacement of Local Practitioners, Mr. Marshall S. Armstrong, who subsequently became president of the AICPA and chairman of the FASB.

Mr. Congressman, when I get my Texas up I really do act. So I had behind me the Chief Accountant of the SEC who said "Mr. Mason, I want you to stay on this account." I had the Chairman of the Committee on Displacement, Marshall S. Armstrong, and he said, "Mr. Mason, I want you to stay on the account."

Mr. Congressman, to make a long story short, we lost the account. It went to a "Big 8" firm.

I pleaded with the managing partner of the "Big 8" firm who was a personal friend, and who will testify here tomorrow. I said to him, "I do not think you should take the account. It means nothing to you but it means a great deal to me, emotionally and professionally." The response that I got was, "We have to take the account."

Subsequently, Mr. Marshall Armstrong visited my office and he is a very fine gentleman. He said, "Eli, you did all you could. You put up a good fight."

Mr. Chairman and members of the committee, sometimes you get tired of fighting and tired of losing.

The profession has resisted the displacement of small by larger firms. Although other factors might render infeasible the audit of a large client by a small firm, the profession has attempted to educate users that competence, ethical standards, and quality of work are common to all members of the profession regardless of the practice unit size (see Carey, 1970: 354).

Second, technological factors dictate that large clients require large auditors. For example, Price Waterhouse has reported that its annual audit of one client requires 72 person-years of effort. Another client whose audit consumes 26 person-years annually has 300 separate corporate entities in forty foreign countries which are consolidated in its ultimate financial statements (Biegler, 1977: E5).

Third, auditors' professional norms of independence and their rational, strategic desire to diversify risk will lead them to minimize financial dependence on any one client. The largest clients of Price Waterhouse and Peat, Marwick, Mitchell account for less than 1 percent of those firms' total revenues (Biegler, 1977: E6); Hanson, 1977: 19). Consequently, firms auditing large clients have incentives to acquire many other clients.

Fourth, regulatory and legal factors are expanding the scope of auditing. Consequently, the level of resources necessary to perform a given audit is increasing.

Fifth, the desire to attract and hold top-quality personnel is a factor contributing to the growth of auditing firms.

For example ("Touche Ross," 1976: 20):

> Mr. Palmer [Managing Partner, Touche Ross] also sees the huge accounting partnerships as committed to growth by the need to keep making room to promote younger partners as they mature. Without that leeway, he said, a firm can't hold its good people—in his view, its true assets.

A similar view has been expressed by Robert E. Schlosser of Coopers & Lybrand. He suggests (1977: 136) that accounting firms have been perceived as having an "up or out" philosophy; to attract and support staff, they should adopt a "stay and grow" philosophy.

A constraint on growth is the increasing cost of coordination and control. Walter Hanson ("When the Auditor Gets Audited," 1975: S3, 1) described this aspect of growth as follows:

> How do you expand a firm from about 300 partners in 1965 to 876 in 1975 . . . without losing control? The answer is sought in personnel training and tight quality control systems—check and re-check all the way up the line.

The profession is painfully aware of some costs of growth. The failure of Equity Funding's auditors to detect that fraud earlier was attributed largely to coordination and control breakdowns related to a merger of auditing firms ("Report of the Trustee of Equity Funding Corporation of America," 1974). In addition, Alexander Grant's former senior partner, Wallace Olson ("To Merge or Not to Merge?" 1977: 59), has stated:

> Virtually every litigation problem we had arose from audits that spanned the merger period.

At least one observer expects that the currently litigious environment will reduce the growth of large firms via merger ("To Merge or Not to Merge," 1977).

Finally, there are factors contributing to the growth of specialization of auditing services (or intraindustry concentration). Those same factors, however, counteract overall concentration. The acquisition of expertise in the accounting, economic, and managerial characteristics of an industry is a type of fixed cost which, up to a certain point, results in declining average costs in the supply of that expertise. Just as first-time audits of a client involve certain familiarization costs that will not be incurred in subsequent audits, so an auditor who already has experience in an industry can offer more efficient (lower-cost) audits to other firms in that industry. Further, the legal and regulatory environment encourages industry specialization. For example, in *Accounting Series Release* No. 173 (an inquiry into certain auditing failures by Peat, Marwick, Mitchell & Co.), the SEC (1975) concluded that:

> In considerable measure this [audit deficiency] occurred because the auditors were not sufficiently familiar with the business context to assess the representations of management. Auditors should be particularly careful when the client asserts that special circumstances require unusual accounting or auditing solutions and should either possess or avail themselves of sufficient industry knowledge to judge the substance of the situation.

The increasing returns available to firms by means of specialization within an industry have an opportunity cost of the returns available from specialization in other industries—returns which one can be sure will be exploited by competitors. Consequently, it is rational to expect that some specialization will occur (as it does) and that no one firm will have a competitive advantage in all industries (as Tables 1-8, 1-9, and 1-10 show).

It is unclear how the proposed regulatory reforms will mitigate these technological, geographical, and regulatory pressures and constraints, nor is it possible in a free society to dictate to financial statement user groups their preference and selection of auditors.

Furthermore, the reforms will not clearly mark the perimeters of the profession. The *Staff Study* defined the public accounting universe as consisting of services to publicly held companies, but this definition omits the tax and bookkeeping services which constitute the bulk of the small practitioner's business as well as nonpublic and not-for-profit organizations in which the small CPA firm has a relatively larger share of the business.

Through the arbitrary selection of perimeters, a devious reformer can do injustice to the situation as it really exists.

An indication of the fixed costs of a practice offering services to public corporations has been given by the senior partner of Peat, Marwick, Mitchell & Co. (Hanson, 1977: 29):

> The types of expenditures necessary to maintain high quality practice are essentially independent of firm size. These include expenditures for the development of firm policy and procedure on accounting and auditing; liai-

son with FASB, the Auditing Standards Executive Committee, and the SEC; research on policy and practice issues and publication of results; development of staff training materials; and professional libraries. As an illustration, the eight largest auditing firms employed in their national offices (as of March 1976) an average of 40 of their most highly skilled technical partners and management personnel solely to support accounting and auditing technical policy. A firm with 500 to 1,000 partners can support this level of overhead, but a small firm could not afford this commitment of resource. It should be mentioned that smaller firms do not necessarily have lower quality practice because they lack these extensive organizations—rather they benefit by formally and informally sharing the output from the large firms. Of course, if there were no large firms, there would be no output to share.[23]

The area of continuing education is one instance where small firms "share the output" of large firms. A significant component of the fixed costs of a large practice is the development and maintenance of contemporary knowledge and expertise. Price Waterhouse spent over $9 million in 1976 on continuing education and technical services, excluding compensation. The inability of a small firm to develop its own training program could place it at a disadvantage when competing for clients and for recruits. This potential disadvantage was recognized after World War II, and the AICPA became active in professional development, service "... serving as a catalyst to enable local firms, on a cooperative basis, to do what none of them could afford to do alone" (Carey, 1970: 294). Many of the resources needed for the early continuing education programs were donated by the large, national firms (Carey, 1970: 298). The Commission on Auditors' Responsibilities (1977: 87) noted that small firms are still at a disadvantage with respect to training programs. Formal continuing education (mandatory in many states), however, has had the effect of reducing the gap between small and large firms in professional capability and expertise. A recent survey (Kreiser, 1977) found that CPAs would prefer to see the profession adopt a program of required continuing education while users generally preferred a system of required reexamination. Table 1-12 summarizes the preferences of CPAs, financial analysts (CFAs), corporate financial officers (FEIs), and bank loan officers (RMAs) in this regard.

Product Differentiation

Product differentiation is another element of market structure which has potential relevance to the performance of public accounting. Caves (1977: 20) has summarized the significance of this element as follows:

>   Differentiation greatly expands the market strategies open to the producer ... it makes his demand curve less elastic. In reacting to whatever

Table 1-12

CONTINUING EDUCATION PROGRAMS PREFERRED BY CPAS AND USERS

Program	CPA (%)	Total Users (%)	CFA (%)	FEI (%)	RMA (%)
1. Required continuing education	41	15	9	22	11
2. Voluntary continuing education	15	7	7	13	3
3. Required quality review	15	12	8	13	13
4. Required assessment examination	11	23	29	13	28
5. Voluntary continuing education with recognition award	7	10	16	11	7
6. Strict enforcement of the code of ethics	7	9	9	8	9
7. Required minimum score reexamination	2	18	15	13	25
8. Voluntary quality review	2	6	7	7	4
Total	100	100	100	100	100

Source: Kreiser (1977: 435).

change in market conditions may come along, he has less incentive to reduce prices and more incentive to increase them. Another important difference in his behavior arises because he can now react to changing market conditions by changing the traits of his product as well as its price.

The audit product and the standards followed in conducting an audit examination are similar for all CPAs. The audit product can be defined as: "... the probability of detection of material errors and nonconformity with GAAP, given that these conditions exist" (Ng, 1978: 12). There is no evidence that significant differences exist among auditors with respect to either the probability of undetected errors and nonconformity with GAAP or compliance with auditing standards.

Although output and standards might be similar for all firms, the pressure to control costs has resulted in the development of different techniques and audit systems. Examples of such systems are Arthur Anderson's TFA (Transaction Flow Auditing), Coopers and Lybrand's CAAG (Computer Audit Assistance Group), Touche Ross's TRAP (Touche Ross Audit Process) and Deloitte, Haskins & Sells's AuditSCOPE (Audit System of Coordinated Objectives, Procedures and Evaluations). It appears, however, that clients are sensitive to differentiated audit techniques only to the extent that they result in more attractive fees ("Competition," 1978: 92).

An indication of the extent of product differentiation in audit services can be obtained from an analysis of the reasons companies give for chang-

Table 1-13

REASONS FOR AUDITOR CHANGE BY TYPE OF CHANGE[a]

	Prior Auditor Was National Firm		Prior Auditor Was Nonnational Firm		
	New Auditor Is National Firm (%)	New Auditor Is Nonnational Firm (%)	New Auditor Is National Firm (%)	New Auditor Is Nonnational Firm (%)	Total (%)
The auditor's fee was too high	46	83	18	4[b]	47
Investment bankers insisted on a national auditing firm	0	0	39	0[b]	8
Banks or creditors insisted on a national auditing firm	0	0	11	0[b]	2
We disagreed with the auditors on certain accounting matters	16	4	4	1[b]	11
We were not satisfied with the services provided by the auditors	43	48	36	5[b]	44
Management wished to have a national CPA firm	0	0	54	0[b]	11
Merger of our corporation with another corporation	20	4	7	0[b]	14
We wanted the parent corporation and all subsidiaries to have the same auditor	6	0	0	0[b]	3
We felt we might get better service if we rotated auditors	4	0	0	0[b]	2
The former auditors trained their juniors at our expense	0	13	0	0[b]	2
Other reasons	7	9	7	1[b]	8
	(n = 83)	(n = 23)	(n = 28)	(n = 7)	(n = 141)

[a]The percentage in the table exceeds 100% since each respondent was invited to give more than one reason for the auditor change. Percentages are rounded.
[b]This amount is the frequency. Not enough replies were received in this category to compute a meaningful percentage.
Source: Bedingfield and Loeb (1974: 68). Copyright © 1974 by the American Institute of Certified Public Accountants, Inc.

ing auditors. Table 1-13 summarizes the results of a study of auditor changes which occurred between November, 1971 and February, 1973 (Bedingfield and Loeb, 1974: 68). The most frequent reason given by corporations for changing auditors is that the previous auditor's fees were too high. This evidence does not support the contention that there is extensive product differentiation in public accounting which allows auditors to trade on their differentiated "images" to charge abnormally large fees. In fact, our discussion of specialization suggests that if firms do have differentiated images, it is largely because of their ability to provide lower-cost services to particular industries.

The selection of auditors primarily on the basis of fees could increase in the future. For example, an emerging market sector is the auditing of municipalities which receive federal funds. Such governmental units are under strong pressure to accept the lowest bidder for services ("Competition," 1978: 94).

Competition

Is the practice of public accounting competitive? Alternative sources claim that it is becoming increasingly competitive ("Competition," 1978: 88; "Touche Ross," 1976: 20), increasingly uncompetitive (*Staff Study* generally; "Accounting Profession," 1978: 33), or that it is already excessively competitive (Commission on Auditors' Responsibilities, 1977: 106). The Cohen Commission concluded that the pressures of excessive competition led to underreporting of hours worked, underbidding for engagements, and even omitting necessary auditing procedures. The number of corporations switching auditors is increasing and the number of auditors bidding for engagements is increasing ("Competition," 1978: 88).

A recent survey by the Financial Executives Institute found that the average audit fee paid by manufacturing companies fell from 0.40 percent of sales in 1971 to 0.033 percent in 1977 (FEI Studies, 1978: 11). This indicates that purchasers of audit services are receiving more favorable relative prices than they did in the past. The range of audit fees in 1977 is shown in Table 1-14.

The AICPA's decision in 1978 to permit advertising was motivated in part by legal pressure from the Justice Department and the FTC towards greater competitiveness in the profession (Ostlund, 1978). It is interesting to note that part of the reason for the Institute's prohibition of advertising in 1922 was that the Treasury Department indicated its displeasure with the advertising practices of CPAs engaged in tax work (Carey, 1970: 232). At that time, lawyers were also extensively involved in tax practice and it is possible that they felt disadvantaged by the competitive edge advertising gave public accountants.

Charges of anticompetitive practices by large firms have been made by smaller ones. Some of these charges concern the issue of displacement referred to earlier. Other recent charges concern the AICPA's plan of self-regulation, specifically the creation of the "Division of Firms" consisting of an SEC practice section and a private companies' practice section (see AICPA, 1978). A report in the *New York Times* ("Accountants Adopt Self-Regulation," 1977: 57) on an earlier proposal of the self-regulation plan stated:

Table 1-14

RANGE OF AUDIT FEES

	1977	
	Low	*High*
Manufacturing: *(in millions)*		
Under $50	$ 6,000	$ 125,000
$ 50– 99	26,000	200,000
100–249	29,000	462,000
250–499	40,000	782,000
500–999	54,000	1,600,000
Over $1 billion	130,000	10,795,000
Nonmanufacturing: *(in millions)*		
Under $50	2,000	128,000
$ 50– 99	15,000	188,000
100–249	8,000	400,000
250–499	19,000	700,000
500–999	33,000	725,000
Over $1 billion	35,000	5,000,000

Source: *Journal of Accountancy* (1978: 12).

Many small firms objected to the proposal, claiming it created first-class and second-class memberships within the institute. They maintained that the rules for membership in S.E.C. division would be so onerous and costly to comply with that they would, in effect, be prevented from successfully competing for the lucrative business of auditing public companies.

Eighteen members of the AICPA (U.S. House of Representatives, 1978: 222) have taken legal action against the creation of an SEC section, contending

... that sectionalization, as promulgated, will severely restrict the abilities of smaller local and regional CPA firms to secure and retain audits of publicly held companies.

One national non-Big Eight firm stated in Congress (U.S. House of Representatives, 1978: 204) in opposition to the institute's plan that

... it intensifies current excessive concentration of major corporation audits in the so-called big eight ... it will cause an erosion in the practice of small firms and force unwanted mergers with larger organizations.

The net competitive effect of sectionalization, however, is not obvious. Many small firms with no current SEC clients have joined, as have hundreds of sole practitioners (U.S. House of Representatives, 1978: 201). It is possible that they believe membership in the section will enhance their practice with private clients and possibly help them compete for small SEC clients.

The problem between large and small firms is particularly vexing. Although the small firms are complaining about the inordinate power and advantage accruing to the large firms, an argument can be made to the contrary.

In a bifurcated group such as the AICPA, no large member has an incentive to provide more of the collective good, and the distribution of the burden of providing the public good is not in proportion to the benefits conferred by the collective good. Thus, the large firms carry a disproportionate share of the burden. In situations such as this, Olson (1977: 29) observes that "there is a systematic tendency for 'exploitation' of the great by the small."

Elsewhere, this is referred to as a type of "free rider" effect (Stigler, 1974); and certainly any careful observer of the accounting scene can cite innumerable instances in which the large firms have been subsidized, aided, or tyrannized by the small firms and individual practitioners who account for 63 percent of the AICPA suffrage. Carey (1970: 339–373) provides some examples: (1) the initiative for most mergers has come from local firms citing the problems of succession, retirement benefits, escape from administrative work, and so on as reasons; (2) the State of Florida prevented out-of-state firms from establishing offices in Florida because of the "snowbirds"—the invasion of solo Northern accountants who combine a holiday in the sun with the practice of accounting in Florida for four or five months a year; (3) local practitioners have dominated the state societies and resisted efforts to implement a "common membership" plan with the Institute. Others include the resistance of small firms to elimination of the experience requirement, to specialization, and to many other Institute initiatives.

Finally, even though employment in the largest ten firms increased from 2,950 to 11,850—a 401 percent increase in the twenty-year period from 1946 to 1966—employment among the small firms in the same period rose from 11,828 to 82,434—an increase of 462 percent (Carey, 1969). The small accounting firm does not appear to be suffering.

The Performance of Public Accounting

The structure and conduct of an industry have importance in economic analysis primarily to the extent that they are related to the performance of that industry. It is not enough merely to say that some structural elements are undesirable and should be changed. Valid reform should be grounded on:

1. Evidence that some aspects of performance are incongruent with broadly accepted norms of social welfare
2. Evidence that those performance shortfalls are related to certain elements of that industry's structure and conduct
3. Evidence that the existing market, judicial, and legislative forces are inadequate in achieving desired industry performance
4. Evidence that the proposed reforms will achieve the desired outcome in a benefit-effective way

Performance has been described as "our normative appraisal of the social quality of the allocation of resources that results from a market's conduct" (Caves, 1977: 14).

The performance of an industry or an aggregation of industries (economy) is a multidimensional construct. Some dimensions may be conflicting; the relative weights given to each dimension in evaluating overall performance may vary over time and between evaluators. Nevertheless, the following dimensions of performance are generally thought to define the economic welfare space, and any valid rationale for regulatory intervention in an industry would have to be made in terms of them.

Efficiency

Efficiency requires the utilization of factors of production so that they yield the highest possible real income. Efficiency is indicated by movements from Pareto-inferior to Pareto-optimal positions, where production of a good or service can only be increased at the expense of foregone production of other goods or services.

A distinction is sometimes made between *allocative efficiency*, which requires that resources can move freely within an economy so that a "normal" rate of return prevails in each industry, and *technical efficiency*, which requires that all resources and production economies be fully utilized.

Are CPAs earning abnormally higher returns? (If so, what is preventing the abnormal returns from being competed away?) The *Staff Study* did not question the reasonableness of partners' income, but it did attempt to show that partners had a large financial stake in the status quo. The *Study* estimated that the net profit margins of Big Eight firms are in the range of 25 percent, while average CPA partnerships are 40 percent and sole proprietorships are 50 percent (1977: 46–47). Table 1-15 shows profits on business receipts for partnerships and proprietorships in selected occupations for 1971,

Table 1-15

PROFITS ON BUSINESS RECEIPTS (%) FOR SELECTED BUSINESS PROFESSIONS—
PARTNERSHIPS AND PROPRIETORSHIPS

Profession/ Business	1971		1972		1974–75	
	Partner-ship	Proprietor-ship	Partner-ship	Proprietor-ship	Partner-ship	Proprietor-ship
CPA practice	28.50	45.19	29.63	47.41	28.41	47.11
Engineering, architecture	20.25	33.38	19.32	34.65	16.51	33.08
Law	52.75	53.11	52.88	54.12	50.54	51.21
Insurance brokerage	26.49	42.45	28.80	42.74	15.06	41.26
Physician and surgeon	55.43	59.86	50.15	58.65	48.34	53.33
Other medical		44.56		44.02		39.08
Security brokerage	19.87		30.55		2.94	
Real estate brokerage	15.30	38.07	11.36	41.72	(4.75)	36.68

Source: Dun & Bradstreet (1975, 1976, 1978).

1972, and 1974–75. These figures are reasonably consistent with the *Staff Study*'s estimates. The margins for CPAs are well below those for lawyers, physicians, and surgeons.

By themselves, these profit margins give no indication of return on investment, which is the relevant consideration in assessing resource allocation. Information on resources invested in public accounting is not available. Even if such information were available, the omission of human capital from the investment base would make comparisons difficult. The *Staff Study* gave no evidence of abnormal returns or of blockaded entry into the profession.

In addition, conventional return and profit measures take no account of the value of services provided voluntarily by the profession for government, community organizations, and public interest groups. In 1977, ten large firms performed a comprehensive review and audit of ACTION, the federal government's volunteer service agency ("White House," 1977: 36). The donated services were estimated to cost the firms $250,000. Free services have also been provided to the government administration in developing budget systems and designing reorganization plans. Acting in groups (such as Accountants for the Public Interest) and individually, accountants have provided valuable services for parent-teacher associations, antipoverty groups, legal aid associations, and environmental groups ("Accountants Join," 1978: 24).

Competence

The *Staff Study* (1977: 67) claimed that "many examples of improper, faulty, and incomplete accounting and auditing practices have been brought to public attention." In countering this criticism, the profession has argued that its auditing and accounting standards are the highest in the world, and certainly higher than those in countries where standards are set by governmental bodies (Hanson, 1977: 3–5). In addition, many of the problem areas discussed by the *Staff Study* have already been dealt with by the profession. After reviewing the record of the federal government in setting accounting and auditing standards, Hanson (1977: 45) concludes:

> In short, there is little or no evidence that the Federal government would or could do a more effective job in the establishment of accounting and auditing standards, even if it were a legitimate government function. In fact, there is substantial evidence to the contrary.

Federalization of standard setting is already complete in the minds of some. The *Congressional Record* of September 23, 1975, shows that one congressman referred to the FASB as the Federal Accounting Standards Board. He explained to his less well-informed colleagues that the FASB is the board which develops accounting standards, and these standards are then submitted to the SEC, which publishes them (cited in Sprouse, 1976: 26).

The existence of accounting alternatives is seen by the *Staff Study* as evidence of incompetence. Yet the issues of accounting for investment tax credits and oil and gas exploration costs are examples of government intervention overturning the profession's uniform solutions and permitting alternative treatments.

Independence

The *Staff Study* (1977: 7) observed that

> the most important requirement of independent auditors is that they be regarded by the public as truly independent from the interests of their clients.

Carey (1970: 175) hypothesizes that the term "independent auditor" was originally used in the sense of "independent contractor," simply to indicate that the auditor was not an employee of the client. Since then, the term has accumulated numerous connotations and is taken by some to mean that the auditors' value and incentive system should be at least orthogonal to their clients' and, preferably, diametrically opposed.

Although the abstract concept of independence is universally supported, it can only be evaluated by looking at decisions made by auditors in particular choices that arise in day-to-day practice. In *Accounting Series Release No. 126* (1972), the SEC gave thirty-nine illustrations of situations in which an auditor may or may not be independent. For example:

> From the books or original entry, client personnel prepared printed tapes that could be read on an optical scanner and sent the tapes to the accountant's office. The accountants forwarded the tapes to a service bureau. The accountants received the print-outs of the financial statements and general ledgers and sent them to the client. The accountants did not edit the input data prior to transmission to the service bureau. The accountants provided this service in addition to the audit.

One study (Lavin, 1976) obtained judgments from CPAs, bank loan officers, and financial analysts on the independence of auditors in these situations. The study found that judgments of independence of financial statement users agreed more with the CPAs and with AICPA ethics than they did with the SEC, indicating that the SEC may be misperceiving users' opinions.

Critics argue that independence of auditors is impaired by the performance of management advisory services (MAS) for corporations and government agencies and by the presentation of arguments on current issues in taxation, accounting and regulation. The *Staff Study* (1977: 52) claimed that positions taken by CPAs on these issues are primarily directed at advancing the interests of clients. The managing partner of Touche Ross ("Touche Ross," 1976: 20) has been reported as indirectly lending some support of this claim:

> As a young firm, Touche Ross has tried to make a virtue of its relative paucity of old-line clients. Without stable utility companies clients, the firm is building a specialty of doing rate studies for regulatory commissions, in 16 states thus far. "We don't have the conflicts of interest," Mr. Palmer said.

Although it is frequently asserted in general terms that MAS impairs auditors' independence, the Cohen Commission was able to find only four cases where specific allegations have been made (Yale Express, National Student Marketing, the "Wall Street Back Office Mess," and Westec). The Commission concluded (1977: 95) that in the first three cases, its analysis ". . . does not support the conclusions that other services weakened the audit function." In the case of Westec, the criticized service was "... an unavoidable part of the audit function. It is certainly not in the category of peripheral services" (1977: 96).

Some legislation has the effect of encouraging the provisions of MAS by auditors. For example, the Foreign Corrupt Practices Act requires that corporations devise and maintain a system of internal accounting controls sufficient to provide reasonable assurances that certain specified control objectives are met. The objectives are taken from the AICPA's *Statement on Auditing Standards No. 1.* Reviews of internal control currently made in conjunction with annual audits do not necessarily satisfy the provisions of the act. It is unreasonable to expect that CPAs will provide some additional services to management in facilitating compliance with the act.

Although the profession has been able to defend itself successfully on factual grounds against most charges of lack of independence, it has come to recognize that public perceptions of independence are often unrelated to the substance of the matter. Consequently, the AICPA (1978) has taken a number of steps to provide independence in appearance as well as in fact for auditors of public companies. These steps include encouraging the formation of corporate audit committees, auditor attendance at shareholder meetings, greater disclosure of fees received from clients, rotation of partners in charge of audits, and limitations on the types of MAS offered.

Auditing as a Public Good

The consumption of a public good by one person does not reduce the amount available for consumption by others. A free market system cannot adequately allocate resources to the production of public goods for two reasons. First, since it costs no more to supply additional consumers, production tends to devolve into a monopoly. Second, consumers have incentives to understate their real desire for the goods: they can be "free riders" if someone else pays the costs of production. Consequently, a suboptimal amount of public goods will be produced. The regulatory solution is to produce goods by public enterprise and to allocate costs to all beneficiaries (for example, through taxation.)

The *Staff Study* refers to accounting and auditing standards and the practice of auditing as public goods. It implies that Congress largely created the demand for auditing, that these services are properly performed by the public sector, but because of various historical aberrations they were temporarily delegated to the private sector. For example, the *Study's* (1977: v) major finding, according to the letter of transmittal is:

> the extraordinary manner in which the SEC has insisted upon delegating its public authority and responsibilities on accounting matters to private groups with obvious self-interests in the resolution of such matters.

Again, the *Study* (1977: 8) states:

> It appears that the "Big Eight" firms are more concerned with serving the interests of corporate managements who select them and authorize their fees than with protecting the interests of the public, for whose benefit Congress established the position of independent auditor.

Some within the profession (Loebbecke, 1972: 3) have acknowledged their delicate position:

> Public accounting as it is known today was the direct result of legislation—that is, the Securities Acts of 1933 and 1934. Birth by legislation implies the possibility of death by legislation.

On the other hand, Watts and Zimmerman (1979: 11) give evidence

> ... that the development of the auditing firm was a market phenomenon, not one induced by regulation.

In the United Kingdom and the United States (Hunt, 1935: 454):

> ... practice has generally outrun legal minima. The stiffening of the requirements over the years has, in fact, merely translated into statute the best of current professional practice.

Carey (1969: 58) states that many companies engaged independent auditors long before it became mandatory. Agency theory has been utilized to show that it is rational both for shareholders voluntarily to incur auditing costs and for managers voluntarily to contract to accept audits and to act in the owners' interests.[24]

Even though there is historical evidence and theoretical justification for the voluntary incurrence of auditing costs, auditing does appear to have some characteristics of a public good. Everyone in society shares the output of an audit (defined by Ng [1978: 12] as "the probability of detection of material errors and non-conformity with GAAP, given that these conditions exist"). Consequently, mandatory auditing may possibly be justified on the grounds that otherwise actual and potential stockholders would not be willing to pay for audit costs, even though the benefits of the audit may exceed the cost.

The foregoing examination of the structure, conduct, and performance of the public accounting profession leads us to the conclusion that the criticisms made during the congressional inquiries are largely unfounded, or at least unproven. Even if some criticisms were justified, however, it would be necessary to establish that the proposed regulation would be effective in achieving a net improvement in social welfare, however defined. The effectiveness of regulation will now be briefly examined.

Part IV — Regulatory Effectiveness

Market Failure vs. Regulatory Failure

The justification for many regulatory interventions rests on the existence of market failures which prevent efficient and equitable free market solutions to resource allocation problems. It has become evident, however, that the regulatory process itself has inherent weaknesses and often causes a different class of failures. Some of the particular regulatory failures that have been observed are:

1. *The "zero-cost" phenomena.* Regulators do not bear the costs of their failures. If a party charged by an agency with violations is acquitted, the agency is not liable for that party's costs or for any damage to its reputation. Stigler (1975: 171) suggests that:

> at a minimum, the regulatory agency should be required to reimburse direct expenses after every acquittal and insert a quarter page ad in 10 national newspapers and magazines withdrawing all accusations with apology. This practice should, of course, be associated with an increase in agency appropriations—the purpose of the scheme is to place the cost of error on the society rather than on the victim. Error is inevitable, but regulators should be given incentives to minimize it.

Consequently, parties charged by regulators may see little to be gained from exercising their legal rights and may tend to enter into consent agreements more readily than they otherwise would. This *de facto* deprivation of rights is discussed further below.

2. *Regulatory lag or nonfeasance.* An effect of such regulation is the deferral of change. These delays are thought by some to be desirable from an equity standpoint. Nevertheless, the time lags have costs. For example, disabilities caused by the premature clearance of some drugs by the FDA must be balanced against illness prolonged by delays in the clearance of other drugs. Delays in rate-of-return regulation during periods of inflation can cause prices to constantly lag behind costs, resulting in supply shortages which have forced the FPC (for example) to extend its activities into rationing as well as pricing (Joskow, 1975: 55).

3. *"The regulatory trap."* This phrase refers to the difficulties of effecting deregulation. Frequently, regulated firms and their employees fear the up-

heavals that would result if a free market were restored. Even if regulated firms are receiving returns at or below the competitive level, anticipated transitional costs and capital losses could be sufficiently high as to make them resist deregulation.

4. *"Tar baby effect."* The tendency of regulation continually to expand its scope has been described by Joskow (1975: 57) as follows:

> A regulatory agency may attempt to implement some policy using a particular regulatory instrument, but the effect of the application of the instrument is not what is expected or is undesirable in terms of some other objective of the regulatory commission. The agency then tries to correct its initial inadequacy or mistake by extending its regulations to other aspects of firm or industry behavior or even to other industries ... Regulating competitive market structures is like trying to plug a leaky dike. The hand of regulation plugs up one hole only to find that a leak springs up somewhere else. Regulation in the U.S. often seems to be at least one leak behind.

The SEC's involvement in accounting and auditing matters is ancillary to its primary objectives of protecting investors from losses caused by fraud, unfair competition, unethical behavior, and effecting the proper functioning of capital markets. It is relevant to consider whether in fact the SEC has been successful in meeting its objectives, or whether its performance indicates the presence of regulatory failure.

Stigler's (1964: 124) conclusion from his analysis of the performance of securities markets before and after the 1933 and 1934 acts is:

> These studies suggest that the SEC registration requirements had no important effect on the quality of new securities sold to the public ...
> ... grave doubts exist whether, if account is taken of costs of regulation, the SEC has saved the purchasers of new issues one dollar.

A former chairman of the SEC, Roderick Hills, acknowledged ("SEC Seeks," 1976: 5) that:

> while the SEC's regulatory efforts have proven their value ... I cannot easily dismiss the conclusion of Professor George Stigler that "the SEC did not (in over 30 years of effort) appreciably improve the experience of investors in the new issues market by its expensive review of prospectuses."

Another empirical study, by Benston, found that the Securities Acts had no effect on security returns or the amount of risk faced by investors, and that the acts may have had a perverse effect on the financing of capital expenditures (Benston, 1973; see Gonedes and Dopuch, 1974, for an extensive criticism of Benston's study). In a later study comparing a private system of disclosure regulation (as in the United Kingdom) to the regulation activities of the SEC, Benston (1976: 497) concluded:

> the evidence reviewed provides little reason to believe that the U.S. system gives the public greater benefits, on the whole, than does the U.K. system. The cost of the U.S. system, though, appears considerably greater. On balance then, there is little (if any) evidence that the disclosure regulations promulgated by the SEC provide a benefit, net of costs, to the public.

In addition, there is some indication that the SEC has tended to expand its activities. The Commission has become less a repository and coordinator of publicly available information and more the authority which determines what information should be disclosed and the form that information should take. Increasingly, the purpose of new disclosure regulations is not only to aid investor decision making, but also to influence the conduct of corporate management. For example, the Foreign Corrupt Practices Act of 1977 uses accounting disclosures and auditing requirements to discourage certain payments to foreign officials to obtain or retain foreign business. Another example is provided by the congressional hearings in 1975 on the extent to which banks should be required to report loans made for certain "national priority" areas (such as small business, farming, etc.), with the purpose of "influencing loan allocations to those areas" (" 'Sample' of Banks to File Loan Data, House Panel Decides," 1975: 13).

The expansion of the SEC's domain has a type of "reverse capture" effect where the agency is able to impose its own values on industry and to reduce the likelihood that firms will challenge its legitimacy. Manne (1974) has described how difficult it is to be a successful securities lawyer without a friendly, noncritical relationship with the SEC. The necessity for firms to maintain favorable relations with the regulator can result in a *de facto* surrender of rights by the regulated firms. An instance of this effect of regulation is given by the senior partner of Peat, Marwick, Mitchell, when he explained ("When the Auditor Gets Audited," 1975: S3, 1): why his firm settled with the SEC over charges of auditing deficiencies:

> More and more ... we saw that you cannot, so to speak, fight with mother. We have day to day relations with the SEC, and we cannot fight with it with one hand while dealing with it operationally on the other.

Although the public interest initiatives represented by the "new" regulation in accounting are largely cast in economic terms, it seems clear that the initiatives will not stand or fall on the results of economic analysis alone, but will ultimately be adjudicated in the political arena.

Two themes which emerge from the congressional inquiries and the regulation literature are the importance of due process and procedural fairness to the legitimacy of economic decision making, and the apparent distrust of the pursuit of private interest to maximize public welfare. The intellectual successors of Adam Smith, while individually prominent, appear to play a relatively minor role in shaping the collective expectations of the public or the private economic sectors.

A recent study of regulatory behavior (Owen and Braetigam, 1978) argues that regulatory agencies interpose norms of procedural fairness and due process between abrupt, impersonal market forces and individuals who are generally risk averse and whose adaptation to change is not instantaneous. Further, it is rational for individuals to pay considerable costs, in terms of lost efficiency, for this procedural fairness. A major effect of regulation "... is to attenuate the rate at which market and technological forces impose changes on individual economic agents" (Owen and Braetigam, 1978: 1). Regulation gives individuals equity rights in the status quo. All affected parties are entitled to delay change and to have their "day in court" to argue for or against change. As economic survival is one measure of the fairness of a system and because of the administrative and judicial norms of fairness, regulatory policies shield individuals from losses and give them greater leverage when losses do occur than a free market system would. The critical issues, from Owen and Braetigam's perspective, are whether in fact regulation does reduce risk and increase economic security and justice, and whether the costs in terms of lost efficiency are acceptable.

Without attempting to evaluate the merits of alternative economic paradigms, it is reasonable to suggest that the public accounting profession and the FASB, as private bodies whose decisions are perceived to have broad economic impacts, be receptive to the signals transmitted by a social norm which can be characterized as being "public interest/equity" oriented rather than "private interest/freedom" oriented.

The major implications of this orientation are:

1. The process of accounting and auditing standard setting must be open, with emphasis on due process and procedural fairness. This will not guarantee that the right decisions are made, but it will guarantee that decisions are made in the right way. The Cohen Commission (1977: 134) recognized that participation by outsiders in setting standards requires not only granting them the right to observe and the right to present their views, but also the right to directly influence decision outcomes.

2. The profession has incentives to maintain the legitimacy of standard setting by the private sector. Given these incentives, the criteria for evaluating standards are primarily (a) whether the standard will be accepted by the interest groups it affects, (b) whether the standard is consistent with public policy objectives, and (c) whether it increases, or at least does not reduce,

the probability that legitimacy will be maintained in the future. Because these criteria require estimates of the future, it is logical that policy should be consequence oriented. There is a growing recognition of the importance of impact analysis in deciding accounting policy, and the literature reviewed in this chapter reinforces the need for such analysis (for a fuller examination of the social consequences of accounting policy, see the American Accounting Association, 1977).

Moreover, the types of consequences that appear to be crucial for policy acceptance are equity impacts rather than efficiency impacts. The regulation literature suggests that society is prepared to pay significant costs in terms of lost efficiencies to maintain perceived equity levels. Nor are only equity impacts important. Wilson (1974: 139) suggests that, politically, individuals are more sensitive to impacts involving decreases in equity rather than increases. That is, individuals are more threat oriented than opportunity oriented. Since economic survival is an important gauge of equity, policies which are perceived to have negative impacts on the income and financial position of cohesive, influential constituent groups can be expected to meet with opposition. FASB 19 is an example of such a policy, where (Solomons, 1978: 68):

> there can be little doubt that the Securities and Exchange Commission would not have acted as it did at the end of August to overrule this standard if there had not been political pressure from certain oil and gas companies which felt that they would be injured by the mandatory use of the "successful efforts" method of costing.

Important functions of accounting research are to provide policy makers with assistance in estimating the probable impacts of policy alternatives, both in real and nominal terms; to assess the probable reaction of users, suppliers, and government agencies; and to assess the probable feedback effects on the policy-setting body. For example, Hicks (1978), Newton (1978), and Sharp (1978) draw on the sociological literature dealing with the diffusion of innovation to predict or explain the pattern of responses to various accounting policies. Abraham (1978) utilizes a variety of futures research methodologies to identify and prioritize the problems facing the profession.

3. The profession should attempt to educate external groups in the consequences of accounting policies, so that the efficiency costs of satisfying equity constraints can be reduced. For example, policy proposals might be objected to by a firm because it anticipates that the accounting numbers reported in compliance with the proposal would invoke negative stock

market reaction. Security price research might indicate that there are no grounds for anticipating a negative reaction. The purpose of this education should be to remove misperceptions of impacts so that resources will not be unnecessarily consumed in circumventing what can more readily be surmounted.

4. The profession and the FASB, as private sector groups, should identify the areas where they have a competitive advantage over public regulatory agencies, and maximize their advantages in those areas. Some possible areas are flexibility, proximity to suppliers and users of financial information, sensitivity to their needs, the ability quickly to identify emerging "hot spots," the ability to discard outmoded policies, and the ability to admit and rectify mistakes.

5. To eliminate the loss to investors as a public policy issue, the large accounting firms should consider the feasibility of insuring investors to the extent of actual losses incurred as a result of audit failures.

6. Large and small accounting firms are really not in the same profession, and considerable controversy could be avoided by having two professions. For lack of better words, the large firms should be members of the *auditing profession* because their chief occupation is auditing, while the small firms should be in the *accounting profession* because their chief occupation is bookkeeping and write-up services. The current divisions of firms is only a partial solution to the bifurcation within the profession as it is now defined.

While admitting to the current overriding concern with equity or fairness we are reminded of the words of Milton Friedman (1977: 4) who, in commenting on the inevitable tension between fairness and freedom, wrote that "when 'fairness' replaces 'freedom,' all our liberties are in danger." He points out that there is no mention of fairness in the Declaration of Independence, the Constitution, or the Bill of Rights.

If it is correct to observe that society appears to accept considerable restrictions on private interests and free markets in order to enhance equity and security, the crucial issue is, what are the limits of those restrictions? It is well to bear in mind the comment of Edward Gibbon on the fall of Athenian democracy:

> In the end they valued security more than they valued freedom, and they lost both.

But that message is for another time and another place.

Notes

1. This law conveyed the title of "certified public accountant" upon qualified persons and provided use of that title by others (Carey, 1969: 44). It also restricted the practice of public accounting to those licensed. Similar legislation was swiftly adopted in other states, notably Pennsylvania (1899), Maryland (1900), California (1901), Illinois (1903), Washington (1903), New Jersey (1904), Florida (1905), and Michigan (1906). According to Wilson (1974: 142) over seventy-five occupations in the United States require state licenses, an average of twenty-five such laws per state.

2. Elsewhere, Rep. John E. Moss referred to the accounting profession as an "oligopoly" (*Wall Street Journal*, January 31, 1978, p. 33). For reports of the Senate Subcommittee study (known as the "Metcalf Report" after its late chairman, Lee Metcalf of Montana), see *Accounting*, April, 1977, p. 51, an article entitled "How the 'Big Eight' Firms Control the Accounting Establishment"; also "Senate Committee Report Blasts Accounting Industry: Self Reforms Urged or Legislation May Be Needed" in *Business Week*, January 31, 1977, p. 76; and the profession's response in "Accounting Firms Challenge Senate Accusations of Large Firms Controlling Market," *New York Times*, April 1, 1977, p. D1.

3. See "Accountants Adopt Self-Regulation in Revamping Plan," *New York Times*, September 19, 1977, p. L57; and "Rep. John Moss Assails Self-Regulation Plan for Accountants," *New York Times*, September 15, 1977, p. D1. See also "AICPA Attempts to Regulate CPAs in order to Forestall Government, Especially SEC, Regulation," in *Daily News*, August 8, 1978, p. 12.

4. See "SEC to Push for Independence, Self-Regulation of Accounting Firms," *Wall Street Journal*, June 14, 1977, p. 10; also "SEC Wants to Give Accountants Year to 'Reform' Profession," *Daily News*, July 6, 1977, p. 12; and for a summary of the SEC's first annual report of the self-regulation effort in accounting, see "Details of SEC's Report on Accounting Profession," *New York Times*, July 11, 1973, p. D4.

5. The AICPA's mandatory peer review program is reported in *New York Times*, June 20, 1978, p. D7.

6. See "American Institute of CPAs Votes to Permit Advertising," *Advertising Age*, April 17, 1978, p. 4; "CPA Advertising Okayed," *Business Week*, April 24, 1978, p. 38; "Big 8 Accounting Firms Begin Ad Campaigns after 50 Year Ban on CPA Advertising," *Business Week*, May 15, 1978, p. 106. Also "How CPAs Sell Themselves," *New York Times*, September 25, 1977, p. F1. This follows the trend in other professions: "American Bar Association Clears TV Advertising for Attorneys," *Advertising Age*, August 14, 1978, p. 3; "National Society of Engineers Amends Its Ethical Code to Allow Competitive Bidding and Advertising," *Engineering News-Record*, August 10, 1978, p. 15; also *Advertising Age*, July 3, 1978, p. 23, regarding advertising by architects.

7. The results of a survey on why 293 companies changed their auditing firm are reported in *Journal of Corporate Action* 1 (1977): 51.

8. For a discussion of some of the "public interest" issues involved, see "Should CPAs be Management Consultants?", *Business Week*, April 18, 1977, p. 70.

9. See "Deliberate Management Fraud Hard to Detect by CPAs; Audit to Catch All Would Be Too Expensive," *Accounting*, May, 1977, p. 25; and "Social Trend Seems to Be Developing to Hold Auditors Responsible for Uncovering Corporate Fraud," *Accounting*, July 1977, p. 29. See also "Recent Fraud Cases Leave Lawyers and Accountants Vulnerable," *Wall Street Journal*, July 9, 1975, p. 1. Also "Accounting Profession Issues Formal Standards on How Auditors Should Deal with Illegal Acts by Client Companies," *Wall Street Journal*, January 31, 1977, p. 8.

10. Also see the discussion in "Some Experts Contend Accounting Profession Needs Further Changes," *Wall Street Journal*, February 2, 1978, p. 22.

11. HR 13175, the "Public Accounting Regulatory Act," introduced on June 16, 1978, by Congressmen Moss, Waxman, Gore, and Moffett. The legislative proposal is summarized in *American Banker*, June 16, 1978, p. 2.

12. See an account of the SEC's action on oil and gas accounting in the *Wall Street Journal*, August 30, 1978, p. 8.

13. For a summary of the SEC's first annual report on the profession, see the *New York Times*, July 11, 1978, p. D4.

14. See the report in the *New York Times*, March 25, 1977, titled "Accounting Inquiry Is Set by FTC on State Anticompetitive Practices." Also "FTC and Justice Department Apply Antitrust Laws to Professionals," *Wall Street Journal*, August 7, 1975, p. 1; and Arthur Andersen & Co.'s annual report, August 31, 1977, p. 9.

15. See U.S. Congress, 1978: 343–349.

16. Eli Mason is managing partner of Mason & Co., an accounting firm based in New York City. He was formerly a vice president of AICPA, president of the New York Society of CPAs, and now serves on the board of directors of the AICPA. Eli Mason is part of the "Group of 18" AICPA members who have brought a proceeding against the AICPA to challenge the "Division of Firms."

17. Harris, Kerr, Forster & Co. can be described as a regional CPA firm with twenty-seven offices and ninety partners in the United States.

18. Remarks of Joseph A. Califano, Jr., Secretary of Health Education and Welfare, commencement exercises, the University of Michigan, Ann Arbor, Michigan, Sunday, December 18, 1977.

19. *Penguin Dictionary of Quotations* (Harmondsworth: Penguin Books, 1960), p. 332. Another source attributes the remark to Georges Clemenceau (1886): "La guerre! C'est un chose trop grave pour la confier à des militaires," *A Book of French Quotations* (New York: Doubleday, 1963), p. 332.

20. For a discussion of this and other theories of economic regulation, see Posner (1974), Joskow (1975).

21. Briloff's statement before the Metcalf Subcommittee in U.S. Senate (1977: 1609). Also his books, *Unaccountable Accounting* (New York: Harper & Row, 1972); and *More Debits than Credits* (New York: Harper & Row, 1976).

22. Stanton & Gilling (1977: 8–11):

> The Gini coefficient has been used to provide an index of the relative dimensions of each structure. This index of dispersion has the extreme value of zero when all firms are of equal size and with increasing size inequality the coefficient value approaches united. The values are broadly similar between countries and they confirm a tendency towards a high degree of size inequality when all auditors in each country are taken into account.
>
> A composity concentration measure reflecting both aspects of market power and size distribution was calculated using the Herfindahl Index . . . The index reaches its maximum value of unity in the case of pure monopoly. In general, its value declines towards zero with an increase in the number of firms and a decrease in inequality between firms in the market. The values for all countries are relative low . . .
>
> The reciprocal of the Herfindahl Index [is] the 'numbers equivalent.' It can be interpreted as the number of equal sized firms in the profession which can generate a specific Herfindahl value. . . . The values suggest that in terms of an effective competitive impact there are relatively few firms in the profession when compared with the actual number of auditing firms.

23. At the other end of the scale, a recent study (Fay, 1976) found that the minimum capital recommended for the establishment of a new practice was $10,000 plus ample funds for living expenses for two years.

24. For a discussion of "agency theory," see Ng (1978) and Watts and Zimmerman (1979).

2

Structural Theory and the Accounting Profession

Michael E. Granfield

Associate Professor of Business Economics
Graduate School of Management,
University of California, Los Angeles

In analyzing the current status of the structural theory of industry/firm performance, I feel like a monetarist discussing the causes and cures for domestic and international inflation before a convention of Keynesians. From an intellectual perspective, all the advantages would seem to be mine: After twenty-five years of vigorous debate and innumerable empirical studies, the collective weight of theory and evidence clearly supports the monetarists. Despite this firm intellectual grounding, however, I am extremely pessimistic about predicting any real possibility for curbing U.S. inflation in the near future. The obvious reason for my pessimism is that the challenge has moved from that of economic ignorance and political instability to one of pure "political will." For the United States, the situation is particularly grim; after thirty-nine months of continued vigorous economic recovery, inflation is still running in excess of 13 percent per year ("Inflation Hits," 1979). More critically, the size of the budget deficit, a key causal factor in our inflationary difficulties because of its impact on accommodative monetary expansion, is already projected to be in excess of $40 billion, with new programs such as welfare reform and an MX mobile missile system (in exchange for a Salt II treaty) likely to push the ultimate deficit above $60 billion for fiscal year 1980 ("Inflation Remains," 1979). In short, curbing inflation has become a purely political problem which, despite the warnings of Proposition 13 in California and the balanced budget forces, has not yet engendered a sufficiently strong consensus to reverse previous trends.[1]

Similarly, structural theory remains a viable political and legal force even though its intellectual base has eroded over the last decade because of the failure of its predictions to come true and the shallowness of its basic causal factors. The structural approach to firm performance continues to exert its influence in proposed legislation, such as the Kennedy conglomerate merger bill, and in the legal arena, such as the FTC's "shared monopoly" case against the three leading ready-to-eat cereal manufacturers. Therefore, it would be naive and foolishly sanguine to ignore the potentially harmful application of structural theory as it applies to a given industry or set of select industries.

What Is Structural Theory?

Although structural theory is easy to describe and is testable empirically, it is not a theory in the sense that it was arrived at by a logical set of interlocking assumptions. Rather, it was and is the product of an *ad hoc* construction based upon certain perceived empirical relationships. The structual approach is much like the proverbial chameleon in that it has changed its complexion and complexity to accommodate its critics while attempting to remain a credible force for public policy.

Briefly put, "structural theory" contends that we can determine whether the firms in a given industry are acting in a competitive or collusive manner over any extended period of time by concentrating not on the dynamic processes of competition or collusion, but rather on certain parameters of the industry itself, such as its concentration ratio together with the alleged existence and level of barriers to entry.

For example, an industry characterized by: (1) a concentration ratio in excess of 70 percent; (2) an average weighted rate of return (net income to net worth) in excess of 15 percent; and (3) no successful entry over the last five years which would imply potentially significant barriers to entry, would be accused of having experienced these profit results due to successful tacit collusion. Furthermore, it would have protected said returns via certain offensive and defensive actions which cumulatively and artificially raise entry barriers or costs. Such an industry should be regarded as a *per se* violator of U.S. antitrust policy (as, for example, contained in Section 1 of the Sherman Act) and should be a prime candidate for such remedies as divestiture, mandatory licensing of trademarks, and other sanctions.

Political and Economic Origins of Structural Theory

Economic History

Given the obvious popularity and impact of the structural approach, it must be at least partially grounded in some perceived base of historical facts that reveal the kinds of abuses likely to stem from industries dominated by large corporations. Although large, privately held corporations are a familiar fact of American industry today, this was not the case as recently as a century ago. Between 1880 and 1910, however, American industry began to take the form that we see today, due in part to: (1) the growth of combinations or trusts which tended to dominate certain industries, such as the Standard Oil Trust, the Tobacco Trust, and the Gunpowder Trust; (2) the decline of transportation costs as a barrier to regional expansion, which permitted the first quasinational markets to emerge; (3) increasing use of the corporate form of organization with the concomitant issuing of public stock offerings; (4) a significant merger movement in many major industries as firms sought to take advantage of various economies of production, shipping, and distribution; (5) rapid entry and exit from industries where successful competitors grew and the unsuccessful exited—but often to reappear under another banner (Clark and Clark, 1901).

Accompanying this rapid industrial growth and formation of large firms were various commercial practices. Some constituted obvious abuses by being anticompetitive in nature; others were obviously procompetitive. In addition, a plethora of more complex arrangements emerged which are still not fully understood.

Some real abuses were: (1) innumerable attempts and certain successes at formal collusion; (2) use of political power or influence to generate complete or partial monopolies via the generation of tariffs, nontariff barriers, exclusive transportation franchises, and so on; and (3) sporadic employment of such devices as predatory price wars, tie-in contracts, exclusionary trading, and so on (Clark and Clark, 1901).

Potential pervasive abuses that did *not* occur were: (1) wide-scale employment of predatory price cutting; (2) erection of successful barriers to entry; (3) persistence of dominant market shares; and (4) persistence of supranormal profits over any extended period of time (Kirkland, 1961).

In addition, the period was characterized by wide divergences in macroeconomic activity, with growth rates varying from +10 percent to −5 percent, as revealed by at least three major recessions and perhaps as many as five (Kirkland, 1961). A major alleged cause of these recessions was the large stock frauds perpetrated on the public by these newly established national corporations. Subsequent investigations, though, have revealed that despite certain notorious scandals, most stock offerings were fairly presented and, more to the point, the fluctuations in economic activity can be more accurately traced to errors in monetary policy (Friedman and Schwartz, 1964).

Nonetheless, despite historical and empirical evidence to the contrary, a "dominant" folklore or mythology arose regarding the formation, growth, and dominance of large "robber baron" firms allegedly characterized by the following behavior patterns: (1) employment of predatory price cutting as a key instrument in eliminating smaller competitors (known today as the "deep pocket" theory); (2) blockading of entry for small firms by the erection of real and artificial barriers to entry; (3) use of stock manipulations to enrich a small number of owner entrepreneurs at the expense of the general public, both directly and indirectly as the by-product of business recessions; (4) use of interlocking directorates and other devices to promote long-term collusive agreements, particularly of a price-fixing nature; (5) manipulation of the political mechanism essentially to exclude competitors and thereby insulate gains; (6) avoidance of accountability, either to the voters through their representatives or to the courts through adjudication procedures.

As stated previously, there was undoubtedly some anecdotal evidence for most of these beliefs; the practices, however, did not seem to be pervasive, nor did the underlying dynamic nature of the U.S. economy at the time (or perhaps at any time subsequent) allow the practices to succeed for any extended period. Yet this system of beliefs, it is argued, formed the foundation for modern views of today's large corporation and its behavior and therefore, in at least a political context, must be countered.

Economics Theory

Although many scholars in the history of economic thought are prone to trace the current roots of economic thinking back to the ancient Chinese or even further, this author will follow the tradition of Joseph Spengler in limiting it to those authors who seem to effect policy at the time of their writings or just subsequent to this period. I will also limit myself to those authors who had the most *subjective* impact on the development of the structural theory.

Alfred Marshall. Although entry barriers were apparently hinted at by Adam Smith, Alfred Marshall was one of the first major modern economists to concern himself with the seeming lack of entry into certain major British industries (e.g., steel) as they were maturing at the turn of the century, even though no legal entry barriers existed. Thus, he began to contemplate the conscious erection of such barriers by the member firms in the industry (Ornstein, 1977).

Berle and Means. During the depression, Berle and Means (1933) examined the pricing behavior of large firms. They concluded that these firms were setting prices independent of the underlying quantities demanded and supplied, since they seemingly failed to lower prices in the face of declining aggregate demand. Thus, said firms must possess some form of market power, which Berle and Means termed the power to "administer" prices to preserve profit margins.

Bain. In examining accounting rates of return for a set of firms for the period 1936–1940, Bain (1965) found a certain subset of industries which simultaneously (1) were dominated by four or fewer firms (their concentration ratio was above 70 percent), (2) had earned above-normal returns, and (3) had experienced no new entry. Although qualifying his analysis and recommendations, he felt these industries and their member firms should be investigated for evidence of possible tacit collusion as protected by substantial barriers to entry.

Bain's subsequent work sought to enlarge the sample of potentially tacit collusive industries by estimating the size of barriers to entry for various industries, with the source of barriers being economies of scale in production, product differentiation, and capital barriers.

Mason and Caves. Building on the work of Bain, Mason and Caves generated a causal paradigm to predict industry behavior (Caves, 1977: 50–80). Specifically, they developed a formal paradigm of structure, conduct, and performance which states that long-run industry performance (profit levels) can be predicted by first examining industry structure which meets certain predetermined criteria (e.g., concentration ratio in excess of 50 percent and substantial barriers to entry) and thus will lead to anticompetitive conduct (tacit collusion). Therefore, if valid, the paradigm leads to a shortcut method, as opposed to lengthy antitrust litigation, for determining those industries which would yield the greatest benefits from various antitrust remedies such as divestiture.

Blair and Mueller. Although of obvious academic importance, the structure-conduct-performance approach to antitrust enforcement might not have reached its level of impact via antitrust policy without the combined efforts of John Blair and Willard Mueller. As Chief Majority Economist for the U.S. Senate Antitrust and Monopoly Subcommittee, Blair was instrumental in the formulation of innumerable Senate studies and testimony that gave support to the structural approach. Similarly, Willard Mueller pressed the application of the structural approach in voluminous studies and especially in formulating complaints brought by the Federal Trade Commission.

Policy Formulation

In its final policy-oriented formulation, structural theory became an aberration of even the simplistic structure-conduct-performance paradigm. Namely, it tended to subsume the conduct portion and proceeded to judge industry performance essentially based on industry structure. Thus, the structural approach tended to ignore the critical operational function or process of conduct, which is hypothesized as one of "tacit" collusion, with the price of the product (i.e., uniformity among competitors) being the facilitating device.

Policy Impact

Legislation. Although no divestiture legislation based on the structural approach has yet been passed by Congress, it has been proposed in several different forms and has been recommended by a major presidential commission.

The Neal Commission, established in 1968 by President Johnson, recommended the forced divestiture of leading firms in various key industries based essentially on structural parameters as an alternative to lengthy antitrust procedures. This policy recommendation was ultimately incorporated in the proposed Industrial Reorganization Act, S 1167, in 1973, which would have forced seven major industries (e.g., steel, autos) to deconcentrate unless they could demonstrate that they were actually competitive or that significant efficiency losses would result. In other words, contrary to a legal antitrust case, the major firms in these industries were being convicted *a priori* of tacit collusion with divestiture as the prescribed remedy.

The structural conditions that would lead to a finding of divestiture were (U.S. Congress, S3832, 92nd Congress, 2nd Session; reintroduced as S1167 in 93rd Congress, 1974):

1. A concentration ratio in the top four firms in excess of 50 percent
2. No significant entry in the past five years
3. An absence of effective price competition
4. An above-average accounting return (greater than 15 percent) of net income to net worth in five of the last seven years

Although originally Title I of the Omnibus Antitrust Improvements Act (Scott-Hart-Rodino Bill), it was abandoned largely due to a hearing record that failed to support its conclusions and recommendations. Much of its general approach, however, has reappeared in Senator Kennedy's proposed antimerger bill, which would bar conglomerate mergers involving assets in excess of $100 million.

In terms of the accounting profession, the Metcalf *Staff Study* (U.S. Senate, 1977) alleged that the Big Eight accounting firms were engaged in anticompetitive behavior as revealed by such factors as:

1. A lack of entry into their ranks, particularly in large-scale auditing firms

2. A lack of formal price competition
3. A relatively high concentration ratio in certain functions
4. An estimate of increasing and above-normal profits

Although the Big Eight have responded in detail, to all of these allegations, they still appear, on some grounds, to be an ideal candidate for a structural attack based on the factors listed.

Court cases. Even though many antitrust cases have employed the structural approach, it has been most prominently and successfully used in merger cases following the passage of the Cellar-Kefauver Act of 1950.

In 1968, for example, the antitrust division of the Department of Justice issued the following antimerger guidelines; that is, it would challenge:

1. All horizontal mergers if the merged firms would control more than 10 percent of industry output
2. All vertical mergers if either firm had 10 percent or more of that segment of industry output

Some of the major cases in which mergers have been blocked, revealing the Court's thinking, are:

1. Various bank merger cases, such as Manufacturers-Hanover (later allowed under Bank Merger Act)
2. Bethlehem-Youngstown Steel
3. Procter & Gamble-Clorox
4. Brown Shoe-Kinney
5. Vons-Shopping Bag

In the latter two cases, the Supreme Court extended the structural approach to industries that were currently unconcentrated but were forecast by the Court to be tending toward greater concentration if the proposed mergers were allowed. Even more convoluted reasoning arose in subsequent merger cases (e.g., Ford-Auto-lite) involving the issue of potential competition by means of potential increases in concentration, effectively preventing most large firms from making horizontal or vertical mergers. In effect, the courts have applied the structural approach in cases where the structural evidence of the type produced by Bain, Mann, and Weiss was totally lacking, on the grounds that it would be present in the future if the mergers were not blocked (Steiner, 1975: 257–287).

Shared monopoly case. In the ready-to-eat cereal (RTE) case brought by the FTC, a new and complex variant of the structural approach has been developed—"shared monopoly." The cornerstone of the case remains the issue of "tacit" collusion but is expanded to include variables other than price, such as the granting of brand-name monopolies and concerted actions regarding new product introductions. Advertising is seen as a key strategic variable which is deliberately enlarged beyond commercial necessity to create an excessive barrier to entry. Thus, the shared monopoly case or theory is an attempt, albeit *ad hoc* in part, to incorporate more of the decision variables that firms can actually alter to increase profits with a simultaneous attack on the alleged monopoly-generating effects of advertising.

Popularity of Structural Theory

Economics

Why was the structural approach so readily adopted by the economics profession and why has it proven difficult to unseat as the dominant view of large firm behavior?

Its popularity seems to stem from a variety of sources:

1. There was not then, nor is there now, a generally accepted theory of oligopoly behavior. Hence, an intellectual vacuum existed which this approach could potentially fill.
2. There was no initial concerted opposition, as most economists were opposed to the growth of large firms and/or monopolies although not necessarily for similar reasons. (e.g., Stigler [1952] expressed concern over the growth of large firms because he feared it would lead to large government needed to regulate large business).
3. There was then and still remains a great deal of ignorance about the actual, dynamic workings of competition among firms, a process which involves a great deal more than price, the standard textbook approach.
4. The generally superficial evidence presented tended at least weakly to confirm the structural hypothesis.
5. It was not generally recognized (and still is not) that the various researchers were not seeking a comprehensive explanation of differential firm profitability but rather were seeking to demonstrate that industry profitability was correlated with various structural factors.
6. Despite repeated warnings about the lack of comparability between accounting and economic measures, the accounting data were generally treated as adequate.

Legal: Court Cases and Antitrust Agencies

Antitrust agencies and the courts found the structural approach appealing because:

1. It was easy to *comprehend* in its approach and the superficial evidence appeared to be consistent.
2. The exact impact and nature of various business practices as they affected the competitive process were largely misunderstood or misinterpreted.
3. It appeared to be consistent with at least some aspects of congressional intent as revealed especially in the debate and hearings surrounding the passage of the Celler-Kefauver Act.[2]

Political

The political popularity of the structural approach, as revealed in congressional hearings and proposed legislation, stems from a variety of important sources:

1. Populism, or the "corporate bigness is antidemocratic" view, has long been an American philosophical political factor and was in part instrumental in the passage of the Sherman Act, the ICC, SBA, and Celler-Kefauver Amendment.
2. Although it remains an undemonstrated hypothesis (except by selective anecdote), many believe a direct correlation and causation exists between the exercise of political power and the ownership of large amounts of financial assets by corporations (e.g., preamble to the Industrial Reorganization Act).
3. Large corporations are often blamed and used as scapegoats for essentially macroeconomic problems of recession, unemployment, and inflation.
4. Limiting the size and effectiveness of large firms removes an obstacle and potential opposition to the desires of large government to implement its policies whether for good or otherwise.

Criticisms of Structural Theory

Empirical

Although numerous critical tests have been made of the structural approach, I will confine myself to those which appear most effectively to refute its major presumptions and conclusions:

Demsetz. Recalling that the structural approach is essentially a hypothesis regarding successful tacit collusion, it would seem critical that the direct implications of this hypothesis be tested for *all* member firms in an industry rather than just the leaders.

Demsetz (1973) did this by comparing the rate of return for smaller firms (by asset size) in concentrated industries versus the profitability of smaller firms in unconcentrated industries. If successful tacit collusion is occurring, we would expect that small firms in concentrated industries, protected by the price umbrella of collusion, would outperform small firms in unconcentrated industries where results were dictated by vigorous competition. The empirical evidence, however, revealed just the opposite. In addition, the large firms in concentrated industries outperformed their counterparts in unconcentrated industries. Thus, the combination of these two findings not only tends to refute the structural approach but also indicates that the dominant firms in concentrated industries achieved dominance via superior efficiency.

Brozen. Brozen (1971, 1970) questioned the empirical results cited by the Neal Commission (Neal, 1968) by posing the key question of whether disequilibrium levels of profits were being sampled, which would be bid away both over time and across industries if capital markets were at all efficient.

By extending the time period of the initial industries and/or by including additional industries, Brozen presented extremely consistent and pervasive evidence that excess profits or quasirents overall were bid away either by new entry or by competition among a stable number of firms in the industry.

Ornstein. An obvious flaw in virtually all the initial structural studies was the simplicity of their specification of the critical hypothesis or model which sought to relate industry profitability to industry concentration. Clearly, if we wish to explain differential profitability, we must include other potentially causal variables simultaneously with the concentration ratio. This more appropriate estimation technique was employed by Stanley Ornstein (1972) for 131 firms and 33 SIC four-digit industries for the years 1950, 1955, and 1960. Furthermore, in addition to expanding the independent variables to include such factors as firm size, economies of scale, and changes in demand and cost conditions, he attempted to remove various accounting biases by using return on stockholders' equity as his dependent variable.

The results from this superior specification reveal that the concentration ratio is not statistically significant. Rather, such factors as firm size, the capital-labor ratio, and changes in demand conditions are the critical causal variables in explaining differential firm and industry profit rates. Hence, previous results may be purely due to a classic "identification" error in which concentration and profitability were related via spurious correlation, not economic causality.

Granfield. In a similar vein to Brozen, the present author found, in a special study for the U.S. Senate Antitrust and Monopoly Subcommittee, that the concentration hypothesis as revealed in Bain's and Mann's work was extremely sensitive to the sample chosen and the time period examined. For example, by adding the next ranking firm in the industries selected by Bain and Mann, the results break down for most time periods chosen. Or, by extending the original ten-year period to fifteen years, the results are confirmed for some samples of firms but not others. Hence, the initial results appear highly sensitive to the sample chosen and the time period examined.

Moore and McCracken. These investigators found that the structural approach was in actuality a confirmation of the superior performance of the top two firms in the industries chosen, in that all the previous results broke down if the top two firms were systematically excluded from the industries sampled.

Empirically, this same result has been duplicated at the FTC by John Kwoka (1979) for a much larger sample of industries. Not surprisingly, however, he has a different interpretation for his results.

Carter. Rather than examining rates of return, Carter (1978) examined price-cost margins, which many regard as a superior test of the presence of monopoly (i.e., a divergence between price and marginal cost). Unlike the previous results Collins and Preston found of low but significant correlation, Carter (for a larger sample of industries) finds no statistically significant systematic difference between price and marginal cost, which indicates the superior performance may well be a quasirent to the managerial function.

Inferential Criticisms

Tacit vs. actual collusion theory. The structural approach postulates tacit collusion based essentially on uniformity of price. Theoretically, however, this is an extremely inadequate approach. Economic theory tells us that other elements or factors are equally if not more critical in the formation of a stable collusive agreement. If certain factors are not present, the probability of the agreement's breaking down is enhanced due to cheating or the transactions costs of detection and enforcement. Briefly, these factors are:

1. A method of successfully restricting output, since this ability, not the fixing of price *per se*, will generate the monopoly returns.
2. Uniform marginal cost functions for the participants. Otherwise, there is no unique collusive solution, which, if absent, will significantly raise transactions costs of bargaining via side payments, and so on.
3. The existence of a policing device to punish cheaters who expand output beyond the agreed-upon level.
4. A low-cost method of detecting and measuring nonprice competition, such as service, warranties, quality control, and so on, so as to detect cheating.
5. The control of substitute products being developed by other industries.
6. Aggregate demand must be relatively stable, for significant growth will facilitate cheating on new customers whereas a precipitous decline would encourage price cutting to cover at least variable costs.
7. New entrants must somehow be blocked or instability will result from constant renegotiation.
8. Imports must be prevented to prevent a fall in demand.
9. Buyer power must be lacking or the market situation will quickly evolve into bilateral monopoly.
10. Other related marketing factors, such as transport costs and customer requirements, must be only minimally important.
11. Mutual trust and confidence must exist among the participants.

Given the likely absence of at least one if not more of the previous factors, we would not expect explicit, let alone tacit, collusive agreements to experience a long, stable history, particularly if the goal is the maximization of joint monopoly profits.

Historical Evidence on Collusion

Most of the earlier and more famous alleged collusive agreements, such as Addyston Pipe in 1899, Sugar Refining in 1899 and Trenton Potteries in 1927, were apparent commercial failures, since prices fell dramatically during the conspiracy period due to falling demand and imports. More recently ("Collusion," 1962), the infamous electrical equipment conspiracy appears to have been characterized by such factors as:

1. Widely fluctuating profits and losses due to periodic successes and failures of the conspiracy
2. Wide-scale cheating due to fluctuating aggregate demand

3. Significant buyer power
4. Increasing complexity, mandating such devices as quotas, rotating of territorial restrictions, and so on
5. Competition from foreign imports and domestic entry, which generated instability

Just as informative is the fact that despite the legal fixing of prices and the blockading of entry by the CAB, U.S. domestic airlines never attempted to close the "collusive" loop via the sharing of revenues, as their European counterparts have done (and as permitted by CAB regulations), due to an apparent mistrust and/or perceived instability in their business. Similarly, legal cartels in Europe have repeatedly failed because of such factors as differing cost structures and differences over an optimal long-run pricing strategy (Armentano, 1972).

Two separate but recent analyses of price-fixing cases brought by the Department of Justice (Asch and Seneca, 1976; Hay and Kelley, 1974) reveal that colluding firms were characterized by:

1. Geographical concentration of the relevant market due to high transport costs
2. A homogeneous product
3. High fixed to variable costs, generating wide fluctuations in "acceptable" prices
4. Below-normal returns which were lower than non-colluding firms.

In short, the historical evidence would seem to imply that most conspiracies are short-lived, unstable, and engaged in by firms who are, by nature of their product and cost structures, subject to wide earnings fluctuations due to excessive price competition.

Barriers to entry. If, indeed, successful tacit collusion is to occur over any extended period, it is necessary, as we mentioned previously, that the successful entry of new firms be precluded due to legal or other forms of barriers to entry. In point of fact, the proponents of the structural approach hinge much of their arguments on the existence of three types of barriers to entry:

1. Production economies of scale, which necessitate a given minimum percentage of national output needed to be cost competitive
2. Product differentiation, particularly as produced or generated by advertising
3. Financial capital barriers

Over the last decade, economists have intensively studied these alleged barriers, particularly with respect to their anticompetitive role. From these studies, we have learned the following about entry barriers:

1. *Economies of scale.* Production economies of scale undoubtedly exist, but it is extremely difficult, if not impossible, to measure them precisely. We must standardize not only for costs at different levels of output but also for planned versus actual volume, and the rate of output.

In addition, firms have shown an incredible ability to adjust to various economies by employing regional plants and distribution systems, differing technologies, and so on.

More critically, since such economies obviously lower costs, it is not clear whether consumers are better or worse off due to their existence (see next section).

2. *Advertising.* The most comprehensive evidence to date does not suggest that advertising is in fact a barrier to entry, since it apparently is not characterized by cost economies, does not create brand loyalty, and does not generate lower price elasticities of demand (Brozen, 1974; Ornstein, 1977). Rather, advertising appears to facilitate competition since:
   a. New brands are more heavily advertised than established brands.
   b. Lower prices result from greater advertising.
   c. There is lower price dispersion when advertising is permitted.
   d. Advertising tends to alter established market shares.
   e. Advertising aids in overcoming economies of scale of established products by increasing demand for new products.

3. *Capital barriers.* Extensive work in financial economics has demonstrated that financial markets are extremely efficient. Hence, the extent to which different firms confront different market costs of capital is a reflection of their differential risks, irrespective of their asset or sales revenue size. Therefore, if a smaller firm is charged a higher cost of capital than a counterpart large firm, this is not due to size *per se* but to relative efficiencies in overcoming various entrepreneural risks.

Internal implementation. It is often assumed by structuralists that the desire to collude tacitly when a few firms are involved is tantamount to success. We have already noted the many interfirm conditions that must simultaneously be met for successful collusion to obtain for any extended period of time. What about intrafirm variables that are likely to disrupt or increase the complexity of such an arrangement?

Some of the variables or factors that would affect the behavior of a large, diversified firm if successful tacit collusion is occurring are the impacts on:

1. Any transfer pricing system that would dictate a different internal (marginal cost) than external price, which would be disallowed by tax law if independent subsidiaries were involved.
2. Divisional ROI requirements which would have to be modified by the nature of competition (or lack of it) for each division, thus blunting the efficiency role of such a criterion.
3. The capital budgeting system which would favor, all things being equal, a growth of the collusive division(s) contrary to their explicit goal of restricting output.
4. Modification of cost accounting for overhead charges, which tends to allocate costs on a standardized output basis.
5. Modification of the personnel system so as to restrict the knowledge of the "collusive game" to a manageable number of people.

In short, if we compare the interfirm and intrafirm implementation conditions, the structuralists seem to believe that these large firms are virtually "superhuman" since they can accomplish the most complex of tasks at the lowest possible levels of cost.

Summary of criticisms of the structural approach. Having examined the structural approach from several perspectives, let us now summarize our findings:

1. There appears to be no theoretical basis for the structural approach. It is actually a model of tacit collusion with no formal counterpart (as, for example, Stigler's theory of oligopoly has). In fact, structural theory lacks most of the elements present in an explicit collusion theory. Recent modifications merely serve to emphasize its *ad hoc* chameleonlike development.
2. The empirical evidence offered in support of the structural approach is at best superficial when compared to the more sophisticated approaches taken by its critics, who were sensitive to such critical factors as an appropriate specification of interfirm or interindustry profitability, the nature of the sample regarding all the relevant firms in the industry, as well as a suitably extended time period.
3. The key causal factor of barriers to entry, particularly with its recent emphasis on advertising, may not even exist or may well work opposite to its hypothesized role.

4. Inferential evidence on actual conspiracies and the problems of implementation—both inter- and intrafirm—seems to indicate that the probability of successful "tacit" collusion being carried on for decades is very low.

In short, although not proving that successful "tacit" collusion is not occurring, the collective and consistent evidence considered earlier would seem to indicate that the probability of such a phenomenon is extremely low. The evidence indicates further that antitrust endeavors should possibly be directed other than where the structuralists have pointed.

Net welfare guidelines. Having just indicated the unlikelihood, but not proof, that successful "tacit" collusion is occurring where the structuralists say it is, let us now take the role of devil's advocate and assume the opposite: namely, that successful tacit collusion occurs that is being protected collectively by cost-related barriers to entry, such as production economies of scale, advertising cost economies, and lower costs of capital for successful established firms. Would such a result warrant the policy prescription of divestiture or deconcentration? The answer, from the perspective of net societal welfare, is no! Briefly put, the gain in consumer surplus from the price reduction and output increase associated with enhanced competition must exceed the loss in producer surplus due to the higher costs generated by deconcentration.

Given that all rational collusive agreements will result in price setting in the elastic portion of the industry demand curve, any cost increase in excess of 5 percent will wipe out the benefits from an increase in consumer surplus, thus rendering society worse off (Liebler, 1978). This result seems likely if we accept (1) most estimates of the probable cost efficiencies of current firms, or (2) Leonard Weiss's estimate that concentration overall leads to profits that are 1 to 2 percent higher than they would be in a purely competitive situation (Liebler, 1978).

From the perspective of sound economic reasoning and application, therefore, it would appear that the case for deconcentration or divestiture is not viable, given the fact that it is based on a paucity of theory and evidence and given its likely net impact on societal welfare.

Structural Theory and the Accounting Profession

If indeed the structural approach is gradually being eroded away as an intellectual force within the economics profession, does this mean that the accounting profession may blithely ignore it? The answer to this query is an unequivocal no, since the assault on the accounting profession comes from the political arena, where the structural approach remains alive and well!

Elements of a Structural Approach to the Accounting Profession

Although the Hart Bill (S 1167) was never enacted into law, its basic tenets still provide the framework for policy judgments within Congress in assessing industry competitiveness.

Unfortunately, the auditing portion of the Big Eight firms' activities appears to fit those legislated conditions extremely well:

1. The top four firms are at or close to a 50 percent concentration ratio.
2. There have been no new significant entrants in the past five years (or longer, for that matter).
3. A certain economy of scale exists which may be construed as a barrier to entry.
4. There has been a ban on overt price competition.
5. It is likely that net income to net worth exceeds 15 percent.

Although the Big Eight may feel that sound commercial reasons exist for these results, it will not be a sufficient explanation without more accompanying in-depth research on the competitive processes within the accounting profession.

Political Vulnerability of the Accounting Profession

Given the ease with which the Big Eight fit structural conditions, can we determine the extent of the accounting profession's political vulnerability?

On one hand, the vulnerability is evident:

1. The profession has been made the scapegoat for such problems as corporate payments abroad, even though the fundamental causes for such payments bear little relationship to the accounting profession.
2. There is widespread ignorance about the nature of what the Big Eight actually do, for example, in conducting an audit or setting up a cost control system.
3. Congress tends to take a risk-free approach to regulation; any error is condemned even though it is patently inefficient to attempt to eliminate all errors.
4. The Big Eight firms have no obvious constituency which would support them except their major clients; support from this quarter is likely to be counterproductive, as it would seemingly confirm the allegation of mutual interdependence.

5. The general public is unaware that the costs of overregulation would be indirectly imposed on them.

On the other hand, it is not clear what a congressman or senator would gain by launching a frontal attack on the Big Eight, since his constituents presumably are ignorant of their existence.

We need to recall, however, that vigorous congressional staff personnel now initiate and conduct much of the investigative work of Congress, a factor which, together with the increasing size of these staffs, may lead to further actions simply because it does generate headlines in the increasingly important business media.

Reform: An Economist's Perspective

Potential Cartel Behavior

For this economist, the structural characteristics of the Big Eight are not matters of concern. Traditional institutional barriers to competition which resemble cartel behavior, however, are. These include:

1. Restrictions on advertising
2. Restrictions on the solicitation of customers
3. The ban on the solicitation of employees (similar to the old reserve clause in baseball)

In addition, the following issues should be probed to determine the role of the Big Eight as further evidence (or denial) of cartelization:

4. Generation of accounting standards that increase the minimum size of a firm needed to perform an audit but do not significantly improve the quality of the audit
5. Continued support of separate state certification of CPAs, thus making it more difficult to assemble a nationwide audit team (i.e., a complete team would be necessary in each state)
6. Support and/or initiation of efforts to promulgate tougher standards in states where larger clients reside

Investor and Customer Welfare

A related set of issues involves the usefulness and the necessity for the basic balance sheet data provided for public perusal by the accounting profession. This profession still largely determines the nature of this information and initiates virtually all major changes in definitions and standards.

The following is a "shopping list" of issues the accounting profession does not seem to be paying sufficient attention to. These issues could be areas of self-regulation that would improve the overall value of the information provided by the accounting profession:

1. Conducting thorough empirical tests on whether changing accounting rules actually enhances the measurement of firm performance (e.g., some contend that FASB No. 8, intended to impart a uniform standard for the reporting of foreign earnings and assets, has in practice been counterproductive [Burns, 1976])
2. Adopting and implementing reforms that have been urged by financial economists, such as the use of replacement cost or historical depreciation rates, a more accurate evolution system for inventories, and the exploration of methods to reflect a risk-adjusted profit measure
3. Collecting more information on how professional financial analysts employ accounting data and what modifications must be made in their interpretation
4. Examining the fact that many firms have developed managerial accounting systems as a method of monitoring their activities more effectively—systems that often depart dramatically from "accepted accounting principles."

Congressional and Regulatory Response of the SEC

Based on this list, it seems apparent that both Congress and the SEC are embarked on a path of reform which will probably add to a firm's accounting costs but will not improve either the quality of information provided investors nor the audit process. Simply stated, they are examining the wrong set of problems. To wit:

Audit Failures

Although obviously a spectacular and by no means trivial matter to their investors, the audit failures of Equity Funding, Penn Central, and National Student Marketing hardly point to a systematic failure of the audit system as such but rather indicate that this system is not error free. In fact, as stated previously, error-free systems (if at all possible) can only be achieved at prohibitive cost and thus are extremely inefficient. In terms of sheer probability, the focus should not be on the few exceptions but rather on the many successes which may, in fact, imply current overstandardization or regulation.

Even if problems did exist, however, Congress in particular, given its innumerable oversight budget failures, seems technically incapable of comprehending what reforms are necessary and what method it should use to implement them. Nor do the SEC's recent meanderings on petroleum reserve evaluation inspire confidence, either in their abilities or in their capacity for remaining apolitical.

Corporate Payments Abroad

As noted previously, the root causes for such payments (nonmilitary) lie in an ambiguous and often schizophrenic attitude toward foreign countries together with a host-country attitude which either encourages such payments or does nothing to eradicate them.

As the SEC's own documents reveal, such payments were often no more than a normal commission, thus making concealment extremely easy. In addition, unless indicative of other forms of mismanagement, it is not clear their mandatory revelation serves anyone's interest.

Complexity of Financial Statements

Rather than questioning the complexity of financial statements, why not pose the more fundamental question of the *usefulness* of the data, clear or unclear?

Uniform Standards

As related to point 3 on our shopping list, by what criterion do we measure the appropriate amount of uniformity? For example, some have argued that a serious defect of public accounting is its lack of flexibility from one municipality to another, thus paradoxically making comparisons meaningless as accountants are forced to translate from one set of terms to another. Similarly, in tax accounting, flexibility has been mandated due to the different "facts and circumstances" which impact various taxpayers.

Conclusion

Altering or "tightening" current federal regulations will not change the allocation of political "property rights" or authority structure via rulemaking, nor will it change the growth of the accounting bureaucracy that benefits most from this system. In short, not much *substantively* will change, although paradoxically accounting costs may rise appreciably. Rather, real reform will have to come from the users of the information or those who ultimately pay for it (the shareholders). Given the enormous transactions costs involved, however, this seems unlikely at the present time.

Therefore, I do not expect current pressures for "reform" to change the fundamental nature of the largest public accounting firms which I believe are best viewed as the group which seemingly has "captured" the SEC more for its benefit as opposed to the greater good of the investing public (Benston, 1976; Reed, 1978). Hence, we should view the growth and behavior of the public accounting firms as we would any government bureaucracy which essentially adopts and reverses all attempts at fundamental change. This is not to say that the information provided in legally mandated financial statements is totally useless or harmful (although it may be, in some limiting circumstances). Rather, the opportunity cost of the current system is twofold: (a) information that may be more useful to investors is not provided; and (2) far too many resources are devoted to the reporting of seemingly redundant information.

Notes

1. This view may be overly pessimistic. The rate of increase of government expenditures (federal as well as state and local) has slowed in the last two years, but it is too soon to determine if this is a discernible shift.

2. See the citations of this act in the Brown Shoe and Vons-Shopping Bag merger cases (Stelzer, 1974: 127–226).

II

Competition in the
Accounting Profession

A significant amount of the criticism leveled at the accounting profession charges that a lack of competition exists, as shown through the existence of the Big Eight firms and their alleged monopolistic practices.

Is there a relationship between having a large share of the market and being anticompetitive? If so, does this relationship apply to the accounting profession? In their chapters, Dopuch, Simunic, and Kripke address these questions in a variety of ways.

Referring to several studies of concentration statistics, Dopuch and Simunic in Chapter 3 find no systematic market allocation by the Big Eight over any period of time, since it appears that the market share decreases along with the size of buyers of accounting services. The lower fees of the Big Eight and the lack of proof that barriers to entry exist show that the market is competitive, they say. They conclude by discussing the need for economic models to help determine appropriate allocation of auditing services.

For Kripke in Chapter 4, the nature of the competition in the profession means that its members must deal with the antitrust question. He points out that since accounting is a human construct, in contrast to professions based upon natural or social law, its operating principles represent contractual restraints among its practitioners. Drawing from court decisions to make his point, Kripke relies heavily upon four recent Supreme Court cases, to explore the impact of self-regulation by the accounting profession. For him, the cases show the importance of accounting and auditing to be so great in terms of social benefit that unification of principles seems "clearly sound in terms of serving the genuine public interest."

The profession is running a risk by not bringing public accounting into compliance with government proposals, Kripke believes, because of the danger that antitrust laws could be applied to the formulation of principles. Even though SEC has failed to exercise its delegated powers for regulation of the accounting industry, he contends, that fact does not give rise to a legitimate antitrust exemption.

3

The Nature of Competition in the Auditing Profession: A Descriptive and Normative View

Nicholas Dopuch

Graduate School of Business
University of Chicago

Dan Simunic

Faculty of Commerce
University of British Columbia

To judge best where the auditing industry falls along the spectrum of monopoly and competition, some preliminary statistics may be useful. Two approaches were possible in collecting these facts. We could have cited the indictments of the auditing industry by congressional and other blue-ribbon committees, or we could have turned to economics literature for previous studies on competition. We chose the latter path, but anyone familiar with the committee reports will note that several of their conclusions also appear in our discussion.

This chapter will examine only the nature of competition in the audit services market. These services, together with other work not related to auditing, are supplied alike by individual public accountants and by public accounting firms; consequently, such features of the industry as entry barriers must be analyzed at both the individual and the company levels. We will look at supplier concentration, entry barriers, and price performance of auditors. Finally, we will present a normative overview and some arguments for standardization.

Concentration of Suppliers

Much of the criticism of the auditing industry (the entire Metcalf subcommittee *Staff Study*, for example) has been couched in the traditional

77

structure-conduct-performance framework of industrial organization. The usual argument[1] is simply that the more concentrated an industry becomes, the easier it is for firms which account for the bulk of that industry's sales to collude in setting prices, allocating markets, and, in the case of the dominant auditing firms, to influence the regulators of the accounting and auditing process. While the concentration doctrine may not be valid,[2] the reliance placed on this doctrine in criticizing the auditing industry provides a motivation for concentration-performance studies of that industry. The issue, then, is how to proceed.

The typical concentration study consists of an attempt to compare relationships between profitability rates, variously defined, to measures of concentration across industries, adjusting for other variables which might lead to differences in observed rates of profitability (such as capital intensity or durables versus nondurables). Unfortunately, the bulk of auditing firms' investments in capital—that is, *human* capital—is generally not recorded as such, so that it would be difficult to compare meaningfully profitability rates in auditing with other industries, including other service industries. The problem would exist whether we tried to use rates of return or profit margins, since both ratios could be biased to the extent investments are not capitalized and then amortized over time. In addition, the rates of return reported by firms are based upon different sets of accounting conventions and principles, and enough has been said already about the potential biases which may exist in treating accounting measures of profitability as surrogates for economic concepts.[3] A survey of some thirty-two concentration studies completed prior to 1969 by Weiss (1971) leads one to the conclusion that the results are mostly inconclusive due to shortcomings in theory, operational definitions, and profitability data.

An alternative approach would be an intraindustry comparison of the profitability of the Big Eight versus "other auditing firms." The public accounting profession is typically regarded as consisting of these two tiers of firms, where significant differences exist in firm size and types of services provided by the two tiers. Measuring size by number of professional employees, the Financial Executives Institute (1973) reported that the smallest of the Big Eight firms was more than twice as large as the largest of the other firms. Moreover, the mix of services varies considerably as we move from the Big Eight to the smaller firms. According to the *Staff Study* (U.S. Senate, 1977), the Big Eight firms derive on average approximately 70 percent of revenues from audit fees, with the balance earned from tax services (18%) and general management consulting (12%). By contrast, a recent regional survey conducted by the Texas CPA Society (1978) found that a typical larger nonnational firm derives 31 percent of revenues from bookkeeping and the preparation of unaudited financial statements, 35 percent from tax services, 5 percent from management consulting, and only 29 percent of revenue from auditing. As the size of the firm decreases, the percent of revenue derived from auditing continues to decrease, becoming a relatively minor source of revenue for the smallest firms. Thus, the eight largest firms appear to be the dominant suppliers of audit services and subject to criticisms under the concentration doctrine. In contrast, the large number of non-Big Eight firms which can and do supply audit services may be assumed to be sufficiently competitive so that their profitability could be regarded as a competitive benchmark against which profitability of the Big Eight could be compared.

This test, however, would also be subject to the unrecorded human capital problem if, on average, the human capital investment of the two classes of firms is different. In addition, the risks associated with the contrasting mix of services, such as audits of large public firms versus audits of "local" firms, are different, requiring some adjustment to the rates of return earned by the two groups of firms before one could start to assess whether monopolistic returns were earned by the dominant tier. Finally, the results could be inconclusive to the extent the Big Eight firms maintain an effective "price umbrella" in the market for audit services.

Another alternative would be to assess the time series properties of profit numbers for the Big Eight versus the "other auditing firms" on the assumption that the autocorrelation functions of a typical competitive series differ from those of a monopolistic series.[4] The theory underlying such tests, however, is not well developed, and we may not have a sufficient number of observations to obtain reliable estimates of autocorrelation functions for either group of firms.

Another critical problem in performing any of these profitability tests is simply that profitability data for public accounting firms are not publicly available, except in isolated cases. At this stage it seems that the best we can do, then, is to look at preliminary statistics on the current level of concentration and changes in concentration over time.

To construct concentration statistics, we must first specify a base measure of the size of firms as well as some limit of the boundaries of the market. Sales revenue is probably the most commonly used size measure, although numbers of employees, firm assets, and value added have also been used (Asch, 1970). The definition of the market must be sufficiently broad to include substitutes yet sufficiently narrow to exclude nonsubstitute services.

Because public accounting firms are private partnerships, data on the typical measurement bases of firm revenues, number of employees, and so on are not publicly available. The quantity of audit services rendered, however, and the revenues of an auditor can be expected to vary positively with the size of the company audited (auditee), other things being equal. In fact, Simunic (1979) and Elliott and Korpi (1978) found that audit fees are a linear function of the square root of auditee size measured either by total assets or sales. In principle, then, we may construct concentration statistics by identifying the buyers of audit services and use the square root of buyer size, a proxy for the revenue from a given audit, as the basis for computing the share of market for various CPA firms. The approach is conceptually sound since the proxy measure of revenue is limited to audit services and is therefore unaffected by other services (which are clearly not audit substitutes) and the observed difference in service mix across suppliers.

Using this approach, we compared the market shares of each of the Big Eight firms and of the non–Big Eight firms as a group for the "Fortune 500" list of companies (auditees) in 1977 and other selected post–World War II years. The results are shown in Table 3-1.[5] Although the total market for audit services encompasses other buyers as well, these large corporations constitute a significant subset of companies, a fact which is of interest in itself.

Evidence on concentration such as that displayed in Table 3-1, which shows the Big Eight firms to be the dominant suppliers of audit services to the largest corporations, led the *Staff Study* (1977: 46) to conclude:

> The information which this subcommittee has received from the "Big Eight" firms and other sources clearly shows an excessively high concentration of auditing influence among the "Big Eight" firms. The degree of concentration in providing independent auditing services to major corporations is so great that it constitutes evidence of a serious lack of competition.

Table 3-1

MARKET SHARES OF AUDITORS FOR THE FORTUNE 500 INDUSTRIALS

	1977	1966	1955
Arthur Andersen & Co. (AA)	15.2%	10.7%	9.6%
Coopers & Lybrand (CL)	10.9	10.9	10.6
Ernst & Whinney (EW)	11.1	11.3	11.5
Haskins & Sells (HS)	11.7	13.4	12.9
Peat, Marwick, Mitchell (PMM)	10.9	10.3	8.4
Price Waterhouse (PW)	21.6	22.8	22.0
Touche, Ross (TR)	4.8	4.8	5.3
Arthur Young (AY)	10.6	9.5	8.1
Other auditors	3.2	6.3	11.6
	100.0%	100.0%	100.0%

Table 3-2

MARKET SHARES OF AUDITORS WHEN BUYERS ARE CLASSIFIED BY SIZE

	Auditee Sales (in millions)						
	$1 to $25	$26 to $50	$51 to $100	$101 to $250	$251 to $500	$501 to $1000	Over $1000
AA	10.2%	15.6%	19.6%	16.0%	18.5%	16.9%	15.8%
CL	8.3	8.6	9.0	9.8	10.8	8.8	9.2
EW	6.7	12.3	13.7	14.4	9.8	12.7	9.8
HS	5.3	7.3	7.3	9.6	12.2	12.3	12.1
PMM	11.1	11.4	14.1	12.5	12.2	16.1	14.6
PW	6.8	7.8	8.5	11.8	13.9	16.5	19.4
TR	5.5	7.5	7.2	6.5	5.7	3.8	7.6
AY	5.5	6.1	6.1	7.3	7.7	6.5	7.9
Others	40.6	23.4	14.5	12.1	9.2	6.4	3.6

This assertion may not be justified, both because no evidence was provided on audit firm performance (rates of return, margins, prices, and so on) and because the "Fortune 500" companies and the companies examined by the Metcalf Subcommittee (firms listed on the American and New York Stock Exchanges) are arbitrary subsets of buyers. A much broader set of concentration statistics (for a single year) can be constructed using such data as collected by Harris (1976), which describe the size and auditor identity of 8,077 publicly held corporations.[6] As shown in Table 3-2, market shares of the Big Eight firms as a whole vary significantly across this group of buyers.

Anyone who does not subscribe to the traditional concentration doctrine would view such evidence on concentration alone as merely descriptive. In effect, this evidence shows that the Big Eight firms' collective share of the audits of the largest industrial corporations has increased over time and that this share varies across the market with the size of buyers. Benston (1979) suggests that the utilization of large public accounting firms by large corporations is due to scale economies of multioffice operations or, alternatively, the diseconomies which would be faced by a consortium of small CPA firms trying to perform a large audit. This is a reasonable hypothesis which could be tested further.

Note also that any computation of market shares which is restricted to the largest buyers will yield upward-biased concentration ratios. In addition, such ratios are further biased if the absolute size of auditees (e.g., company sales) are used as weights in computing market shares, since the relation between audit fees and auditee size is nonlinear.[7]

Some insight into the competitiveness of the industry using concentration data alone might also be obtained by examining the stability of market shares of the dominant suppliers over time. If the Big Eight firms behave as a cartel and either explicitly or implicitly allocate customers to specific auditors, the market shares of individual firms should be highly stable. Table 3-1 provides some tentative evidence on this issue, indicating that the shares of three Big Eight firms—Arthur Andersen; Peat, Marwick, Mitchell; and Arthur Young—of the market of audits for the largest industrial corporations increased the most between 1955 and 1977. An extension of these statistics to a larger set of buyers might provide more evidence of market share changes.

To obtain additional evidence on the stability of market shares, we replicated the study by Zeff and Fossum (1967) which examined auditor concentration for over 600 major corporations classified by industry. Controlling for the industry of buyers may be of interest because the industry of the client is a reasonable criterion on which a cartel might allocate customers to specific auditors. Thus, highly stable auditor shares and limited auditor entry in the various industry categories might be evidence of market sharing arrangements. The results for those Standard and Poor's Industry Survey categories which are consistently defined between 1965 (the Zeff and Fossum data) and 1975 (our data), are shown in Table 3-3. In computing market shares, the sales of auditees are used as weights. Comparing the two years' data does not suggest any systematic market allocation. For example, in twenty-three instances during the period, a Big Eight firm was a new entrant into a specific industry, and in twenty-four of the thirty-two industries, the dominant auditing firm in 1965 lost part of its market share during the next ten years.

Given the difficulty in obtaining profitability and other performance data for public accounting firms, further evidence on changes in firm market shares, together with hypotheses to explain such changes, could prove useful in assessing the stability of market shares of audit services. This evidence should pertain to all firms, not just the Big Eight.

Barriers to Entry

Monopolistic practices are generally hypothesized to occur in industries where potential competitors face significant barriers to entry. Stigler (1968) defines an entry barrier as a "cost of producing . . . which must be borne by a firm which seeks to enter an industry but is not borne by firms already in the industry." The evidence on product mix variations across different-sized CPA firms suggests that, in this context, it is necessary to distinguish between barriers to entry of *individuals* into the accounting profession as such, and barriers to entry of *firms* into the market for audit services. The entry of an individual into the profession as a certified public accountant is only a necessary condition which must be satisfied if the individual is to render audit services as a sole practitioner or firm partner. The sufficient condition is the existence of demand for that individual's audit services. On the other hand, an individual may perform audit services as a firm employee without satisfying this necessary condition. Thus, the relative ease or difficulty of individual entry into the accounting profession may be irrelevant to the market for audits which, available evidence indicates, is dominated by the larger CPA firms. One could argue, for example, that a group of colluding oligopolists would support easy entry into the profession to maintain a flow of motivated employees, while smaller firms and sole practitioners would be motivated to erect barriers to individual entry. The outcome would then depend on the relative political power of the two groups, but the cartel would appear to support competition!

The dominance of large firms in public accounting distinguishes this industry from medicine or law and blurs the significance of any entry barriers at the individual level. Nevertheless, since charges that entry barriers restrict the available supply of CPAs have been made by critics such as Pichler (1974), we discuss and provide some evidence on barriers to entry to both individuals and firms.

At the individual level, entry barriers commonly associated with "professional" service industries such as auditing are licensing or certification requirements which limit the right to perform service to "qualified" individuals. Such restrictions are entry barriers in the Stiglerian sense if, for example, more stringent education requirements are applied to newcomers.

More severe licensing requirements for a profession exist in the medical profession. Not only are practices restricted to those who pass the final licensing examinations, but the training in preparation for the examination is limited to a number of accredited schools.[8] The principal argument supporting these requirements is the need to protect the general public from the injuries persons would suffer if improperly trained (and licensed) individuals were allowed to practice in this industry. Of course, an alternative explanation with some support[9] is the need to protect physicians' income.

The conduct of audit services is also limited by licensing and certification requirements. As of this date, however, the training in preparation for the CPA examination is not restricted to a small number of schools. This condition currently is being threatened by the wave of professional schools of accounting. There is a legitimate concern that eventually only those who graduate from schools of accounting will be allowed to sit for the licensing examination.[10] So those in favor of encouraging competition in the auditing industry should vote against any proposition that only professional schools of accounting should be accredited.

Table 3-3

PERCENTAGE OF INDUSTRY SALES AUDITED BY VARIOUS CPA FIRMS—1965 vs. 1975

	AA 1965	AA 1975	AY 1965	AY 1975	EW 1965	EW 1975	HS 1965	HS 1975	CL 1965	CL 1975	PMM 1965	PMM 1975	PW 1965	PW 1975	TR 1965	TR 1975	All Others 1965	All Others 1975	Total Number of Firms 1965	Total Number of Firms 1975
Aerospace	11.4	5.7	16.2	12.5	22.7	23.0	21.2	16.5	–	7.5	–	–	8.9	13.0	14.3	17.3	5.2	4.4	15	13
Air transport	24.5	27.1	14.7	11.1	8.7	7.4	19.1	23.3	16.3	10.4	5.5	9.1	11.2	10.5	–	–	–	1.1	11	16
Amusements	19.6	11.9	16.4	11.2	7.1	3.6	–	–	–	12.9	–	17.5	51.2	42.5	–	–	5.7	–	6	15
Autos	.7	–	.9	–	1.7	2.4	51.0	48.0	29.0	30.4	–	–	–	–	16.8	19.1	–	–	8	8
Auto parts	4.8	6.1	14.8	7.7	35.2	32.3	2.2	20.1	5.5	–	22.6	22.4	6.8	8.8	4.1	–	4.0	2.6	20	14
Building	21.7	43.1	13.2	7.1	8.2	13.0	15.8	1.5	22.4	16.3	8.5	5.9	5.6	7.3	2.6	3.4	1.9	2.4	22	25
Chemicals	7.7	2.7	3.9	6.7	–	0.6	35.3	26.4	2.7	5.5	14.9	14.2	24.1	31.0	–	–	11.3	12.7	28	33
Containers	7.7	–	13.6	17.9	2.6	–	37.3	27.0	24.1	22.0	–	–	9.9	23.6	2.9	6.3	1.9	2.8	14	12
Drugs—health care, cosmetics	3.5	20.8	2.0	2.6	4.3	8.6	1.7	3.1	23.6	12.0	11.6	14.9	23.6	24.5	3.3	–	26.4	13.6	21	24
Electronics	13.2	22.5	12.0	15.8	5.9	7.7	3.8	1.1	9.8	1.1	32.4	28.9	2.4	11.7	4.8	6.5	15.8	4.5	23	34
Food products, canners, packers	8.5	19.2	4.0	–	4.9	1.6	10.9	8.9	2.8	4.1	9.4	25.6	38.2	37.8	–	2.3	21.2	–	15	15
Food products, meat, dairy	17.7	12.5	20.6	16.8	3.2	3.3	13.5	1.1	–	3.4	9.8	16.8	35.1	28.5	–	14.2	–	3.3	15	26
Home furnishings	–	20.4	–	–	–	–	–	–	64.7	22.4	35.3	28.9	–	–	–	–	–	28.4	3	4
Liquor	14.4	14.2	–	17.3	–	–	11.9	–	–	–	–	–	73.7	68.6	–	–	–	–	5	7
Machinery—agricultural	–	–	–	–	–	–	78.0	85.2	–	–	–	–	22.0	14.8	–	–	–	–	4	3
Machinery—industrial	11.0	23.3	12.0	1.9	5.4	3.8	–	1.3	4.9	6.7	15.3	12.7	40.1	40.2	8.7	2.5	2.6	7.7	25	38

	AA		AY		EW		HS		CL		PMM		PW		TR		All Others		Total Number of Firms	
	1965	1975	1965	1975	1965	1975	1965	1975	1965	1975	1965	1975	1965	1975	1965	1975	1965	1975	1965	1975
Metals	–	6.0	–	2.2	12.7	11.3	9.7	15.5	50.0	41.1	5.8	3.0	21.6	18.8	–	–	–	2.3	24	19
Office equipment	–	–	–	–	–	–	2.4	9.8	–	1.9	7.6	18.8	90.0	69.5	–	–	–	–	8	10
Oil	10.9	18.8	20.5	17.7	4.0	4.9	1.8	0.6	6.0	8.4	2.8	3.0	53.0	46.0	–	0.4	0.8	0.2	29	35
Paper	35.7	26.1	–	–	36.5	47.0	28.6	26.0	14.9	12.3	–	3.0	12.8	20.8	8.0	8.7	–	3.0	14	13
Publishing	–	10.3	8.2	11.0	26.9	11.9	5.8	18.0	–	–	16.9	7.3	22.6	6.3	–	–	10.0	–	11	9
Rail equipment	9.6	12.1	–	42.0	–	–	20.3	–	20.1	–	–	11.5	23.1	22.5	–	–	–	–	5	6
Rubber fabricating	–	–	–	–	15.3	14.9	16.5	14.2	22.0	24.2	–	–	46.2	46.7	–	–	–	–	6	6
Shipping, shipbuilding	50.2	66.3	10.9	–	–	–	–	8.4	–	–	10.1	–	28.8	25.3	–	–	–	–	7	6
Soft drinks and candy	13.5	9.3	7.9	43.6	54.4	47.1	24.1	–	–	–	3.4	9.0	–	–	–	–	–	–	5	4
Steel, coal	.8	7.6	.8	–	17.2	15.5	9.8	8.9	–	1.0	–	16.6	66.1	55.0	1.9	3.0	–	–	22	22
Sugar	62.1	55.9	–	–	–	–	37.9	–	–	–	–	–	–	13.3	–	–	–	14.2	3	4
Telephone	11.3	14.9	19.9	17.3	–	–	–	–	66.9	66.5	1.9	–	1.9	1.3	–	–	–	–	5	6
Textiles	–	–	4.0	25.7	4.0	–	14.5	20.0	2.7	–	39.2	32.5	2.7	–	–	–	31.3	21.9	16	12
Tobacco	–	–	34.0	7.5	34.0	34.9	20.7	6.7	40.3	50.8	5.0	–	–	–	–	–	–	–	6	5
Utilities—electricity	24.1	25.2	1.5	–	–	–	25.8	37.1	12.3	13.1	–	2.1	27.0	22.5	–	–	9.2	–	35	34
Utilities—gas	50.2	41.5	–	–	–	–	18.4	8.8	–	–	12.7	15.8	8.5	7.8	–	15.0	10.2	11.1	12	11

In addition to a certification examination, state laws may impose additional requirements on those who wish to practice within their jurisdictions. Several years ago, the state of California was toying with the idea of limiting tax practices, even of the storefront type, to CPAs. One of the authors has a brother-in-law who is a CPA doing tax (and auditing) work as a partner in his own firm in San Jose, and a second one who is not a CPA who does tax work out of his garage in Merced. As you might guess, the first is for and the second is against the proposition.

There are several aspects of the regulations restricting entry into the auditing profession we might study. The first is obvious: the extent to which the licensing examination limits entry into the profession. The general rule is that a candidate who wishes to sit for the CPA examination must possess a bachelor's degree with a major in accounting, be of sound mind and character, and possess $50–$100. Many individuals seem capable of obtaining a bachelor's degree from an accredited business school which offers an accounting major, so this requirement does not pose a major obstacle. Indeed, it may take more self-discipline to meet the accounting requirements than the degree requirements.

To measure objectively the soundness of a person's mind and character is not an easy task, so we usually give him or her the benefit of the doubt. And since many auditing firms will reimburse the $50–$100 fee to their employees who take the examination, the significant hurdle for initial entry into the profession seems to be passing the exam. But to what extent is the examination a barrier?

Statistics on the pass-fail rates across different states are not easy to come by, and the available data are difficult to interpret. At the national level, the pass rate is approximately 30 percent. In 1921, it was about 13 percent. These rates usually include those who pass all parts of the test at their first sitting and those who are writing off conditions. The latter rate is generally greater than the former. In Illinois in 1976, for example, the two rates were 12 percent and 18 percent, respectively.

A more valid assessment of the pass rates may come from studies such as the one conducted by the Florida State Board of Accountancy, which indicated that 86 percent of the "serious candidates" taking the exam for the first time passed all four parts within three years or less.[11] Serious candidates were defined as those who take and retake the exam for three years. Over 60 percent of those candidates who did not pass all four parts quit after their first try.

Colorado provides an interesting set of statistics for its candidates for selected years from 1948 through 1976. These are reproduced in Table 3-4. Note that over 70 percent of those who originally took the exam in 1959, 1968, 1969, and 1971 eventually passed the examination by 1976. Such statistics hardly support a conclusion that the CPA examination is a significant barrier to entry into the accounting profession.[12]

Table 3-4

CPA EXAMINATION SUCCESS RATES IN COLORADO

Original Exam Date	Number Sitting Nov. 1976	Number Passing Nov. 1976	Cumulative Results		
			Number Originally Sitting	Total Passing to Date	Percent Passing
May 1948	1	0	91	55	60
Nov. 1955	1	0	35	19	47
Nov. 1956	2	0	47	22	46
Nov. 1959	1	0	62	45	73
Nov. 1964	1	0	81	38	47
Nov. 1968	1	0	99	77	78
May 1969	3	1	110	76	69
Nov. 1969	2	0	145	110	76
May 1970	2	0	119	81	68
Nov. 1970	2	0	126	92	73
Nov. 1971	4	1	137	89	64
May 1972	10	0	206	130	63
Nov. 1972	6	1	155	107	69
May 1973	11	3	245	159	65
Nov. 1973	10	2	202	138	68
May 1974	22	4	267	182	68
Nov. 1974	32	8	215	130	60
May 1975	57	25	278	156	56
Nov. 1975	83	27	233	116	50
May 1976	145	43	305	92	30
Nov. 1976	238	41	238	41	17
Total	634	156			

In addition to the requirement of CPA certification, a number of states also impose restrictions in the form of experience requirements on those who wish to perform auditing services within their boundaries. The experience requirements are varied, ranging from two to six years with certain substitutional privileges, such as substituting the teaching of accounting courses for auditing work. The restrictiveness of these laws varies from states in which only CPAs are allowed to perform the attest function to those labeled as states in which the attest function can be performed by licensed non-CPAs as well. As of 1976, eleven states fell into the latter category.

One feature of state licensing laws which might inhibit competition among professionals is the extent to which individuals who qualify in one state can practice their profession in other states as well. In a study on the mobility of lawyers, Pashigian (1977) notes that mobility across states might be restricted because (1) complete reciprocity is not practiced between states; (2) a heavy investment in reputation is required to obtain "sales"; and (3) states may impose specific laws and procedures which require lawyers to invest in additional educational costs in moving from one state to another.

Regarding auditing, complete reciprocity among all the states does not exist. Except for Florida and New York, however, which impose special restrictions on "new" immigrants, auditors who qualify in one state have little difficulty in meeting the rules imposed by other states. Moreover, those who work for large firms can move freely to other states merely by transferring to their firm's branch offices. All that is usually required for a firm to audit company records in a particular state is that one of the partners qualify to practice within its jurisdiction. These loose restrictions also suggest that Pashigian's third class of restrictions would not be significant in reducing individual auditors' mobility.

The second restriction noted earlier does apply to auditing, although it is not clear whether we should approach the issue at the individual or firm level. Service industries in general rely upon reputation to obtain "sales," perhaps because of the difficulty in assessing the quality of services (an unobservable). Brand names in service industries may perform the same function under conditions of uncertainty as they do with other products. New firms, however, may have difficulty developing brand names given the code of professional ethics of accountants. The restrictions contained in the AICPA code attained legal status through the state accountancy laws, which typically incorporate a code of ethics modeled after the AICPA rules of conduct. Although the AICPA code has been recently revised to eliminate restrictions on advertising, solicitation, and encroachment, these provisions may persist in some state laws.[13] Of these restrictions, the historic prohibition of advertising has probably been the most significant one in shaping the structure of the industry. The rule was adopted in 1922 following much debate (Chatfield, 1974). It is interesting to note here that the formation of each of the Big Eight firms preceded the adoption of this rule; alternatively, no other firm has since joined the dominant tier.

The prohibition of advertising eliminates a relatively inexpensive means by which a firm could develop brand name recognition. The potential significance of such recognition is illustrated in a casual survey conducted by Dow Jones (1978) in which 89 to 99 percent (depending on the size of the company) of corporate chief executive officers or presidents responded "Yes" to the question, "Do you consider it important that your stockholders be somewhat familiar with the name and reputation of your company's CPA firm?" In a subsequent question, which attempted to establish the respondent's own familiarity with various CPA firms, 10 to 70 percent replied that they had "never heard" of each of the various non-Big Eight firms included in the list, whereas all had some familiarity with each of the Big Eight.

We should be careful, however, not to attribute too much significance to the "brand name" restriction of entry into the profession. The local contacts of large well-known firms are the partners and managers in charge of the audits and the assigned staff personnel. Lucrative audits are a constant inducement for these local contacts to start their own firms, using as their base their clients taken from the large firms. Of course, once these local firms become established and profitable, they become targets of mergers with large firms, starting the cycle again.

A possible barrier faced by a firm seeking to render audit services at the national level, especially to publicly held companies, is the cost of acquiring the necessary knowledge of federal government regulations. Such costs are not true entry barriers, however, if they must be incurred by both present and potential suppliers and each firm is free to acquire the level of expertise consistent with the importance of the related audits to its own service mix. In response to government prodding, however, the AICPA recently created a separate SEC firm Practice Section with "oversight" responsibilities. The limitation of SEC practice to members of that section and the imposition of practice standards upon its members may create entry barriers if the imposed standards force smaller firms to acquire "excess" expertise. In fact, a group of accountants from eighteen small and medium-sized firms sued to prevent implementation of the plan on the grounds that it violated Institute bylaws and would decrease competition.

Evidence on Price Competition

Recently, the Financial Executives Institute (1978) conducted a survey of its members and reported the following ranges of audit fees paid by a sample of 631 manufacturing companies:

Auditee Size as Measured by Sales (in millions)	Low Fee	High Fee
Less than $50	$ 6,000	$ 125,000
$50 to $99	26,000	200,000
$100 to $249	29,000	462,000
$250 to $499	40,000	782,000
$500 to $999	54,000	1,600,000
Greater than $1,000	130,000	10,795,000

The results indicate that significant variability in fees exists, even when we roughly control for the size of the buyer.

Simunic (1979) examined the determinants of audit fees for a sample cross-section of 397 publicly held companies in various industries. An objective of this study was to test the effects of market structure upon the pricing of audit services. Recall from Table 3-2 that the market dominance of the Big Eight firms varies considerably with the size of auditees. In his study, auditees were divided into classes of two sizes: companies with sales less than $125 million and companies with sales greater than $125 million. The assumption was that the submarket for the audits of the "smaller" companies was competitive. The determinants of fees in the two submarkets were then tested by fitting separate regression functions which included a (0,1) independent variable to identify audits performed by the Big Eight versus other auditors.

Before discussing the results of this study, we should note that audit fees represent revenues, or the product of the unit price of the service (p) and the quantity of service purchased (q). Unfortunately, only this product, pq, is observable in a transaction, not both the separate price and quantity components. Initially, it may seem that the quoted hourly billing rate schedule of a CPA firm is the observable analogue of p. Many state CPA societies (e.g., Arizona, 1973; Ohio, 1972 and 1976; Florida, 1978) have collected data on quoted rates from their member firms. These surveys consistently show that mean rates for a given category of staff personnel increase as the size of the CPA firm increases. Such evidence, however, is not in fact meaningful because quoted rates are subject to discounting and are affected by interfirm differences in audit production functions.

Monopoly pricing through collusion among the Big Eight firms would increase p above the competitive level, and in the absence of external audit substitutes, would increase the fee, pq. Other resources, however, particularly the services of internal auditors, are likely to be substitutable for external auditing, at least to some degree. Therefore, the observable effect of monopoly pricing upon the auditors' revenue will depend upon the price elasticity of the demand for external audit services which itself depends on the goodness of available substitutes. As a result, in order to interpret any observed systematic difference in audit fees across classes of suppliers (such as Big Eight versus other firms), it is necessary to test for substitution toward or away from external audit services by auditees.

Turning to the results, Simunic found that after controlling for various factors which were hypothesized to affect the difficulty of an audit (that is, the level of q), the fees paid to seven of the eight dominant firms were, on average, lower across the entire market than the fees of non–Big Eight firms. The control variables included in the study were:

1. Size of the auditee as measured by the square root of total year-end assets

2. Degree of decentralization as measured by the number of consolidated subsidiaries
3. Industry diversification as measured by the number of two-digit Standard Industrial Classification industries in which the auditee operated
4. Ratio of foreign assets to total assets
5. Ratio of receivables to total assets
6. Ratio of inventory to total assets
7. Certain industry classification variables

Overall, the two market segments were found to be homogeneous in audit fee determinants; that is, the observed difference in Big Eight concentration across the market, as shown in Table 3-2, was not found to be relevant to the formation of audit prices.

Although the fees of seven of the Big Eight were, on average, lower than those of non-Big Eight firms, the average fees of one of the Big Eight firms were significantly higher than those of the other seven. The test for substitution of internal auditors for the services of external auditors, which is necessary for the interpretation of any observed fee difference, yielded no evidence of such substitution by clients of the seven. Companies utilizing the services of that Big Eight firm, however, also utilized significantly greater amounts of internal audit services. Thus, the higher average fees may be due at least partially to a greater quantity of external audit services demanded by that firm's clients. Alternatively, they could be due to the existence of a differentiated product for which companies are willing to pay a higher price.

Overall, the study concludes that the hypothesis of price competition throughout the market for audit services cannot be rejected and that Big Eight firms may, in fact, enjoy certain scale economies which at least partially are passed through in the form of lower prices to clients.

Scale economies to large firms in auditing are most likely to arise from opportunities for staff specialization through division of labor. The issue of whether the growth of the Big Eight firms and the decreasing market shares of the non–Big Eight firms over time (see Table 3-1) can be attributed to the efficiency of firm size deserves further research. Given the criticism and charges made against the dominant firms, the importance of the issue is obvious.

Competition in the Auditing Industry — Some Normative Views

We turn now to a brief discussion of some normative views on competition in the auditing industry. To set the stage, let us first consider some characteristics of the profession that condition the extent to which auditing can function like other competitive markets.

Recall that in many service industries the quality of the product is not observable. Rather, what we observe are inputs into the production of the service—hours worked by various levels of skilled personnel, number of tasks performed, and so on. This holds for auditing as well. In a sense, those who perform audits have a superior knowledge of the quality of their product than those who pay for it. In recent years, this type of asymmetry of information has received attention in the design of optimal incentive contracts when a party operating on behalf of another has superior knowledge of the quality of his actions. One possibility in such situations is to base incentives on input characteristics of the production process that are assumed to be highly correlated with quality of output (Harris and Raviv, 1978).

In the area of auditing, this could take the form of proof of specialized training (such as passing the CPA exam), accreditation by some reputable agency, and peer reviews of the production process. Unfortunately, we do not know what mix of input characteristics (if any) will actually lead to optimal incentive contracts for auditors. Presumably, over time, those who participate in an auditing contract would be able to determine which input characteristics seem to be correlated with higher quality of output (i.e., "better audits," assuming these can be defined). Those auditors who possess more desirable input characteristics would then command higher fees (rewards).

An important point here, though, is that a competitive market exists in which prices can be assigned to those input characteristics which, over time, can be correlated with output quality. In this way, participants in the process can decide on whether the costs of obtaining these characteristics will be returned in the form of higher returns. One way to achieve this is to provide for the means by which those who possess desirable input characteristics have proof of their acquisition which can be offered to potential buyers. Degrees and various other forms of certification are examples of such proofs.

Note that this does not argue for licensing, which prohibits those who do not possess certain input characteristics from performing auditing or other services. Such strict licensing requirements would eliminate a competitive market in which prices could reflect the desirability of possessing various input characteristics.

Consider next the context within which the audit contract between management and the auditor occurs. Management and the auditor wish to minimize their respective costs, but the output of the process is primarily of benefit to a third party. This leads to the possibility of an externality. In the absence of outside influences, there is no guarantee that the third party's interests will be served by the auditor and management. One outside influence, of course, is the threat of a lawsuit. Standards of performance to which auditor and management are to be held accountable facilitate the establishment of liability on these two parties.

Finally, the outcome of an audit has the characteristic of a public good, since one person's reliance on the results of an audit does not reduce its availability to serve other parties as well. The typical argument is that rational agents will not reveal their preference for a public good via a pricing mechanism, since it is to their advantage to "freeload" on someone else's purchase of that good. This is one condition under which government intervention into the rules governing the production and distribution of a good may be justified.

It is well known, however, that a demand existed for audit services in this country before there was a pervasive requirement for audits such as that contained in the various SEC acts and rulings. This demand was met by audit firms which sold their services for a fee, and the issue is whether such a "free market" setting which existed some fifty years ago and earlier was more efficient in terms of resource allocation than our present regulatory system. It is difficult to design a controlled experiment in which this issue can be resolved, and what evidence exists on the efficacy of the SEC is, in general, inclusive.

Summary

The preliminary evidence on competition in auditing presented here can be summarized as follows.

Structurally, the Big Eight firms are the dominant suppliers of audit services to large corporations, but the aggregate market share of these firms decreases significantly as the size of buyers decreases. This suggests that auditee-auditor pairing may be influenced by economies to auditor size. Although the present structure of the industry may have been affected by the restrictions on price and nonprice competition formerly contained in the AICPA rules of conduct, these restrictions have now been essentially eliminated.

There appear to be no real barriers to entry of individuals into the profession, and the typical state licensing laws are far less restrictive on practice and mobility than in the case of physicians or attorneys. In fact, the education and certification requirements which characterize auditing practice are consistent with a market in which quality uncertainty and information asymmetry exist.

Available evidence on the pricing of audit services is consistent with the hypothesis that the market is competitive.

Finally, both the public good aspect of an audit and the possibility that the value of audited information is not internalized by the market participants suggest the need for further economic modeling of the audit service under both existing and alternative institutional arrangements.

Notes

We wish to express our appreciation to Paul Caster and Patricia Libby, who gathered most of our data on concentration. We also benefited from comments made by S. Acosta, N. Gonedes, R. Kormendi, and S. Sunder on an earlier version of this chapter.

1. As Demsetz (1973: 1) states, "The doctrine . . . holds that the structure of a market gives a reliable index of monopoly power . . . "

2. See Goldschmid, Mann, and Weston (1974) for a discussion of the issues and evidence.

3. See Gonedes and Dopuch (1979) for a review of this issue.

4. As an example, see B. Lev (1979).

5. In computing market shares, the size of buyers is measured by total sales as reported in Moody's Industrial Manuals for the indicated years. A number of corporations are excluded from the statistics because their auditors could not be identified (1955, eleven companies; 1966, twelve companies; 1977, thirty-five companies).

6. This list still does not encompass the entire market, since closely held corporations are not included.

7. See, for example, pp. 39–40 of the *Staff Study* (1977).

8. Similar restrictions pertain to the legal profession as well.

9. See, for example, E. Rayback (1977).

10. Although not stated explicitly, this seems to be a desirable evolution by the Commission on Auditors' Reponsibilities (1978: 90–91).

11. The statistics reported here are taken from "CPA Examination" (1978).

12. Add to this the fact that thirty-two states now cooperate in a program sponsored by the National Association of State Boards of Accountancy and designed to help unsuccessful CPA candidates in subsequent tries at the exam.

13. The provisions concerning direct uninvited solicitation and encroachment were officially removed in May, 1979.

4

The Nature of Competition in the Accounting Profession: A Legal View

Homer Kripke

Chester Rohrlich Professor of Law
New York University School of Law

The nature of competition in the accounting profession leads to the law of antitrust. Much of what we need to know about antitrust and the accounting profession can be found in recent cases in the United States Supreme Court, which I shall refer to as *Goldfarb*,[1] *Bates*,[2] *Engineers*,[3] and *Ohralik*.[4] To these may be added reports of recent proceedings by the antitrust authorities against the legal, medical, and dental professions as well as the proceedings against the accounting profession itself.

Since *Goldfarb* established that lawyers examining titles for real estate in a local county were engaged in an activity affecting interstate commerce and were subject to the Sherman Act, there can be no question that accounting firms auditing the sizable companies engaged in commerce and required to furnish audited financial statements to the SEC are engaged in commerce and affect interstate commerce.

Within the meaning of the dicta in the antitrust cases about special considerations for professions, accounting is undoubtedly a profession. It has been said (Gaines, 1978): "A search for the distinguishing characteristics of a profession quickly leads to the notion of fiduciary responsibility. Professions achieve their status by virtue of an expertise that requires their clients to trust their judgment." A current proposed draft issued by the American Institute of Certified Public Accountants (1978) draws such a sharp distinction between the function of management and the audit function as to lead to the question of whether a client trusts the auditor or the auditor is an independent judge. This draft obviously overstates the case. The better position is stated in the AICPA Code of Professional Ethics, §51.03 and §52.14: "Ordinarily those who depend upon a certified public accountant find it difficult to assess the quality of his services; they have the right to expect, however, that he is a person of competence and integrity ... CPA's continually provide advice to their clients, and they expect that this advice will usually be followed."

Goldfarb established that a profession such as law is not exempt from the Sherman Act when it engages in such restraints of competition as price fixing, and that a relationship with a state which is not sufficient to constitute state action will not provide a shield for it. *Bates* carried *Goldfarb* further to the question of restraints on competition by prohibitions on advertising, but held that where the restraints constituted action by the state, they were immune from the Sherman Act. But *Bates* also held that advertising was protected by the First Amendment principles of free speech.

Engineers teaches us that even though the rule of reason may apply, it does not carry us to the point of sanctioning price fixing, monopoly, or other restraints on competition unless on balance the total effect of the restraint is procompetitive. The question of the validity of the restraints depends on their impact on competitive conditions. Anticompetitive action will not be saved by other factors, such as the effect of the restraint on product safety or similar factors not directly bearing on competition. Perhaps what survives is permitted regulation by the profession of such egregious activity as ambulance chasing, for which discipline was sustained in *Ohralik*, if there is anything equally blatant in accounting.

Ohralik teaches us that, notwithstanding recent extensions of free speech protection to commercial speech such as the advertising involved in *Bates*, not every action that has a speech element is protected by the First Amendment. But the profession's preclusion of competition by solicitation sustained in *Ohralik* also depends on the existence of state action, and there is certainly no clearly surviving field for limitation of competition by professional action alone.

Engineers tells us that where the defendant was guilty of a violation, the court's power to fashion appropriate remedies permits it to enjoin expressions of opinion to the effect that competitive bidding is unethical. But the Chief Justice dissented on this point, and it may be possible that professions such as accounting which saw the handwriting on the wall and withdrew many of their anticompetitive pronouncements before the antitrust authorities caught up with them[5] may still have the protected freedom of speech to express the opinion—without any teeth—that encroachment, raiding of employees, and other anticompetitive activity is unethical. But that is a subtle point, and I defer to those more accustomed to constitutional and antitrust subtleties to provide a definitive guess.

In light of the recent blockbusters from the Supreme Court, the old belief that professions were immune from the antitrust laws is dead. In the face of *Bates*, architects and accountants voluntarily revised their antiadvertising codes and the American Dental Association settled an FTC action. An FTC administrative law judge has made a ruling of violation with respect to the American Medical Association, and an appeal is pending to the Commission itself. The American Bar Association tried to find an intermediate position on advertising and suffered a suit, which was then dropped when the position was abandoned.[6] The Accounting Code of Professional Ethics, §56.04, and Rule 502 of the AICPA's Statements of Auditing Standards both now merely prohibit advertising which is deceptive, and this may eliminate the advertising problem at the level of generalized pronouncements. Rule 502 has recently been amended to eliminate the prohibition on solicitation of customers. AICPA Rule 401 no longer forbids encroachment—that is, endeavoring to provide a person or entity with professional services currently provided by another accountant except upon request, and this eliminates an anticompetitive prohibition which would have presented problems. Such auditing rules as Rule 302 prohibiting contingent fees based on specific findings or results could be argued to be noncompetitive.

The latest of Milton Handler's annual reviews of antitrust before the Association of the Bar of the City of New York is mandatory reading for anyone interested in the foregoing subject matter. He states (1978: 565–566):

> It is plain that there are social values separate and apart from competition which should be balanced but which under the Stevens thesis may not be . . . I believe that we can maintain full allegiance to the precepts of competition for the private sector and yet in these exceptional cases enlarge the scope of the rule of reason so as to avoid the kind of unhappy results that flow from the unmitigated operation of competition in areas for which it is entirely unsuited and where the social harm outweighs the benefits. In short, I would urge more flexibility in these exceptional cases . . ."

Handler takes an alarmist view of the meaning of the *Engineers* case. He therefore urges more flexibility, believing that he is calling for a change in the law. The Federal Trade Commission's Chicago regional office has announced (1977) "an investigation into whether activities by state accountancy licensing boards *and private accounting associations* [emphasis added] restrain entry into the profession or restrict the competitive behavior of accountants."

The same press release states in part:

> The staff will examine the effects, among other things, of:
> —minimum educational requirements and restrictions concerning age,

character, residency and citizenship imposed by states upon persons seeking
to become licensed accountants;

—prohibitions in codes of ethics against solicitation and advertising,
competitive bidding, and incompatible occupations; . . .

That the approach may be ideologically absolute, without a rule of reason, appears from a letter written by a member of the FTC Chicago office
staff to a state legislator reviewing his state's regulation of accounting:

. . . this letter is only an informal staff opinion, and is not binding on or
attributable to the Commission.

• • •

I commend your findings and recommendations regarding the elimination of prohibitions against advertising, competitive bidding, and encroachment. Your recommendations to eliminate the moral character, domicile and
residence requirements are also steps in the right direction.

However, I would also recommend that the legislature consider adopting what is commonly called a "Practice Restriction" form of regulation,
which would allow individuals to perform the attest function or hold themselves out as being able to perform such a function if they have met certain
statutory requirements. Under this form of regulation, the legislature should
consider eliminating the education and experience requirements and impose
only those requirements which can be shown to be directly related to job
performance. This form of regulation differs from licensing in that there
would be no need for an interim body with the general authority to promulgate rules and regulations, and no specific mechanism for monitoring the
profession on an ongoing basis. Once the individual has met the statutory
requirements, only civil or criminal remedies would be available to withdraw the state's permission to practice accounting. Administration of the entrance requirements, including administration of an examination, if deemed
to be one of the requirements directly related to job performance, could be
delegated to a state agency. This would further lessen the power of the profession to restrict entry.[7]

We shall have to wait to learn what comes of this investigation.

The foregoing analysis of the recent Supreme Court cases presents
nothing that might not have been written by any competent lawyer. In my
opinion, however, there are deeper issues that go to the fundamentals of
the accounting profession's posture of self-regulation. The same press release cited earlier (FTC, 1977) states that another topic of the FTC's Chicago
office examination is: "the establishment and application of accounting and
auditing standards." And so, as for the self-regulation now said to be enjoyed by the accounting profession in the formation of accounting and auditing principles, the fat may be in the fire. I have not been able to learn of
any actual movement in this direction in the FTC's Chicago-based investi-

gation, and I do not mean to encourage any such movement, which I think would be unfortunate. But the language last quoted must have been intended to mean something, and—given my task in this chapter—it seems worthwhile to explore the possible issues.

And here is the notable feature which sets accounting off from the other professions. Medicine and dentistry are rooted in the natural laws of the biological sciences. Engineering and architecture are rooted in the natural laws of the physical sciences. Law is rooted in prescriptions by the state which create social laws. Accounting, however, insofar as it is "self-regulated," has no external referent. It cannot be proved or verified empirically. It is an entirely human construct, and its "principles" represent contractual restraint among its practitioners as to what they will say and how they will say it.

How, then, do accounting principles and their practitioners escape the interdictions of the antitrust laws? When in Ethical Rule 203.1 the AICPA decrees that a member shall not express an opinion that financial statements are presented in conformity with generally accepted accounting principles (GAAP) if they depart from any principle promulgated by the body designated by the AICPA Council, is it not restraining the member? Suppose the member believes not only that a different principle is correct—for example, that value rather than historical cost should be the basis of stating fixed assets—but also believes that there is substantial support for this proposition. Should he not be permitted to attest to the assets on this basis?[8]

Ethical Rule 201E forbids a member to permit his name to be used in connection with forecasts, in a manner leading to believe that he vouches for the achievability of the forecast. Is this not a suppression of competition, serving no apparent purpose of public understanding or reliability?

Or, when Ethical Rule 202 forbids a member to permit his name to be associated with financial statements in such a manner as to imply that he is acting as an independent public accountant unless he has complied with the relevant generally accepted auditing standards promulgated by the Institute, is not this also anticompetitive?

I am not arguing that the antitrust authorities should take action to destroy the FASB's and the AICPA's adherence to FASB Standards, nor that they destroy the developing code of Statements on Auditing Standards. Rather, I am suggesting that it is hard to see why these do not limit competition in a narrow sense. Even though the standards obviously serve important functions, it is superficially difficult to see how the resulting reduction of competition can be supported by the rule of reason as defined in the *Engineers* case, which puts all of the focus on competition and argues that other public benefits are not sufficient to balance the interference with competition.

And yet, although my credentials in the antitrust field are nonexistent while Handler's are unimpeachable, I have the temerity to take a slightly more sanguine position on the application of *Engineers* in other professional contexts than he does. I have the advantage that my opinion is formed after another significant Supreme Court opinion, *Broadcast Music, Inc.* v. *Columbia Broadcasting System, Inc.,* was decided on April 17, 1979. *Engineers* was an extreme case in which that professional organization tried to justify overt suppression of competition. In that context it is permissible for a lawyer to speculate whether all members of an inevitably unanimous court are firmly committed to the broad dicta in Justice Stevens's opinion, whose reach goes far beyond what was necessary to a decision on those facts. This type of speculation is encouraged by the situation in *BMI* v. *CBS,* just cited, where Justice Stevens found himself in a minority of one dissenting from an otherwise unanimous court. Eight justices concluded that what might be called tie-in licensing of musical compositions might be justified under the rule of reason applied to the special circumstances of broadcast performance of copyrighted music, while Justice Stevens found a violation.

From this approach, suggesting that not everything said in *Engineers* firmly commands the support of the full Court, it is possible to express the hope that something still survives of Chief Justice Warren Burger's observation in footnote 17 to *Goldfarb:*

> It would be unrealistic to view the practice of professions as interchangeable with other business activities, and automatically to apply to the profession antitrust concepts which originated in other areas. The public service aspect, and other features of the professions, may require that a particular practice, which could properly be viewed as a violation of the Sherman Act in another context, be treated differently.

Both in *Goldfarb* and in *Bates,* the Court recognized the important status of the law and the importance of state regulation thereof with this language: "The interest of the States in regulating lawyers is especially great since lawyers are essential to the primary governmental function of administering justice, and have historically been 'officers of the courts.' " By a similar token, accountants are essential to the flow and control of commerce, both for the disclosure and regulation controlled by the SEC, and for the factual basis for regulation by the FTC, the Interstate Commerce Commission, and other federal agencies, and the importance of accountants to the flow of commerce cannot be gainsaid.

From this point of view, the unification of auditing and accounting principles seems so clearly sound in terms of serving the genuine public interest that I would hope it can be justified, notwithstanding the limiting tests of the *Engineers* case. The courts might fit it within the language of *Continental TV, Inc.* v. *GTE Sylvania, Inc.,* 433 U.S. 36, quoted with approval in *Engineers:* "The true test of legality is whether the restraint imposed is such that merely regulates and perhaps thereby promotes competition or whether it is such as may suppress or even destroy competition." Indeed, it could be said that these principles and their enforcement promote competition in a larger sense—competition in the business and financial community and in the allocation of resources on the basis of uniform presentation, which encourages accurate perception of realities and the avoidance of fraud.

This is not to say that the result is clear. I have had occasion to state in other contexts that the SEC seems to like to live dangerously in legal matters, and the recent record of its legal positions in the Supreme Court seems to show that it is not a lucky gambler. To rely on reasoning like mine earlier seems foolhardy for the SEC and the accountants when a much safer position is available.[9] The way to avoid these risks would be to bring accounting and auditing within the safe harbor of action required by government. This would not be as recognized in *Goldfarb* and as applied in *Bates* for state action, but as action of a self-regulatory agency implicitly exempted from the antitrust laws in order to carry out the scheme of the federal securities legislation and subject to review by a specific federal agency. This was the basis on which anticompetitive price fixing by the New York Stock Exchange was held to be nonviolative of the antitrust laws in *Gordon*. In contrast, however, where there was no provision for supervision, the antitrust laws were held applicable in *Silver*.[10] Can we make a case that FASB action on accounting principles and AICPA action on auditing standards already fulfills the intent of the securities legislation, and is supervised by the SEC within the meaning of *Gordon?* Or must we apply here the teaching of *Silver* as stated in *Gordon:*

> Repeal of the antitrust laws by implication is not favored and not casually to be allowed. Only where there is a "plain repugnancy between the antitrust and regulatory provisions" will repeal be implied ... Under this principle, "[r]epeal is regarded as implied only if necessary to make the Securities Exchange Act work, and even then only to the minimum extent necessary."

SEC Regulation S-X, §202(b) requires that financial statements be certified and that the auditor in rendering his opinion represents that he has complied with generally accepted auditing standards. No source for these standards is specified, but it is well known that the SEC looks to the standards announced by the AICPA. When dissatisfied, SEC has pressed the AICPA to revise these standards—for example, at an early date after the McKesson and Robbins case regarding verification of receivables and the auditor's presence during inventory; and more recently when it pushed the AICPA into agreeing to the expression of an opinion on interim statements after an examination falling short of an audit.[11] But since the statutes say not a word about deriving auditing standards from auditors' self-governing agencies, and since the SEC has never conceded that it does not itself have power to control the extent of the statutorily required audits,[12] I doubt that the SEC's pressures on the AICPA convert the AICPA into a part of the scheme contemplated by Congress.

On accounting principles, the position is even more dubious. SEC Regulation S-X, §202(c) requires an independent accountant's opinion on the financial statements and the accounting principles reflected therein, but it does not expressly recognize generally accepted accounting principles or any similar concept.

Perhaps this omission is cured by two subsequent accounting series releases. In *Accounting Series Release No. 4* (1938), the Commission stated that financial statements prepared in accordance with accounting principles "for which there is no substantial support" will be presumed to be misleading. The release goes on to state that in case of disagreement between the registrant and the Commission, disclosure will be accepted in lieu of correction only if the registrant has substantial authoritative support and the SEC has not theretofore expressed a contrary opinion. This is the situation that still prevails. The Commission will accept "substantial authoritative support" except in the instances where it has chosen to go its own way in accounting. It is commonly accepted that the reference to "substantial authoritative support" marked an agreement of the SEC with the AICPA that the Commission would defer to the latter in the formulation of accounting principles if the latter would only get on with the job. Chatov (1975) has traced this history at length.

Subsequently, in *Accounting Series Release No. 150*, the Commission announced its support for the newly formed FASB and stated that it would consider the latter's pronouncements authoritative.

More recently, as in the release on reserve recognition accounting for oil and gas (*ASR* 253), the Commission went out of its way to reaffirm its general support for the FASB as the standards setter for GAAP, even though it asserted its own final responsibility and disagreed with the FASB in that instance.

This relationship between the Commission and the FASB, I have long contended, is unsatisfactory. Unlike auditing, over which the Commission neither had explicit statutory powers of control nor has the AICPA ever conceded the Commission's control,[13] the Commission does have express authority and responsibility for the accounting principles used in its disclosure documents under §19(a) of the Securities Act and §23(a) of the Securities Exchange Act. There is no doubt of this. Equally, no doubt exists that these acts contain no shadow of indication that the Commission is authorized to establish the AICPA, the FASB, or any other accounting authority as a self-regulatory agency, in contrast to the express statutory recognitions of the stock exchanges and the National Association of Securities Dealers, Inc. (NASD) as self-regulatory organizations. Without inside knowledge, we cannot know how much is fact and how much is obfuscation in the elaborate assertions both by the Commission and the accountants that the accounting profession is in fact self-regulated and that the Commission exercises only an occasional supervision. The more both parties protest, the weaker would seem to be the accountants' hope for immunity from the antitrust laws in their system of restraints in the use of accounting principles. In my opinion, reliance on the fact that the Commission uses them to do what Congress told the Commission to do and in most cases rubberstamps their conclusions is not sufficient to make them part of the scheme created by Congress. The single exception was congressional recognition of the FASB in the Energy Policy and Conservation Act of 1975. In the other rare cases where the SEC does not rubberstamp FASB or APB determinations, it acts by disregarding them, not by formally reviewing them.

Certainly, the attitudes of the Moss and Metcalf Committees do not indicate that the current congressional committees believe that the Commission's delegation to the accountants' agencies is required by the statute or part of the statutory scheme. I cannot see any antitrust exemption arising from SEC abandonment of its delegated powers. I suspect that there is theoretical antitrust vulnerability. Whether the theory will become actuality depends on how rigidly the antitrust authorities read the assertions of *Engineers* that only the balance of competitive effects weighs in the scale, not other public policy effects.

The antitrust considerations merely reinforce other points made here about this relationship:

1. It is obvious that the Commission does maintain some kind of contact with the FASB and influences its agenda and its decisions, but usually without public knowledge or scrutiny. I question whether this kind of invisible public influence is in the public interest. What becomes of the FASB's vaunted due process if it is subject to Commission pressures *in camera?*

2. When the Commission, by rubberstamping the FASB, makes its pronouncements matters of law, there is a serious question whether the Commission has complied with the Administrative Procedure Act in enforcing FASB Statements as law. The recent Arthur Andersen case was decided on the preliminary question of standing and sheds no light on the question.[14]

3. If the rules which the Commission enforces were adopted under the Administrative Procedure Act, everyone would know his rights to be heard

before the Commission and his rights of appeal. In the present nebulous and symbiotic relationship of the Commission with the FASB, there is no general opportunity for input to the Commission about the suitability of accounting principles, and no right of appeal when the Commission enforces the FASB determination while purporting merely to be applying GAAP. It is equally clear that there is no right of appeal from FASB's promulgation of Statements, which, like those of prior accountants' standard-setting bodies, are in theory only the determinations of a private organization.[15]

We would all be much better off if it were frankly recognized that the Commission is making law when it applies FASB Statements and if *these* pronouncements were adopted simultaneously as Statements of the FASB and as rules of the Commission, after whatever procedures the FASB chooses to follow, and after appropriate procedures under the Administrative Procedure Act by the Commission. This action would require some coordination, but not much delay; it would give clarity to the relationship and status to the pronouncements. A statutorily authorized delegation of the drafting functions to the FASB would solve the antitrust problem.

The narrow topic of my chapter is supposed to be "The Nature of Competition in the Accounting Profession: A Legal View." A lawyer who does not practice but who professes in the ivory tower does not see the competition among accountants sufficiently to comment on the actuality of competition from the authority of personal observation. One hears about the extensive and vigorous "development" operations of the accounting firms and wonders whether the anticompetitive thrust of the accountants' prohibitions against encroachment and raiding other firms for personnel when they existed actually precluded these kinds of competition, and whether the former restraints may still be observed. Some price competition on presentations and estimates seems to exist, as evidenced by the fact that the Cohen Commission found that one of the factors leading to inadequate audits was the time pressure resulting from costs of the accountant in relation to his expected fees.[16]

Theoretically, according to the Cohen Commission, accountants should "compete principally on the quality of their services." Presumably, unless antitrust someday causes a complete revolution in thinking, this should not include competition in accommodating management by accepting its proposed accounting as being in accord with GAAP. Yet some instances of this type have been known and widely publicized, in which the management has discharged one public accounting firm and engaged another which accepted accounting that the first firm had refused to approve. The SEC has an elaborate procedure of required reporting of instances of this type, designed to bring them to the SEC's and the public's attention. [17]

Theoretically, an opportunity should remain for competition among accountants in the extent of their willingness to accept from available alternative GAAP that one which management prefers instead of their own preferences. But perhaps the accountants are afraid of the ruthlessness of any such competition and the manner in which it might cause bad accounting to drive out the good. Therefore, when the SEC required in *Accounting Series Release No. 177* that the accountants express an opinion that a change in accounting principles made by management was to a principle that the accountant deemed preferable, the profession resisted bitterly. It contended that, in the absence of action by the profession, there was no basis for one accountant to determine the preferability of one accounting principle as against another. This was the basis of Arthur Andersen's litigation against the SEC.[18] This contention has never seemed to me to be convincing or even plausible. If accountants as a group can determine legislatively that one or several accounting principles are sound enough to be incorporated into GAAP as permissible across the vast range of potential applications, and others are not, standards of judgment must exist which can be applied in these difficult situations of multiple application. In most cases, it would seem far easier to determine the preferability of one among the limited number of remaining available alternatives when applied to a specific fact situation. The accountants' unwillingness to make this judgment may indicate a determination not to compete for fear of making Gresham's law applicable. Indeed, when viewed in this light, the whole program over the last forty years of institutionalizing accounting principles through, successively, the Committee on Accounting Procedure, the Accounting Principles Board (APB), and the FASB may be thought of as a cartel arrangement by which accountants agreed that they would not compete by accepting any of the accounting principles which the standard-setting body had rejected or not approved.

This question of competition over preferability is not yet ended, both because the SEC has made ASR 177 stick, and because the AICPA's own Commission on Auditors' Responsibilities (the Cohen Commission) went even further than the SEC. The Cohen Commission took the position that reporting accountants ought to consider continually the preferability and suitability of the accounting principles being used by management, not merely on the occasion of a change as required by the SEC in ASR 177.[19] So far as I know, the AICPA has not yet either accepted or rejected this recommendation.

In conclusion, it would seem that the application of antitrust law to the more mundane aspects of the accounting profession is now clear—that is, it forbids restrictions on advertising, price fixing, encroachment by solicitation of customers of another accountant, solicitation of employees of another accountant, and so on. In addition, the unique aspect of accounting, namely that its body of principles has no verifiable existence in the physical world and no clear public command as in law, leaves the principles both of accounting and auditing as contractual restraints which present the-oretically major antitrust problems under the *Engineers* case. It would be in the public interest if the standard-setting process for accountants found the shelter it deserves and needs in more active participation by the SEC in the standard-setting process. In any event, it would not be sound public policy to disturb the formulation of accounting or auditing principles by applica-tion of the antitrust laws. I leave it to the antitrust authorities to figure out a way how not to do it.

Notes

1. *Goldfarb* v. *Virginia State Bar*, 421 U.S. 773 (1975).

2. *Bates* v. *State Bar of Arizona*, 433 U.S. 350 *(1977)*.

3. *National Society of Professional Engineers* v. *United States*, 435 U.S. 679 (1978).

4. *Ohralik* v. *Ohio State Bar Association*, 436 U.S. 447 (1978).

5. The AICPA compilation on professional standards shows numerous suspensions as of March 31, 1978 of interpretations formerly contained in the Code of Professional Ethics. Comparison with earlier editions of the Code shows that the interpretations suspended had anticompetitive implications. Modification in the specific rules on advertising and encroach-ment seems to have had a similar motivation.

6. On this suit, see "F.T.C. to Hear Appeal" (1979).

7. The letter is to a Florida legislator, and it is dated December, 1978.

8. This was indeed the position taken by Beaver in a well-known article (1973) in which he argued that disclosure, rather than adherence to uniform principles, should be sufficient and that uniformity serves to suppress information.

9. When the SEC announced ASR 150 (discussed later in the text), I wrote a Commissioner suggesting that the Commission's legal structuring of its position with the accountants had maximum vulnerability. I urged the position stated here, which I believe is far safer.

10. *Gordon* v. *New York Stock Exchange* (1975); *Silver* v. *New York Stock Exchange*, (1963). See Handler, 1978: 569–571.

11. See AICPA Statements on Auditing Standards Sec. 720A.

12. See discussion in the American Law Institute's (1974) Federal Securities Code, Tentative Draft No. 3, §1503 and Comment.

13. See note 12.

14. *Arthur Andersen & Company* v. *SEC*, (N.D. Ill.). See CCH Fed. Sec. L. Rep. §95720 (1976) for denial of injunction and §96374 (1978) for dismissal.

15. *Appalachian Power Company* v. *AICPA*, 268 F. 2d 844 (2d Cir.) cert. denied 361 U.S. 887 (1959).

16. See Commission on Auditor's Responsibilities (1978: 109–118).

17. SEC Form 8-K, Item 4; Reg. S-X, Rule 3-16(s).

18. See note 14.

19. See Commission on Auditor's Responsibilities (1978: chapter 3).

III

Regulation and the Accounting Profession

Surveillance of the accounting profession grew substantially following 1977 and 1978 congressional hearings and reports that were highly critical of the industry. Probably the most important response by the profession was the formation of a "Division of Firms" by the AICPA, with an SEC Practice Section possessing disciplinary sanctions for firms with publicly held clients.

The following four chapters reach a consensus on the need for self-regulation and the belief that government intervention in the private sector in general and in accounting in particular can cause problems. Beyond that, however, they diverge considerably on such issues as identifying the function of self-regulation and the relation of principles adopted to that function.

In Chapter 5, for example, Nelligan believes the current self-regulatory program doesn't reach far enough; in Chapter 8, Chetkovitch defends it. For Williams in Chapter 6, leadership and the willingness to back that leadership are lacking in the profession. In Chapter 7, Mosso believes accuracy should be the most important benchmark.

The basic issue for Nelligan is ensuring the public's right to expect strong accounting and uniform principles. If self-regulation is to be effective, it must be perceived as effective by the public. Since the membership of the SEC Practice Section represents only a fifth of the firms auditing publicly held companies, Nelligan concludes that the private sector is not fulfilling its responsibilities to the public. Therefore, in his view, the SEC must act.

Chetkovich believes the AICPA has moved quickly and decisively on self-

regulation, as voluntary membership in the Practice Section accounts for firms handling 80 percent of the total SEC practice. The challenge as he sees it is to temper both the government's zeal for regulation and the profession's self-interest.

Although Williams and Mosso are philosophically opposed to government intervention through regulation, they are much less sanguine than Chetkovich about the profession's response to that prospect. Both stress that because of public interest pressure, a lack of positive response by the profession leaves the government with no choice but to undertake "reform" measures itself.

For Williams, the ultimate thrust of self-regulation should be to provide much better investor guidance. He believes the profession, and particularly the Practice Section of the AICPA, can help do so, even without a consensus. Should this not happen, the alternative for Williams is for the SEC to provide leadership—something it is reluctant but not unwilling to do.

Mosso concludes that it is uncertain whether the private or public sector can best set accounting and auditing standards. But, he adds, the profession's primary goal will have to be a commitment to accuracy, tempered by restraints on unfair economic behavior, if standard setting, such as that now done by the industry's Financial Accounting Standards Board, is to be kept from drifting further into the public sector.

5

Regulation and the Accounting Profession: The Congressional View

James L. Nelligan
Operations Director
Oversight and Investigations Subcommittee
House of Representatives
U.S. Congress

To serve the public from whom my authority is derived.

To serve my profession and contribute to its institutions.

To practice at the highest professional level.

To maintain an ethical posture characteristic of a learned profession.

To maintain my technical skills so that the public is served with competence.

To maintain a state of independence at all times so that decisions are reached with objectivity.

To work with my colleagues—for the practice of a profession is an experience in human behavior and mutual respect.

"Credo for a CPA"—Eli Mason, CPA

In what might be described by some as a subtle attack on the nation's leading accounting firm, the Big Eight firm of Coopers and Lybrand, breaking a long tradition of secrecy, announced in November, 1978 "the largest annual volume ever reported by an accounting firm." Hailed as the "new champion" by *Forbes* magazine, C&L boasted revenues of more than $595 million for the fiscal year ended September 30, 1978—up 17 percent from the preceding year and 105 percent over the last five years. Thus, one might get the impression that C&L had dethroned Peat, Marwick, Mitchell & Co., considered by most to be the nation's foremost accounting firm. In a swift counterattack, however, PMM pointed out that its 1978 revenues of $585.9 million were for the fiscal year ended June 30; if it had used a September 30 fiscal year, its earnings would have exceeded $603 million, keeping PMM "number one."

Perhaps it *is* better to be "number one" than "best." To be the best, however, is certainly more in the public interest—an interest which is at least a stated objective of most, if not all, public accounting firms auditing public companies.

At a recent roundtable conference at the University of Florida on the subject of government regulation of accounting and information, a well-known financial reporter criticized the accounting profession for the complexity of corporate financial statements and the confusion and misunderstanding they caused, not only among investors but among other users as well, including accountants. Making a strong pitch for more simplified and informative financial statements geared to greater understanding and use by investors, the reporter was challenged by a partner from a Big Eight firm. He expressed his objection to the reporter's criticism by indicating that if investors were unable to understand and use financial statements as they are presently prepared and were hesitant about investing as a result, then they should put their money in a bank at 5 percent interest.

In an atmosphere where American business is finding it difficult to raise needed capital, such an attitude, in my opinion, has no place in a profession which alleges to have a public interest.

At the same conference, another partner from the same Big Eight firm aired his views on the AICPA's Division of Firms, the self-regulatory mechanism instituted by American Institute of Certified Public Accountants to reform the accounting profession. He strongly implied that no need for such reform existed and espoused the philosophy, "If it's not broken, don't fix it."

Considering the steady stream of exposés which involve large accounting firms and crowd the financial pages of our daily newspapers, and the profession's oft-stated concern that *perception* of impropriety is as detrimental to the profession as *fact* of impropriety, I find it difficult to agree with this Big Eight partner that reform of the accounting profession is not needed. I believe not only that reform is needed and long overdue, but that meaningful reform is not being achieved. It is consoling to know that many CPAs agree with me—or, to place it in proper perspective, that I agree with them.

These are just a few of many observations which indicate to me that for many accounting firms, particularly large ones, phrases such as "serving the public" and "preserving the public interest" are overworked platitudes which shield true motivation. To me, actions really do speak louder than words, particularly in this arena. And although the primary objective and concern most frequently articulated by large firms auditing public companies is "public interest," rhetoric does not appear to be in step with action. Preoccupation with increased revenues and size, status in the profession, lack of concern for investors, retaining the profitable status quo, and meaningless reforms are actions that have become so pervasive they are beginning to leave little room for the public interest.

The public's disenchantment with CPAs over such issues as their relationship to the public, financial statements, and investor needs is not new. It has just been ignored.

For example, a study conducted by Opinion Research Corporation in 1974 disclosed that CPAs *still* had not done enough to make sure there was an adequate flow of reliable, relevant, and understandable information. The study covered some 400 shareholders and a similar number of what ORC called "key *publics"*—business executives, government regulators, securities analysts, lawyers, brokers, business school professors, CPAs, business journalists, and social activists.

More than half the shareholders and almost half the key publics complained that financial statements were complex, difficult to understand, and did not provide enough information. About one third of the shareholders believed the statements were biased and inaccurate, and two fifths of the key publics believed that accountants had not made an adequate effort to ascertain that all relevant financial information was revealed. They also felt that the major public accounting firms gave in too easily to direct pressure, bent accounting rules in management's favor, and questioned whether accounting firms were fair to investors' interests. Also notable in the study was the belief of a majority of the shareholders that a CPA firm's most important function is to detect fraud and the belief of a majority of the key publics that large firms do not accept enough responsibility for their mistakes—issues the profession continues to avoid like the plague.

More to the point here is the fact that congressional disenchantment with the accounting profession is not new.

Contrary to widespread misconception, congressional interest in accounting matters is not recent. It began with the economic slides of the 1930s and gained impetus under the scandals that have shaken our country over the past several years—Equity Funding, Penn Central, Four Seasons Nursing Homes, and National Student Marketing readily leap to mind. In all of those situations, publicly owned companies went bankrupt and caused substantial harm to investors with no prior warning from their independent auditors that anything was amiss. Congress began to wonder where the auditors were during the period these companies were headed for their falls, and, more importantly, where was the Securities and Exchange Commission? Congress gave the SEC broad powers to set accounting standards in Section 13 of the Securities Act of 1934—a power seldom used to date.

Interest was further aroused as Congress began to study particular industries and experienced difficulty working with the accounting methods used. In the securities industry, for example, it found certain capital rules that allowed firms to arrive at eight or nine different capital ratios depending upon the methods they employed. This helped lead to the demise of over a hundred brokerage firms in the late 1960s with resultant harm to their customers. One question frequently asked was this: Could uniform accounting standards have helped to alleviate the crisis? The answer was, yes. Congress felt compelled to legislate in this area in the Securities Acts Amendments of 1975.

As the energy problem became more pressing, Congress discovered that it was unable to obtain reliable data on companies involved in the energy industry. As a result, my former employer, Congressman John E. Moss, proposed a provision in the Energy Policy and Conservation Act calling for development of a reliable energy data base. It was intended that a preferred, uniform accounting standard for recording similar facts and circumstances within the industry would enhance the intercompany comparability which policy makers, managers, investors, and consumers have been denied for too long. Unfortunately, the SEC's recent rejection of the FASB's attempt to establish the uniformity Congress intended merely adds to the list of oversight failures for which the SEC has become infamous in the accounting area.

But Congress's largest impetus to study the profession came with the disclosure of illegal and improper payments made by some of our nation's largest and most prestigious corporations. Bribery, illegal political contributions, kickbacks, slush funds, and secret bank accounts were matters that independent auditors either did not discover or did discover but chose not to disclose publicly.

In response to revelations such as this, the House Subcommittee on Oversight and Investigations, chaired by Congressman Moss, undertook a study dealing with corporate accountability. In October, 1966, the subcommittee issued its report containing recommendations for change. It recommended that publicly owned corporations adopt and enforce codes of conduct; that independent auditors attest to the quality of enforcement of the corporation's code of business conduct and system of internal controls; that corporations have audit committees comprised of a majority of independent directors; and that such committees have available to them independent expert advisors.

The subcommittee concluded that the SEC should play a more active role than it had in the past in the setting of accounting principles and the establishment of auditing standards. As I stated earlier, the federal securities laws have, since 1934, authorized the SEC to ensure that publicly owned companies report financial data in such detail and such form as the Commission shall prescribe, and authorized the agency to prescribe "the methods to be followed in the preparation of reports . . ."

It also concluded that the SEC should prescribe a framework and establish the guidelines within which the private sector determines accounting principles and sets auditing standards. The SEC should also suggest priorities based upon national and international needs and should exercise in a much more vigorous fashion its overseeing of proposed principles and standards and the operation of those already in place, exercising its right of preemption when necessary.

Some months after the Subcommittee on Oversight and Investigations issued its report, the staff of the Subcommittee on Reports, Accounting and Management of the Senate Committee on Governmental Affairs, commonly referred to as the Metcalf Subcommittee, issued its report on the accounting establishment. Its recommendations, which went considerably further than those of the House, called for extensive federal involvement in the accounting profession. In November, 1977, however, the Metcalf Subcommittee, by unanimous approval of its members, issued its report—a toned-down version of the staff report that was substantially in agreement with the recommendations of the House.

The numerous congressional hearings preceding these reports enshrined the problems of the accounting profession in the financial pages of the nation's daily newspapers, and it was not uncommon for such news to be aired on the front page.

Congressional concerns about the accounting profession have been recorded and repeated time and time again during the past few years. The lack of uniformity in generally accepted accounting principles and standards, management fraud and illegal political contributions escaping the detection of accounting firms, financial failures of corporate giants following the publication of unqualified financial statements by Big Eight auditors, and the accelerating trend toward concentration of the profession among the Big Eight, accompanied by the alarming disappearance of some of the nation's most prestigious mid-sized firms—such as Wolf and Co., Clarence Rainess, J. K. Lasser, and S. D. Leidesdorf, are some of these concerns.

Regarding S. D. Leidesdorf, it should be noted that within the last eighteen months, Ernst and Ernst, through a merger with S. D. Leidesdorf, leaped from eighth to a disputed third place among the Big Eight, with 8,000 employees and annual revenues of about $345 million. Just recently, Ernst and Ernst finalized another merger with two British firms to create a network of 304 offices in seventy-one countries with over 14,000 employees and annual revenues of more than $500 million. Clearly, there will never be a Big Nine.

Perhaps the most alarming of congressional concerns, however, is the accounting profession's recognition that reform of the profession is needed and long overdue. Yet the structure and vehicle the profession proposes through its trade association, the AICPA, to achieve this reform is subtly but clearly designed to retain the status quo.

As result of congressional prodding, in September, 1977, the AICPA, yielding to pressures it could no longer ignore, unveiled its self-reform measures and self-regulatory program at its annual convention. Support for the program was far from unanimous, with one third of the members in attendance standing in opposition to the program. They claimed, among other things, that the new Division of Firms, with its SEC Practice Section and Private Companies Practice Section, split the traditionally member-oriented AICPA into first-class and second-class members. The result has been a continuing bitterness within and fragmentation of the AICPA and a basic mistrust in the AICPA leadership that continues to smolder and fester more and more each day. The plight of the dissenters is so severe that several small and medium-sized firms have bound together in what many of them view as a last-ditch effort to survive.

A few months ago, a newly formed association called the National Conference of CPA Practitioners held its first national meeting in Washington, D.C. More than 225 medium and small accounting firms, numbering in excess of 3,000 accountants, have joined the organization to date, and the founders met in Washington to discuss their concern about such threatening issues as bank loan agreements which require audit reports from Big Eight accounting firms, underwriters and investment bankers who insist on audits by Big Eight firms when the client goes public, and the damaging effect of audit committees on smaller firms. The camaraderie and dedication to purpose demonstrated at the meeting can only mushroom as other small and medium-sized firms become aware of NCCPAP's existence. The Conference has established chapters in Albany, Detroit, Indianapolis, and New York City; plans are underway to establish chapters in many other cities, including Los Angeles and Washington, D.C.

Moreover, the group recently submitted to the AICPA's Special Committee on Small and Medium-Sized Firms recommendations which warrant serious consideration. The recommendations included changing the method of amending AICPA bylaws so that Institute members, by legal petition of at least 500 signatures, can require a mail ballot of AICPA membership, changing the method of designating the AICPA Nominating Committee so that Institute members can have more direct voice in the selection of Institute officers, and eliminating lifetime AICPA Council seats for past presidents and past chairmen.

These suggestions strike at the heart of Big Eight dominance. For example, rotation of the AICPA chairmanship between a big firm and small firm and then placing them on the Council for life provides a disproportionate share of influence to the large firms, which number only about twenty-one of the 27,000 public accounting firms. Of the twenty-three past presidents and chairmen of the board presently serving ex officio on the Council, eighteen are from large firms and eleven of those are from Big Eight firms.

In addition to the bitterness and fragmentation within the AICPA, congressional concerns about the organization's self-regulatory program have centered on the control of the SEC Practice Section's committees and sub-committees by the largest accounting firms, the effectiveness of its Public Oversight Board, the voluntary nature of the program, and the effectiveness of its disciplinary procedures. Although many changes have been made by the AICPA during the last eighteen months in response to congressional criticisms of its program, the changes have been mostly cosmetic. Basic concerns have not been addressed.

For example, a close look at the composition of the SEC Practice Section's Executive and Peer Review Committees clearly shows that the AICPA's program is controlled by the large accounting firms. Of the more than 500 members in the Section to date, only the largest sixteen firms with thirty or more SEC clients have automatic representation on the twenty-one-member Executive Committee. The smaller firms are represented by only five members. The imbalance is even greater in the Peer Review Committee, where fourteen of the fifteen members represent large firms, including seven of the Big Eight. And there is nothing in the structure that does not ensure that it will remain so in the future. For each firm that reaches the level of thirty SEC clients and is added automatically, a small firm will also be added. Such a procedure will not only ensure the perpetual dominance of the large firms, it will make the Executive Committee unmanageable as the current trend toward mergers continues.

As for the efficiency of the peer review structure, there are serious questions about the objectivity of the peer review process and willingness of one firm to criticize another, particularly the large firms. The SEC, which has had experience in this area, has expressed similar views. There is also concern that this peer review concept will offer in reality little more than the AICPA's voluntary quality review program, which, after a year, never got off the ground and was considered by many in the profession as sheer "window dressing" instituted to thwart congressional action.

It is envisioned that only large firms will conduct peer reviews of other large firms since the firm being reviewed, rather than the Peer Review Committee, will select the reviewing firm. And should the Committee "pool" be used, it is envisioned that these pools will consist primarily of employees from large firms. Despite an expensive, duplicative system calling for the appointment of quality control review panels which are supposed to ensure the objectivity of the reviewing firm, the "back scratching" implications in the peer review process are inescapable.

And the fact that the firm under review can exclude certain engagements from the peer review and select the one year of three that it wishes to be reviewed subjects the process to further suspicion.

Moreover, the Peer Review Committee can only *recommend* sanctions to the Executive Committee which makes the final determination on whether sanctions should be imposed and publicized. And where sanctions are warranted, it is not mandatory that the Peer Review Committee make such recommendations. Thus, it appears that the AICPA's peer review process includes a subtle safety valve whereby the large accounting firms dominating the Executive and Peer Review Committees can influence or prevent disciplinary actions against deficient firms. Whether this be the case in fact or appearance, it leaves grave doubts about the validity of the entire peer review process.

It is generally believed that the success or failure of AICPA self-regulation may hinge on its Public Oversight Board.

I share this view. I am, however, deeply concerned about the Board's status as a part-time operation, expected to work only thirty or forty days a year, and the ability of its members to sustain the degree of independence essential to achieve the Board's objectives. The five members appointed to the Board are unquestionably men of impressive stature and background, with years of distinguished service and experience. When they appeared before the Subcommittee, however, they seemed to lack the understanding and perception of an effective oversight function. For example, two members will continue to spend most of their time in New York and Chicago law firms and did not feel that the Board's independence would be enhanced if members could be dismissed only with the approval of the SEC. A third lawyer, also a college professor and former SEC Chairman, felt that the SEC's involvement in the AICPA's program should be minimal. The remaining two members are retired chairmen of the board of two of America's corporate giants—Sears and Alcoa—and together have served or are serving on the boards of no less than fifteen other major corporations, not to mention membership in numerous other business associations and societies, including the Business Roundtable and the Business Council. These two gentlemen also shared the view that the SEC's involvement in the AICPA's program should be minimal. From a board comprised of practicing lawyers and big business men espousing such a hands-off attitude, one wonders which members, if any, will emerge as the public protector on this so-called Public Oversight Board.

I believe that the Board should be a full-time job, appointments should be for a period of three to six years, and dismissal should be for cause only after review and approval of the SEC. I also share the SEC's view that the Board should have line authority over the operations of the SEC Practice Section rather than an advisory role. Unfortunately, the AICPA, including the five members of the Oversight Board, do not share this view.

Notable in regard to the Oversight Board's independence is the appointment of the Board's chief staff officer from the same firm as the AICPA president's former firm. It may be pure coincidence, but the fact that the Board's executive director and the AICPA's president are alumni of the same firm certainly casts a shadow over the Board's independence in appearance if not in fact. And on the subject of appearance and fact, I also question the propriety of the chairman of the SEC Practice Section's Executive Committee and the present chairman of the AICPA Board of Directors being the top two partners in the nation's number one accounting firm.

As an inducement to acquiring their services, in addition to the $30,000 to $50,000 they are paid annually, the AICPA has authorized Board members to hire others of their choice to assist them in carrying out their duties. Both the POB chairman and vice chairman have used their law firms extensively for this purpose. While this arrangement may not constitute a legal conflict of interest, it certainly has raised the eyebrows of many in the profession who view it as a moral conflict. Such a pecuniary arrangement can hardly be viewed as typical of an independent body watchdogging the public interest.

Many of my concerns about the AICPA's self-regulatory program are shared by others, including some very powerful clients of Big Eight accounting firms and a Big Eight firm itself.

Robert Morris Associates, a nationwide organization of bank loan officers, recently advised the AICPA that the division between publicly owned and privately owned companies is not in accord with reality and expressed concern that two sets of standards might develop. Following an exchange of correspondence, the AICPA was unable to alleviate the bank lenders' concerns that the second-tier companies could sustain the same high standards it has had. And earlier, in August, 1978, Price Waterhouse expressed strong disagreement with the AICPA's self-regulatory program. Specific areas of disagreement centered on granting authority to impose sanctions and disciplinary actions to those upon whom sanctions may be imposed, firms undergoing peer reviews selecting their reviewers and excluding particular audit engagements, and the lack of line authority for the Public Oversight Board. It is seldom that a Big Eight firm, the SEC, and I see eye to eye on accounting issues, but we are certainly in agreement on these. Moreover, we are in total accord that the AICPA program must not only be effective but must also be perceived by the public as effective.

Congressman Moss's growing dissatisfaction with the AICPA's program culminated in June, 1978 with the introduction of HR 13175, a bill to establish the National Organization of Securities and Exchange Commission Accountancy—more commonly known as NOSA.

The function of NOSA, in essence, would provide for regulation of a profession, under SEC oversight, with a goal of stronger protection for the investor public. The new organization would be managed by a five-person board of directors. These individuals would serve on a full-time basis to ensure the constant involvement of top leaders—in contrast to the AICPA's Public Oversight Board. They would be compensated at a level comparable to similar professional positions in the private sector.

Two members of the board of directors would be from independent public accounting firms and three from other professions or occupations. This representation was proposed to avoid any anticompetitive charges against certain public accountants and to ensure adequate protection for the public and investors. Of the two members of the board from public accounting firms, *one* would be from a firm with thirty or more SEC clients and *the other* from a firm with fewer than thirty SEC clients. We struck this balance to create greater equity between large and smaller firms and to avoid domination by the Big Eight.

Under the bill, the SEC would appoint the initial five directors and the directors would appoint their chairman. In subsequent periods, the members of the board would appoint their successors from lists of candidates approved by the SEC. Directors would be appointed for three-year terms but for no more than two terms or six years, and the appointments would be staggered. These provisions were designed to bring about a balance in continuity of management with fresh faces and insights.

One of NOSA's primary functions would be a continuing program of reviews of registered public accounting firms. These would be independent reviews because they would be performed by NOSA staff and not by peer firms. Further, these reviews would not only include the examination of accounting firms' quality controls but would also closely examine, for selected audit engagements, whether generally accepted auditing standards were followed and generally accepted accounting principles were applied. We feel such reviews would make a strong contribution toward ensuring that satisfactory audits have been conducted by accounting firms.

NOSA's staff could also investigate problems identified in reviews of firms or otherwise brought to the attention of the organization that indicate inadequate audit performance by a registered firm. In response to certain situations which were brought to the Subcommittee's attention, such as targeting and intentional low bidding, the organization would also be empowered to investigate allegations by one public accounting firm of unfair competitive practices by another firm. Refusal by accounting firms or their clients to cooperate with investigations of the organization would be grounds for sanctions or other appropriate action.

The organization would take disciplinary action, as required, against either registered public accounting firms or their principals. These actions would include suspension of or expulsion from registration, fines, censure, or limitation of operations. All disciplinary actions would be made public and reported to the SEC. The SEC would review and either accept or reject all disciplinary actions on its own. All disciplinary actions would be appealable in the United States Court of Appeals. Since expulsion from NOSA results in cessation of SEC work, we think the bill provides for strong sanctions but with adequate provisions for review and appeal.

The bill envisions a significant role for the SEC in oversight over the organization. In the forty-five years since its creation, the SEC has hesitated to use its authority over accountants, deferring in the main to the private sector. Unfortunately, this attitude prevails today. On July 1 of last year, the SEC, in a highly critical report to Congress, stated that there were many elements of the AICPA program which were unacceptable. If these were not corrected, it would have to withdraw its support from the program. Despite strong indications that many of these unacceptable elements will not or cannot be corrected, the SEC appears perfectly willing to wait three or four years—or longer—to determine if the program is successful—or unsuccessful. The risk of another Penn Central and the adverse financial impact on investors, taxpayers, and the nation does not permit us to share the SEC's "wait and see" attitude.

One of the elements which the SEC views as essential to successful self-regulation is that the program must be mandatory for all accounting firms auditing public companies. I agree. Under the AICPA program, however, membership is voluntary. The April issue of *Public Accounting Report* cites some revealing figures on the SEC Practice Section's membership status. Only 210, or 20 percent, of approximately 1,050 firms auditing publicly held companies had joined the Section as of March, 1979. Despite the continuous flow of publicity about the AICPA's self-regulatory program, only ten firms joined the section between October, 1978 and March, 1979.

The March issue of the *Journal of Accountancy* paints a much rosier picture. It boasts an SEC Practice Section membership of 525 firms. What the AICPA consistently fails to publicize is that three fifths of the section's membership consists of firms with no publicly held companies—just another nondisclosure which impugns the credibility of the program. Based on the lack of enthusiasm for the program to date, it is extremely doubtful that optimum membership in the program will ever be achieved.

We have remained firm in our belief that standard setting should be assigned to those who are equipped to do the best job. We believe that is the private sector. But we have also been consistent in stating that where the private sector fails to act, the SEC must.

As for accounting principles and auditing standards, the bill would leave this function in the private sector but defines and strengthens the role of the SEC. The SEC would, in consultation with designated organizations, develop listings of needed principles and standards, set priorities and timetables for their development and, if necessary, develop and issue the principles and standards itself when the private sector fails to act. This arrangement is meant to result in the prompt and satisfactory issuance of uniform accounting principles and strong auditing standards that the investor public has a right to expect.

To avoid the practical difficulties encountered by small public accounting firms in performing audits for SEC clients located in a number of states and to make them more competitive with large firms, a frequently requested innovation was included. The bill would permit public accountants to audit across state lines while performing audits pursuant to federal securities laws.

The bill would also make public accounting firms liable to third parties for negligence in preparation of audit reports in respect to SEC filings. Any person suffering damages as a result of reliance on such audit reports could bring an action in the appropriate U.S. District Court. Although such action can be taken now, of course, the intent of the legislation is to provide greater public protection against accountants' actions beyond that now provided as a result of the Hochfelder case. The legislation would make accountants liable for acts other than those intended to deceive, manipulate, or defraud, to the extent the public is damaged, as determined by the courts.

Finally, NOSA would be open to those public accounting firms and principals with no SEC clients that wish to register voluntarily. This, too, was included in the bill at the request of many small accounting firms and again would make them more competitive with large firms. They would be subject, however, to the same registration, review, and disciplinary requirements as those firms that were required to register with the organization.

A general misconception seems to exist that HR 13175 calls for government regulation of the accounting profession. And, I might add, the AICPA and the larger firms in particular have done little if anything to dispel this misconception.

Late last year, a senior partner in a Big Eight firm told a group of accountants that Congressman Moss wants nothing less than a complete government takeover of the accounting profession. That is simply not the case. If he had wanted that, our bill would have proposed a federal regulatory commission instead of a nongovernment body headed by accountants and public representatives. It would have mandated that this commission or the SEC set accounting principles and standards rather than allowing accountants to continue to do it. And it would have given the federal government much more than just an oversight role over a self-regulatory body of the type suggested in our bill.

What the bill does establish is a self-regulatory body with SEC oversight, meaning that the accounting profession will be given the opportunity to regulate itself, but if it is not effective in doing so, the SEC will step in to ensure public protection. As Allen Brout of the small firm of Brout & Company put it, the issue is not whether government regulation is better than AICPA self-regulation, but whether Big Eight regulation is better than government supervision of self-regulation.

Our motivation is not a complete government takeover of a profession. Our motivation is, for one thing, to improve and clean up the great profession of accounting—which has fallen to the depths in credibility during the past several years. But more important to us than even the accountant is the public, the investor, and the taxpayer. I am sorry to report that there are too many accountants in this country who do not share that concern even half as much as we do.

With the retirement of Congressman Moss and the death of Senator Metcalf, you have probably heard, as I have heard much too often, that all is quiet on the Potomac. I also heard that sigh of relief from the biggies in the accounting profession and their comments that the Moss bill is dead. In my opinion, however, there is little cause for complacency.

The Oversight and Investigations Subcommittee is just that—oversight, and not legislative. And although the Subcommittee provided the forum for highlighting the problems of the accounting profession and Mr. Moss, like any member of Congress, introduced legislation, he was powerless to hold legislative hearings. That jurisdiction belonged to Congressman Eckhardt, the former chairman of the House Consumer Protection and Finance Subcommittee, who showed little if any interest in Mr. Moss's bill. Interestingly enough, Mr. Eckhardt is now the new Chairman of the Oversight and Investigations Subcommittee. Moreover, a man who has shown a great deal of interest in the concerns of small business, Congressman Scheuer of New York, has assumed the chairmanship of the Consumer Protection and Finance Subcommittee. Congressman Scheuer expressed precisely those concerns when he spoke to the National Conference of CPA Practitioners in Washington. Not only can this man reintroduce the Moss bill, but to a great extent he can control its destiny—something Congressman Moss could not do. It will be an interesting matter to follow.

I state these facts not as one who is a friend or foe of the accounting profession; not as one who is for more government regulation or against needed government regulation; not as one who can predict with certainty the future of the accounting profession or whether or not congressional interest in its problems will be sustained. Rather, my intent has been to share my observations on the profession's self-regulatory program, some words of caution, and what I *believe* will be the profession's ultimate fate if a sincere effort is not made to achieve meaningful reform.

Congressional prodding has brought the accounting profession to the threshold of reform. But I firmly believe that Congress and the public will not be fooled by meaningless reforms. With key members of Congress, such as Mr. Scheuer, showing an interest in the subject; with concerned accountants, such as those joining the National Conference of CPA Practitioners, creating a national forum to highlight the profession's problems and inequities; and with people familiar with the issues, such as Mr. Moss, myself and others, continuing to articulate those issues; I believe with the passage of time congressional interest will intensify rather than diminish.

The accounting profession has for many years enjoyed a low profile in the public eye. Now that the profession is in the limelight, a heightened sense of the accountant's role and his responsibility to the public is well underway. There are in excess of 25 million investors in this country who, through their power at the polls, will see to it that the present interest is sustained and interest among more members of Congress is generated. It has been my experience during twenty-nine years in government that legislation involving the broad use of constituents gathers momentum once it is introduced and studied. And—although it may not appear to be the case at the moment—I firmly believe that the type of self-regulation proposed in HR 13175 will sooner or later become law.

6

Regulation and the Accounting Profession: The SEC Viewpoint

The Honorable Harold M. Williams

Chairman, Securities and Exchange Commission

The focus of my discussion will not be the structure of the accounting profession. The SEC does not wish to ignore the structural issues, but its primary concern has always been the ability of the profession to be independent and to provide financial information necessary to enable investors to make intelligent decisions. So long as the structure of the profession does not impair those abilities, it is not the focus of our interest. The real action, in my opinion, lies elsewhere.

Let's start from the perspective of the "public interest." There is a real gap today between financial information and public needs and expectations. This situation embraces a larger territory than simply the accounting profession. It is the difference between the information communicated by financial statements and the true condition of American business. The problem, then, is how to close that gap.

In the late 1960s, many investors became alienated and withdrew from participation in securities markets. They did so, I believe, largely from a sense of having been misled, from a sense that the markets at that time were not what they *appeared* to be. The blame for false appearances should not be laid at the feet of the accounting profession. But accountants should realize that events from the late 1960s, as well as subsequent episodes, have led investors to distrust both financial information and those whose business it is to deliver it.

This distrust has taken the form of dissatisfaction with the performance of the accounting profession. The public is confused about the difference between the information auditors provide in statements and information outside those statements. It is confused about the true meaning of "earnings per share." It is confused by the fact that an auditor's statement can say that earnings were, say, $1.89, and then go on to add that earnings can't be computed with such precision.

In short, a gap exists between reality and what accounting statements tell us. How do we close that gap? First, we should do a better job of educating people about what the numbers really mean. Second, we should have auditors identify the numbers that are currently left off traditional financial statements. Third, we can begin to address the disparities between traditional accounting and economic reality. This does not mean that historical cost can be done away with entirely—only in some instances. In others, we may have to go beyond financial statements and include data that is not based on historical cost, even though it means depriving ourselves of the comfort, security, and objectivity that goes with that tradition.

To accomplish this, we may need to reconstruct our concept of what a financial statement should look like. We may need additional financial statements that include data not currently considered auditable or definitive. But more than this, we must ask where the *leadership* to accomplish the closing of the gap is going to come from. If the gap isn't closed by some means, the credibility of accountants will diminish increasingly. Unfortunately, however, the dynamic of all professions is the status quo. The ability to come together and provide leadership for change is extremely difficult for any group to undertake on its own.

Here the role of government, as well as others outside the profession in the private sector, becomes important. It becomes, in my judgment, far too important. It is easy to increase the degree to which government dictates what the private sector should do. But that action deprives the private sector of its responsibilities, as well as giving the private sector a scapegoat other than themselves. If I wished to do anything in my five years at the Securities and Exchange Commission, it would simply be to hold the mirror up to the private sector and say: "You get what you deserve." And, unless the accounting profession provides its own leadership, it is going to get just that.

Regulation is not a cure-all; the SEC did not overrule the Financial Accounting Standards Board on its Statement 19 with great enthusiasm. Statement 19, of course, concerns methods for amortizing the intangible costs associated with oil and gas exploration and development. Under the mandate of the energy bill, the SEC simply could not accept one of two totally inadequate concepts. Where was the experimentation? Where was the activity in the private sector that should have given it the ability to make a more intelligent decision on Statement 19 than it did? And where were the academics during all the years before this issue became critical who could have anticipated the need for a better accounting method?

Five years have slipped by and we're still trying to do something about inflation accounting. But what response did the profession make to the FASB proposal? "None of the alternatives is good; give us an opportunity to experiment." In reply, I ask the profession: "Where have *you* been? Why do you deserve more time to experiment? Why should we or the FASB have confidence that experimentation or anything else beneficial is going to happen?"

For two years, my theme in speeches has been that corporate earnings are not high enough, and I've explained at great length why they aren't. So, in terms of inflation accounting, I was delighted to see the fourth quarter earnings of 1978. I could factor them reasonably well, I thought, at least in the aggregate, for the impact of inflation. But then the corporate earnings figures were published, unadjusted, without interpretation of the need to reinvest corporate capital. Consequently, the White House, the Teamsters, the rubber workers, and the head of the United Auto Workers all unite in decrying the apparent fact that corporate earnings are too high. From their standpoint, it looks as if people are being asked to sacrifice when corporate earnings are at an all-time peak. They don't really understand what those numbers mean. The *New York Times*, for example, published an article recently that spoke positively about the fact that dividends are increasing more rapidly than inflation. But if those earnings are adjusted for the impact of inflation, for one-time inventory profits, for inadequate depreciation, and for taxes incurred on those inflated earnings, then take a second look at dividends. It would be quite a different figure.

The United States has companies in the process of liquidation that aren't even telling their shareholders what they're doing—frankly, I'm not even sure that management is telling itself. In such a case, of course, sophisticated financial minds know what is happening and the market price of the stock might reflect that fact. But—far more importantly—the American voters don't know it. Neither does Congress or the newspapers. If I remember the figures correctly, the *Wall Street Journal* reported that earnings are up 22 percent, the *Washington Post* reported 27 percent, and the *New York Times* reported 44 percent. All three newspapers were using the same figures. What guidance were they given in arriving at these results?

Here the responsiblity lies as much with the corporate community as it does with the accounting profession. First and last, it is their problem. But accountants share the problem. We all do. Which brings me back to the point: Where is the leadership? The FASB's proposed conceptual framework has the potential to be the most important contribution to this profession's future in a long time. A contributor to this volume speculates that the conceptual framework won't be completed for a decade. I hope he is wrong. He may, in fact, be right, but it is absolutely vital for him to be wrong. The conceptual framework, inflation, changing prices, and the other issues must not be cast in the mold of consensus documents. By the time consensus is reached, the game will be over.

If the accounting profession does not provide leadership on these initiatives, the alternative is for the SEC to do so. The Commission is reluctant but not unwilling to provide that leadership. In the matter of FASB Statement 19, we did provide it. Critics say we did so in response to political pressure. I was there, and I know that we did not. But that brings us back to the old problem of abdicating responsibility. If the accounting profession puts the burden of formulating principles on the SEC, it will always be concerned about the extent to which the Commission is responding to political pressures.

The SEC has also been criticized from the other side, by parties such as Congressman John Moss, for not being tough enough on the accounting profession. This is valid criticism. It's difficult on one hand to be demanding and on the other to encourage, plead, and urge a profession to assume its responsibilities. It is difficult to accomplish all these tasks and still have enough latitude and time to develop remedies.

The SEC's current position toward the AICPA's SEC Practice Section is one of expecting results. The SEC and the Practice Section, as we have told Congress, have reached an agreement on what the objectives of the Practice Section ought to be. Although the SEC believes there is a better way for them to reach these objectives than the way they have chosen, as long as they head for those objectives they can do it their own way. All they have to do is get there, and we are watching their progress closely. The SEC Practice Section is a viable experiment; whatever we learn from it, it must succeed.

The FASB, both in substance and in credibility, is also an important part of the future of the accounting profession. The FASB must move ahead, provide leadership, and develop a conceptual framework. Without the conceptual framework, we will continue to circle around definitions and other trivia at the expense of substantive programs. The emphasis on users and financial information in this framework is extremely appropriate. As I have stressed earlier, there must be broader auditor involvement in all aspects of financial information publicly reported by American corporations.

Increasingly, the SEC is going to involve itself with the concept of "soft" information, which constitutes a major policy shift from the past. (The worst way to project the future, I might note, is to extrapolate from the past.) Only soft information, not traditional hard numbers, tells us the truth about corporations. This information will include such areas as the time value of money and pension liabilities—major areas that American corporate reporting has been extremely deficient in treating.

To move into these new areas of financial reporting, the academic community as well as practicing accountants needs to play a more active and vigorous role. The accounting profession, like any other, needs its loving critics, its conscience, and its experimenters. To derive a degree of comfort from the status quo is the private sector's most devastating and self-deceptive habit, and it is true of the business community at large, not just the accounting profession. Accountants and their academic counterparts must join forces to provide both leadership and "followership" to make the important transition from the status quo to an area of broader responsibility and self-governance.

7

Regulation and the Accounting Profession: An FASB Member's View

David Mosso

Member, Financial Accounting Standards Board

Accounting standards are subject to Murphy's law of thermodynamics: Things get worse under pressure, especially political pressure.

Since Mr. Murphy's law is a muddled mixture of scientific and political ingredients, it captures the two principal strands of thought that run through this chapter and through the history of accounting standard setting. The thermodynamic reference is particularly apt because politics is essentially a thermodynamic process—the generation of power through the application of hot air.

When I joined the Financial Accounting Standards Board a year ago last January, I had spent the major part of my career in government service and had not had much firsthand involvement in setting private sector accounting standards. The notion that accounting standards should be set in the private sector was under massive assault at the time: From the government in the form of the Moss and Metcalf Committee inquiries. From industry in the form of the attack on FASB Statement 19 on oil and gas accounting. From the accounting profession in the form of the Arthur Andersen challenge to the Securities and Exchange Commission's delegation of standard-setting authority to the FASB. I searched for reasons in support of either a private sector or public sector body, but found none that wrapped it up conclusively.

To sum up past discussions of the issue, the following reasons have been advanced for keeping standard setting in the private sector:

1. Government could not attract enough high-quality talent nor devote sufficient resources to standard setting to do a good job.
2. A government agency would be susceptible to undue political influences, both through special interest groups and through reinforcing current government policy objectives.
3. Experience with government accounting regulations supports the expectation that standards would be in the nature of rigid and detailed rule prescriptions, unresponsive to investors and to the realities of the market.
4. The domain of the SEC, and typically of other agencies, is limited to particular segments of economic activity—it does not run to the whole of the private sector.
5. Government standard setting would sap the vitality of the accounting profession, turning off the generous supply of professional talent devoted to standard setting and turning accountants away from independent attestation and toward client advocacy.

From the other side, these arguments have been used to support moving standard setting to the public sector:

1. The public interest at stake is too high to be entrusted to the private sector; it demands direct congressional supervision.
2. A government agency would be free of conflicts of interest, more impartial and more responsive to all interests; it would not become a tool of business interests or of the accounting profession.
3. Government could better summon the variety of intellectual disciplines that should be, but have not been, brought to bear on accounting standards—economists, lawyers, and financial analysts, as well as accountants.
4. Accounting standards have the effect of law and therefore should be legislated by the government.
5. A government agency would act more quickly on pressing problems and would be more responsive to Congress and the President.

With these arguments for a backdrop, I will explore the nature of accounting standards and then relate them to the nature of governance systems to see if any clear indication of bias toward public or private exists.

Views of Accounting Standards

In terms of purpose to be served, there seem to be three ways of looking at accounting standards. First, as instruments developed to guide the measurement of economic activity. Second, as rules of conduct designed to restrain unfair economic behavior. Third, as incentives designed to promote economic behavior in furthering national goals.

Accounting is concerned with measuring economic activity. The subject of economic activity is income and wealth or, in a business context, earnings, investment, and return on investment. The three differing views of accounting standards derive from the inherent complexity of the concept of earnings and the limitations of existing methods of measuring it. Caricatures of the three views are sketched in the following paragraphs.

The first view of accounting standards, that they are guides for the measurement of economic activity, starts from the premise that earnings can be defined and measured. It does not premise precise measurement, only that measurements can be accurate enough to be useful for decision making. The primary objective of standard setting from this viewpoint is to develop guidelines that, when applied in practice, will measure return on given investments during given periods as accurately as possible. The test of a good standard is whether it leads to measurements that are consistently borne out by economic events.

From this view, standard setting is basically a research process aimed at developing a theory of earnings measurement and a set of application guidelines suitable for use in the actual measurement of earnings. Earnings measurement, the argument runs, will get more accurate as experience weeds out the ineffective measurement methods and sharpens the effective ones. The process can be visualized as a diminishing spiral moving from observation of economic activity to formulation of broad concepts, translation of concepts into working guidelines (standards), assessment of application results, reformulation of concepts, sharpening standards, and so on, always tightening the grip on earnings.

As a consequence of shooting for the closest reasonable approximation of income in particular circumstances, this reasoning is likely to lead to standards with broad criteria for guiding measurement applications with emphasis on what is reasonable in particular circumstances. It depends heavily on skillful application, on the judgment of accounting practitioners in the preparing and attesting organizations.

The second view of accounting standards, as rules of conduct to restrain unfair economic behavior, does not totally reject the premise that earnings can be defined and measured. But it finds that the lack of precision inherent in most definitions and measurements leaves too much room for discretion in arriving at reported earnings. Discretion leads, at best, to lack of comparability between good faith measurements of similar facts and circumstances and, at worst, to deliberate manipulation of reported results. By this logic, the primary objective of standard setting is to limit the discretion of practitioners in order to minimize variations in reporting the earnings results of similar facts and circumstances.

Standards reflecting this philosophy are likely to emphasize uniformity of method and verifiability of results. In areas of high uncertainty, they may lean more toward what has been described as "being precisely wrong in preference to being approximately right." To the extent that this view aims for uniformity within a reasonable range of probable error, it is not wholly incompatible with the first view, but when it forces results to fall outside that range or to cluster far away from the central tendency, it conflicts with the measurement view.

The third view of accounting standards, as economic incentives, sees in the inherent imprecision of most earnings measurements an opportunity, perhaps even an obligation, to set standards that will motivate decision makers to act in ways that further social and economic goals. It starts from the premise that accuracy of earnings measurement is an impossible dream, a nonoperational hypothesis. It views the bottom line, reported earnings, as the motivator and assumes that decision makers will react to the reported number even if that number departs from what most practitioners might think is a more accurate measure. This rationale rejects both accuracy of measurement and uniformity of result as primary goals. Earnings is not a measured result of observed economic activity; it is a calculated cause of economic action.

To illustrate the differences among the three views of accounting standards, let me caricature how each might accommodate a hypothetical accounting standard for advertising outlays. The first view, measurement guides, would provide for capitalization of advertising outlays in all cases where the circumstances indicated a clear connection with future revenue increments. The second view, rules of conduct, would more likely provide for mandatory expensing of advertising outlays in all circumstances because of the general subjectivity of linking outlays with revenues in most circumstances. The third view, economic incentives, would expense all or part, capitalize all or part, or do it different ways in different industries, depending upon the perceived effect in relation to goals to encourage or suppress particular industries or activities.

An Artful Science

A dichotomy exists in accounting literature between descriptions of accounting as an art and as a science. There does not seem to be much difference, however, in accounting practice flowing from the two views, and from that perspective the issue is not worth serious debate. But it does seem to have implications as a frame of reference for approaching the standard-setting process.

The first view of accounting standards is consistent with a science of accounting; standards are measurement guides based on scientific laws of behavior derived from observation and experience of economic activities. The second and third views are consistent with an art of accounting; standards are conventions—adopted more or less arbitrarily (the second view) to bring behavioral order into an otherwise undisciplined process, and adopted purposefully (the third view) to bring about desired behavioral results.

The essential characteristics of a scientific discipline are objectivity, measurement, and prediction. By themselves, those characteristics are not very confining because it is possible to approach almost any subject using them as a frame of reference. Even politics goes under the title of political science. What separates the disciplines we usually think of as scientific, especially the natural sciences, from those we think of as intuitive is the existence of data that are susceptible to measurement in quantifiable and verifiable terms and the existence of general laws of behavior (either of physical elements or human actions) that form a basis for reliable prediction.

The objectivity that accountants bring to their discipline is well established, and the quantification foundation of accounting is axiomatic. What is needed to qualify accounting as a scientific process is the existence of some universal laws governing the behavior of the subject matter, earnings. For those laws we have only to look to our allied discipline, economics. There we find universal behavioral forces that have existed from the beginning of civilization, the forces that make up supply and demand—market forces. Those forces are self-activating in any situation involving two or more people in possession of resources and a willingness to trade. They are clearly laws of nature; as immutable within the time span relevant to accounting standards as laws of motion and force—and thermodynamics. They cannot be repealed by governmental fiat, even though governments of all ideological persuasions stubbornly refuse to accept the evidence of history on that conclusion.

Even money, that peculiarly governmental institution, a monopoly of national governments, is not a governmental invention. It develops in every primitive society, in prison camps, wherever there are people with incentives to trade. It springs from those same market forces that are a fundamental part of human behavior. That is not to take anything away from governmental inventiveness. Our federal government did for the dollar what Henry Ford did for the automobile—applied mass production techniques to make it faster and cheaper.

Markets governed by general laws of behavior create the environment in which accountants operate. Markets determine the values that accountants measure, classify, record, and even—a point to which I will return—predict.

The market is also the place where the accountant's measurements are tested. These are objective tests; they are not matters of individual judgment or of political intuition. They are tested when revenues are realized, when assets are sold, when liabilities are liquidated. They are tested at the completion of every business activity cycle. These impersonal forces put severe limits on the accountant's measurement of earnings. No matter how "creative" the accountant gets in the measurement of earnings, there is always a hard market test just ahead.

We accountants have tended to play down the scientific measurement aspect of our business. We have papered it over with an emphasis on recording transactions. We intimate that recording historical cost on a transaction basis is a recording of hard fact—an anchor to reality. We seldom acknowledge that every recording is a prediction. We predict that an expenditure has acquired a future benefit, and we book it as an asset; or we predict that the benefit has expired, and we book it as an expense. Every time we prepare a balance sheet, we predict that every asset will generate enough future cash flow at least to recover its booked cost, or else we predict that it will not and reduce the book value. So historical transaction cost, our anchor to reality, turns out to be an anchor made of wood. That leaves us, like it or not, adrift on a sea of prediction.

We are able to gloss over the predictive nature of accounting for two reasons. One is that we have adopted a wide band of indifference by saying that historical cost is the preferred measure as long as any reasonable prediction of current value is not less than cost nor more than absurd. The downside of the band has been formally drawn with the cost-or-market rule, but the upside is only raggedly drawn through such devices as last-in-first-out (LIFO), accelerated depreciation, selective market valuations, asset revaluations, and indexing (in some countries). The reason is that the market forces on which our predictions are based are indeed stable enough, predictable enough, to keep recorded historical values within that broad band of indifference most of the time, and to give us a discernible path when we are compelled to leave the band.

The dilemma is that, notwithstanding the fact that we are dealing with laws of behavior that make our data subject to measurement and prediction, we are also dealing with data that do not stand still. In the surge and swirl of market forces, the crest of the highest income wave may fall on the reefs of an operating loss. Because we work in a dynamic environment, our measurements and predictions are always tentative and that is what leads people to describe accounting as an art. An accountant might be compared to an oceanographer. Knowledge of the physical dynamics of waves is part of the scientific stock-in-trade of an oceanographer; but if he tries to hang ten on a surfboard, it is not scientific knowledge that prevents a wipeout, it is artistry.

Nonetheless, the dynamics of the market environment carry the risk of accounting standards being washed up on the government shore. Accounting measurements are subject to a varying range of error. Although ultimately testable in the market, they cannot be tested soon enough or precisely enough to substantiate a present measurement in many circumstances. That is why accounting standards can easily be viewed as conventions and why the purpose of standards can be shifted from a scientific frame of reference with a measurement focus to an artistic frame of reference with a behavioral focus. A behavioral focus is an invitation to governmental entry, a subject to which I now turn.

Governance Systems

To get at the issue of whether standard setting is inherently inclined toward the private sector or the public sector, one has to have some notion of how the line is drawn between those two sectors. I draw the line something like this: Governance in any form is a substitute for anarchy and requires that the members of a group give up some rights of individual self-determination, some freedoms.

In a democratic society, the citizens decide not only which individual freedoms they will give up, but also how to organize the governing force. Three levels of organization are discernible. At the first level, the governing force resides in the individual members of a group and governance is achieved by self-restraint acting within the informal ethical code of the group. At the second level, the governing force is located in a private sector body chartered by members of a group. In that case, governance is also achieved by self-restraint but acting within a more formal ethical code and supplemented by whatever economic and social persuasions the group can bring to bear. At the third level, the governing force is located in the state, the public sector, where governance is achieved through a formally structured code of law backed by the police power.

A private sector governing body, the second level, comes into existence when two conditions are met: (1) there is a potential for gain from centrally coordinated action in pursuing a common objective—either through a negative dimension, the resolution of conflicts among individual members of a group, or through a positive dimension, the coordination of goal-centered effort; (2) there is an expectation that for each member of a group the loss of freedoms will be less than the gains from cooperation.

The state, police-powered governance, comes into the picture when a third condition is met: (3) an expectation that some members of a group will be disadvantaged either because their interests will be suppressed in the decision process of the group or because the persuasions available to the group will be inadequate to enforce compliance with group decisions.

One inference that I draw from this analysis of the organization of governing forces is that it must be inherent in the word "civilization" that the highest form of governance is individual self-restraint and the lowest form is the state. The single factor that sets the state apart from all other organizational forms in a society is the police power. If freedom means anything, it means that the application of police power should be limited to matters of vital public interest that cannot be governed adequately by voluntary self-restraint. And it means that the burden of proof falls on those who would transfer governance from a higher to a lower form of social organization, from voluntary restraint to compulsory restraint.

Capital Allocation

A focus of every system of governance is fair play for all persons affected by the governed activity, whether they be active participants or passive. In a market environment, the objective of governance is to see that neither the competitors nor the interested bystanders are dealt with unfairly.

The primary role for accounting standards is in the capital allocation process, the competition among capital suppliers for investment outlets and among capital users for investment dollars. The measure of competition in both cases is income, return on investment. In broad terms, the winners in the competition are the capital users, who get the capital they need at the lowest rate of return commensurate with risk, and the capital suppliers, who find the investment outlets they need at the highest rate of return commensurate with risk. The interested bystander group is the general public, which looks to the economic system to provide support for its standard of living, its income.

But the public interest in accounting standards is much broader than just the capital markets. Or perhaps it would be more accurate to say that capital markets are broader than just the places where money and securities change hands. Income measurements are vital to other capital allocation processes—to the formulation of national fiscal, monetary, and economic policies; to energy, transportation, and foreign trade strategies; to antitrust and other economic competition regulation; to employment, pension, and collective bargaining negotiations; in short, to a vast sweep of economic activities and to all parties, public and private, with interests in those activities.

Many of these broader capital allocations are carried out through political processes where the rationing mechanism is the vote, in contrast to market processes where the rationing mechanism is price. Income measurements are used in a variety of ways in vote-centered political processes, usually less direct and less predictable than in price-centered markets, but still central to allocation decisions.

The entire resource allocation process, then, whether it is carried out through the private capital and resource markets or through the political power markets, is centered on income. The capital allocation process, in fact, can be thought of as a trading in past income accumulations for the purpose of generating future income accumulations, the goal being achievement of the highest possible rate of return on capital—return on investment at the investor level and rate of productivity at the national economy level. If past income is the subject and future income is the object, it is hard to imagine how anything could serve the allocation process better than accurate income measurements. That conclusion previews the following section.

A Matching Up

So the stage is set. I would like now to match up the three views of accounting standards with the three levels of governance, all in the context of a pervasive public need for accurate income numbers and a scientific income measurement process with some notable frailties.

Starting with the view of accounting standards as instruments for use in a scientific process of measurement and prediction, this view fits the need for accurate information on income as just described. This is the essential match-up if the risk of public sector involvement is to be minimized.

The need for some kind of governance system to deal with accounting standards from this view stems from several causes. One is that a basic ingredient of markets is standardization of measures. Standard measures imply a central authoritative body to define and communicate the nature of the measures. Another need for governance stems from the imprecision of our income-measuring instruments, indicating a need for coordinated research and experimentation to develop better instruments. Finally, given the fact of imprecise instruments, there is a need for governance mechanisms to balance the potentially conflicting interests in the outcome of measurements.

The critical question: Is there a need for a governance system backed by the police power? Not, it would seem, for the purpose of conducting research and experimentation. Agencies of the state are indeed capable of conducting scientific research, but the only essential reasons for the public sector to undertake such research is to fill a void in the private sector or to fulfill a national security need. Similarly, the police power is not essential for achieving standardization of measurement. State agencies frequently do promulgate standards for weights and measures of a physical nature, but it is not a uniquely state function and typically does not require the support of police power. Finally, the police power is not necessarily required for balancing the conflicting interests of the various parties in the capital allocation process, including the interests of the state itself. The vast majority of interest conflicts in our society are resolved through systems of self-restraint.

On the other hand, public interest in the capital allocation process is so great than an effective system of governance is essential. It is clear that the state must step in if the private system is injuriously ineffective or injuriously biased and is unable to correct those flaws.

Turning next to the rule-of-conduct view of accounting standards, this view does not serve well the public need for accurate income measurements. Because it is behavior oriented, finding criteria that will provide measurement accuracy is secondary to finding criteria that can function as checkpoints for behavioral conformity. The hallmarks of this view are uniformity and verifiability. Those hallmarks are broadly incompatible with a primary focus on accurate measurements. Accurate measurements require assessment of particular facts and circumstances; the economy is too complex to be abstracted into hard and fast rules that are equally applicable to a wide range of facts and circumstances.

That is not to say conclusively that a broader public interest is not served by this view. On the contrary, on the grounds that the wide range of error possible in income measurements and the consequent ability of accountants to choose, to some extent, an income result, one can argue that the public interest is better served by a high degree of uniformity and verifiability of result than it is by the variability of results that accompany most attempts to achieve accuracy.

A structured governance system is implicit in the rule-of-conduct view, since it is based on an expectation that incompetence or intent will cause some participants to be unfairly disadvantaged by the imprecision of existing measuring instruments. The case for public sector governance is strong because the very essence of the state, of police power, is to establish and enforce rules of conduct, to control unfair behavior. Even so, it is not an open-and-shut case. Setting rules of conduct is a prominent function of any state, but it is by no means a monopoly of the state. The enforcement of rules of fair conduct has been developed in the private sector in connection with the resource allocation process to a high degree of sophistication. The independent accountant's opinion on the fairness of financial statements is the capstone of a uniquely powerful governance system built on the foundation of voluntary self-restraint.

Turning finally to the economic incentives view of accounting standards, the public need for accurate income information is not served at all by this view. It presumes that conscious guidance of economic activity will provide greater actual economic income (however measured) or greater social good of some kind than could be achieved by any attempt to measure income accurately (the first view of accounting standards) or to legislate uniformity of measurement (the second view).

A formally structured governance system is essential for deciding which goals to pursue and how to structure and apportion the behavioral incentives to achieve the goals. A system supported by the police power is also essential to this view because a "measurement" dictum that will benefit (and motivate) one competitor will normally burden another. This boils down to a differential tax and subsidy system, an income redirection mechanism. No system of voluntary self-restraint in the history of mankind could cope with that.

Furthermore, national goals can only be known to the national government. As a practical matter, they can only be known by a particular government decision maker at the moment of a particular decision. Therefore, the process could only be organized so that accounting standards would be legislated as part of any law where they were relevant. In some instances, they would be specified in the law; in others, they would be delegated to an executive agency or commission. A single standard-setting agency would not be possible because no one agency or decision maker below the President could arbitrate the conflicts of goals pursued by powerful departments and agencies of government.

In my view, it is more difficult to identify national goals than it is to measure income. Furthermore, all economic goals and many social goals rest on a foundation of income—gross national product at the highest level of aggregation and many varieties of income and income-based matters at lower levels. If goal achievement were measured by income and if income were measured by rules designed to achieve goals and if goal and rule were connected through the same government decision maker, it is predictable that the resulting circuit would be closed to two national goals—economic growth and economic freedom.

Inconclusions

I started off to explore the issue of whether accounting standards should be set in the public or private sector. I end my own dissertation with the same assessment I made of others—inconclusive. The long windup ends not with a strike but with a balk; no crisp conclusions, only philosophic musings.

Accounting standard setting originated at the first level of governance, individual self-restraint, and most of it continues to be located there in millions of decisions made daily—in applying FASB or other formal standards, in applying the vast body of uncodified standards that exist in common practice, and in coping with the steady flow of new situations that constantly arise.

The imposition of standards through formally structured private and public sector bodies like the FASB and the SEC was a combination of positive reaction to a need for coordination of measurement efforts in practice and, more significant in its political implications, negative reaction to a failure of systems of voluntary self-restraint, failure to deal fairly.

It is not inevitable, in my view, that the central standard-setting function will drift to the public sector, but the currents pull in that direction and it will take steady and alert navigation to keep it from doing so.

The forces that cause the currents to pull toward the public sector do not emanate from Congress or the SEC, as is sometimes intimated. As an astute political analyst once said, "The fault, dear Brutus, is not in our stars, but in ourselves . . ."

Some of the fault lies in the swindlers among us, the perpetrators of spectacular frauds. They are largely beyond control, but whether these frauds involve accounting or auditing standards, they carry a high risk of generating a sweeping public sector response that burns a wheat field to kill a weed.

Some of the fault lies in the fudgers, not lawbreakers but lawbenders, who play all of the flexibilities of accounting standards and the uncertainties of income measurement to their own advantage. Theirs are the actions that generate reactions in the form of accounting standards designed to restrain unfair behavior, the rule-of-conduct type of standard, the kind of standard the state is good at setting.

Finally, some of the fault, and the highest risk, lies in the headstrong, those who insist on getting their own way regardless of the cost to the system of self-governance. They are the ones who hurdle the third condition in the governance hierarchy—refusal to abide by peer group decisions. The two most famous cases of public sector interference in standard setting were not, I surmise, power plays initiated from the government side. The investment tax credit standard was given away by one accounting firm. The oil and gas accounting standard was given away by one company. There will always be somebody willing to carry the flag on major issues like those because of a perception that a specific economic gain is worth more than a general loss of freedom.

The real risk is not wholesale nationalization of accounting standards. The risk is that the private sector will give them away one at a time until there is nothing left worth fighting for. With even minimal showing of responsible performance on the part of the private sector, Congress would not, in my judgment, shift the standard-setting responsibility to the government. Nor do I see any inclination on the part of the SEC to do that, although that is less predictable because the SEC is more susceptible to circumstantial pressures. Individual issues, however, are another matter. Accounting is humdrum stuff for most of the world, and individual accounting issues are inevitably mixed up with nonaccounting issues that are the center of congressional attention. It is difficult to generate a high level of political interest in accounting side issues; therefore, there is a high probability that any standards issue that gets into the political process will slip out of private sector control.

If we are going to be navigating against the current, how do we chart our course? Primarily, I think, by getting a firm fix on two stars, income and freedom. Granted, they may have faults as navigational guides; they may be the dimmest stars in the sky. But things that are perceived only dimly are often the things most worthy of perception, most productive as guiding principles. So it is with income. So it is with freedom.

In relation to the first navigational star, income, the accounting standards goal should be accurate measurement of income, of investment, and of return on investment. Accurate income measurements are vital to economic processes and to economic freedom.

I have stressed the word "accuracy" throughout this chapter because we accountants have tried to bury the word and, as a result, often seem to pursue the wrong goals. We ought not to be seeking income measurements that are "useful," "neutral," "uniform," or "fair." We ought to be seeking income measurements that are accurate, testable in the marketplace, because accuracy is the substance of measurement. Usefulness, neutrality, uniformity, fairness are all attendants of accuracy.

Do not misunderstand. I have no illusions about our present ability to measure income consistently with a high degree of accuracy. My point is merely that we should not give it up as the primary goal and we should not stifle the search.

Before Galileo, nobody had measured gravitational force in relation to the speed of falling objects. Before Newton, nobody had measured gravitational force in relation to the motion of celestial bodies. Before Einstein, nobody had measured gravitational force in relation to time and universal motion. Measurements improve when accuracy is persistently pursued.

Although fixing on stars can help keep accounting on a bearing toward worthy future income goals, fixing present income results may have more immediate payoff for some participants in the capital allocation process. So while we pursue accuracy as a goal, we have to deal realistically with the imperfections of our environment. Within an acceptable range of measurement accuracy, there must be some curbing of the tendency to fix reported results and there must be some emphasis on comparability among competitors for capital.

In sum, the first view of accounting standards, as guides to accurate measurement, must be paramount. But it must be tempered by the second view, as restraints on unfair economic behavioral tendencies.

The third view, as economic incentives, must be rejected totally. No standard can possibly further a national goal as well as a standard that leads to accurate income measurements. That does not mean we can ignore behavioral consequences. On the contrary, behavioral results that defy economic logic are one form of market test; they provide clues that a standard has hit or missed the economic mark.

In relation to the second navigational star, freedom, the accounting standards goal should be to keep as much standard setting as possible at the level of individual self-restraint—with financial report users, preparers, and attestors—and as little as possible at the level of the state.

A proper role for the state, as represented by the SEC or otherwise, is limited and twofold: (1) to monitor the workings of the resource allocation system for the purpose of stimulating corrective actions where it is needed in the public interest, and (2) to deal with criminal conduct bearing on the use, abuse, or absence of accounting standards. The role is to deal with the negatives, the failures, of private sector governance systems.

A proper role for private sector governance bodies such as the FASB is to lead in the positive aspects of self-governance—to coordinate the financial reporting needs and efforts of individual participants and to conduct research for the purpose of developing better income measurement instruments.

A proper role for individual participants is to eliminate the need for the other two levels. This is the nub of the matter. A keen sense of business ethics and a strong resolve to support peer group decisions conscientiously made—to refrain from drawing on political power for narrow private gain, for sustaining a position that has been rejected by peers—are the fundamentals on which accounting freedom stands.

Freedom, like fossil fuel, is finite. What is burned up in the political process is lost; it is not regenerative. When freedom is lost, there are no bystanders, only participants, because freedom is jointly owned. When one person, or firm, or industry, loses freedom, all of us lose some. So there is no need to speculate about whose accounting freedom will be next to stoke the fires under the political boiler; it is yours.

Note

Expressions of individual views by members of the FASB and its staff are encouraged. The views expressed in this speech are those of Mr. Mosso. Official positions of the FASB on accounting matters are determined only after extensive due process and deliberation.

8

The Accounting Profession Responds to the Challenge of Regulation

Michael N. Chetkovich

Retired Managing Partner, Deloitte, Haskins & Sells

School of Business Administration
University of California, Berkeley

The possibility of regulation, or rather of more regulation, of accounting and accountants is not a phenomenon that is unique to this time. We know that the function of accounting, insofar as it relates to the financial reporting of publicly owned companies, has been subject to growing regulation for a considerable period of time—certainly since the 1930s. We should be well aware of the authority of Congress in this area and of the will and muscle of the Securities and Exchange Commission, to say nothing of the involvement of other federal agencies and even of state and local governmental bodies.

There is no doubt, however, that in the past few years the intensity of the challenge has heightened considerably and the possibility of legislation and of more regulation, particularly of the public accounting profession, has increased materially. Congress has paid more critical attention to the profession in these past few years than in all its previous history.

The intensity, persistence, and adversary nature of this attention probably came as more of a surprise, perhaps even of a shock, to public accountants than it need have. It should have been obvious to us that we were in a period of question, challenge, and contention on a broad scale. And, given the negative attitudes toward business, the increasing focus on accountability, and the growing recognition of the importance of accounting, it was inevitable that accountants, particularly those involved in independent audit, would be subjected to critical appraisal quite apart from any of our own shortcomings. This is the kind of environment in which expectations tend to run well ahead of performance, if not reality; the inevitable imperfections are identified and magnified, suspicions grow, motives are questioned and the credibility gap widens.

Part of the surprise and consternation probably came from the fact that many in the profession thought that it *had* been responding to changing conditions and mounting concerns. The American Institute of Certified Public Accountants had mounted a number of initiatives which, at least compared with earlier times and with what was being done (or not done) elsewhere in the world, were rather impressive; in more normal times, these actions might have been met with favorable recognition if not acclaim.

In the span of a few years we had seen the appointment of the Wheat Committee, leading very quickly to the establishment of the Financial Accounting Standards Board, the formation and the report of the Objectives Study Group (the Trueblood Committee) and, most recently, the work and the report of the Commission on Auditors' Responsibilities (the Cohen Commission). In addition, the pace of other Institute activities had accelerated, especially in the auditing standards area.

But these actions, significant though they might have appeared to us, were by no means sufficient to satisfy the critics nor to discourage congressional attention, as we well know. In 1977 and 1978, this attention reached a peak, beginning with the publication of the *Staff Study* ("The Accounting Establishment") of the subcommittee chaired by Senator Lee Metcalf, followed by the hearings and report of that committee. In the House, the subcommittee chaired by Congressman John Moss held its own hearings, which were followed by a legislative proposal to set up a regulatory structure for accounting firms. The attention continues in both houses of Congress, and the SEC has heightened its surveillance of the profession.

The criticisms and concerns expressed and the remedies proposed were numerous and varied, covering substantially the whole range of possibilities. This made it difficult, to say the least, to respond quickly and effectively to all points. In some instances, the nature of the criticisms was such as to call for conflicting remedial actions.

Nevertheless, the profession, principally through the AICPA, focused on the principal issues and developed a comprehensive program of response. While there has been a considerable difference of opinion (to put it mildly) within and without the profession concerning the propriety, adequacy, effectiveness, and even legality of the program, even the critics had to be amazed, if not impressed, that this broadly based membership organization could move so rapidly. I confess that *I* was amazed and still am. The

AICPA often has been characterized as a slow-moving or do-nothing organization. On this occasion, many of its critics complained that it was moving too far, too fast.

As mentioned, we were confronted with a list of shortcomings calling for reform "or else." The standard-setting processes, both for accounting and for auditing, were alleged to be seriously deficient in effectiveness and in objectivity. The role and performance of the independent auditor were subjected to the severest scrutiny and criticism, and this became the most important area to be addressed by the AICPA. Weaknesses, deficiencies, and improprieties were cited. It was alleged, among other things that the profession:

- was not giving adequate consideration to the needs and interests of the public, nor was it fulfilling its obligation as "public" accountants
- was ineffective in audit performance
- was engaged in activities which were incompatible or in conflict with its primary function
- lacked independence and objectivity
- had failed in and was incapable of self-regulation and self-discipline

Besides citing these nominal shortcomings relating to the conduct of the audit function, there were allegations of undue influence or "domination" of the AICPA and the accounting standard-setting function by the Big Eight firms, that these firms monopolized audit practice, particularly as it related to large companies, that there was a lack of competition within the profession, that there was unfair competition, that the needs of the smaller firms and of small business were inadequately served or ignored, and that the processes and decision making of the Institute were conducted behind closed doors and were not open to public scrutiny. At the same time that these charges were being voiced, the Department of Justice and the Federal Trade Commission were looking into the activities and rules of the profession, just as they were looking at other professions, the concern being that certain proscriptions in our code of ethics and the requirements for entry into the profession might be anticompetitive and/or unduly and unnecessarily restrictive.

How does a profession—and particularly one embracing such a variety of practitioners, large and small, with an ever broader variety of views and interests—address such a litany of challenges? How does it come up with the "reforms" which are said to be necessary? It would be a formidable task given years to accomplish; to do something meaningful and practicable in a matter of months seemed almost hopeless. It is not surprising, then, that some in the profession maintained that we should do nothing and others concluded that, given these circumstances, we should let government do it—that there was no effective alternative to further governmental involvement and control.

Nonetheless, the profession, primarily through the AICPA, moved with surprising and perhaps unprecedented speed on a broad front. I will mention only some of the actions taken and then only briefly, so that I may concentrate on what I consider to have been the most important feature of the program—the establishment of a division of firms within the structure of the Institute. This approach should by no means suggest that the actions which are not mentioned, or are mentioned only briefly, were insignificant, for they were not. Some of them may well have set in motion forces which will have a profound impact on the profession in years to come. Further, some were highly controversial within the profession.

To meet the criticisms of the financial accounting standard-setting process, the Trustees of the Financial Accounting Foundation directed their Structure Committee to review the structure and processes of the FASB and to recommend changes as appropriate. The Committee moved quickly and effectively; its major recommendations were approved and implemented by the Trustees and the FASB in short order. Significant changes were effected in the structure and processes of the Board and in its funding, and its meetings were opened to the public. To blunt the allegation that the Institute and the Big Eight firms dominated the FASB, the role of the AICPA was significantly reduced.

Within the Institute, the changes effected were numerous and far-reaching. Our time-honored proscriptions on advertising, solicitation, and encroachment were eliminated; the participation of Big Eight firms in the activities of senior committees was reduced; meetings of Council and of senior committees were opened to the public; three non-AICPA members were added to the Board of Directors (in effect, as "outside directors"); and the auditing standard-setting function was restructured and strengthened. In addition, standing and special committees were directed to evaluate all the major recommendations emerging from the congressional hearings and the Cohen Commission report and to suggest means for their implementation. For example, a special committee was established for the purpose of examining whether the Institute should establish rules requiring audit committees as a precondition to independent audits.

The establishment of the Division of Firms, however, was certainly the most important feature of the program. It was designed to provide a vehicle for effective response to the major area of complaint—that the regulatory and disciplinary processes were inadequate, that the profession was unable to do anything about it, and hence that outside (governmental) intervention was necessary.

Self-regulation within any profession, insofar as it has to do with the disciplining of errant members, is at best limited, if not ineffective. The disciplinary processes are agonizingly slow and the penalties, when imposed, are of limited severity. The record, when judged in terms of cases successfully prosecuted (which to some critics means the number of hangings), is not impressive. But the disciplines and penalties imposed by a profession, in our case through the AICPA, are but a small and rather insignificant part of the total system of disciplines and penalties to which the certified public accountant is subject. There are, to begin with, the State Boards of Accountancy, which are the licensing authorities. Much more significant, however, are the SEC and the courts, to say nothing of the impact of unfavorable publicity on the individual and the firm. All this is, of course, in addition to the individual's own sense of professional pride and commitment.

Nonetheless, it was recognized that, under the circumstances, more needed to be done to ensure quality of performance and to strengthen the Institute's disciplinary processes. A major weakness of the existing system, besides the long delays inherent in the process, was that it could be directed only at individuals (since membership in the Institute was on a individual basis), whereas accounting practices were carried on, for the most part, through firms. Therefore, some structural change was necessary which would involve firms. This thinking led to the proposal to form a Division of Firms within the structure of the Institute.

At a tumultuous meeting in Cincinnati in September, 1977, the Institute's Council adopted this hotly debated proposal. A Division of Firms was created, composed of two sections, one for firms whose practice included companies which reported to the SEC, the other for firms whose practice was largely confined to privately owned companies. Any firm, however, could belong to either or both of the sections or neither. Opponents of the proposal carried the fight to the floor of the subsequent membership meeting of the Institute where Council's action was sustained. Later, a number of practitioners challenged the action in court but were unsuccessful.

I will deal here primarily with the SEC Practice Section, inasmuch as it is the one which relates most closely with the regulation issue. Although the purposes expected to be served by the two sections differed, they are similar in many, if not most, respects. Response to the new sections, in terms of applications for membership, has been far from universal. Only a small proportion of the total number of practice units have become members. As of last fall, however, the membership of the SEC Practice Section included firms which audit approximately 80 percent of the number of companies registered with the SEC; in terms of total assets or aggregate revenues represented by these companies, the percentage would, of course, be much higher.

Firms joining the Section agree to abide by its membership requirements and to submit to its disciplinary processes and sanctions. These membership requirements, as established through the enabling resolution and subsequent actions of the Executive Committee of the Section, include the following:

- adherence to minimum standards of continuing education for all members of the professional staff, including partners (a minimum of 120 hours in a three-year period with no less than 20 hours in any one year)
- a mandatory peer review of the firm at least once every three years
- mandatory rotation of partners in charge of SEC client audits
- adherence to limitations on the scope of practice which may be established by the Executive Committee

These are representative of the more important requirements for initial and continuing membership, but the listing is far from complete.

To provide independent assessment of the structure and, hopefully, to enhance its credibility, provision was made for a five-member Public Oversight Board to monitor the activities of the Section and to express publicly its views thereon. The initial members of this Board, all persons of high standing and impressive credentials, include three eminent attorneys, two of whom have served as chairmen of the SEC, and two retired chief executive officers of major corporations. While the Board does not have line authority, it does have the right to examine into any and all activities and actions of the Section and to report publicly its findings and recommendations; its own staff assists in carrying out its responsibilities. Given the character and reputation of the members of this Board, the attention focused on its role, and its right and responsibility to "go public" with its findings, I have no reservations about its independence or its potential effectiveness.

As you might expect, the establishment of the Division of Firms with its two sections did not meet with universal acclaim and approval, either from within or without the profession. From within, the opposition was vocal and persistent. It came largely from the smaller firms of the profession, who saw the move as being motivated by the interests of the large firms. There was also criticism, however, from members of some medium-sized firms, and significant reservations were expressed by one of the Big Eight firms. From without, the critics ranged from those who saw the action as totally cosmetic and lacking in any real commitment and effectiveness to those who focused on what they saw as specific deficiencies. Most of these latter criticisms had to do with the role of the Public Oversight Board, particularly its lack of line authority and its part-time character, perceived deficiencies in the peer review process, and the structure and authority of the Executive Committee.

I will not attempt here to evaluate these criticisms. Certainly, there is room for differences of opionion about what would make for the most effective program. The leadership of the Institute and of the Section are mindful of those reservations and, already, some fairly significant changes have been made—to strengthen the position of the Oversight Board, to provide at least the possibility for greater representation for smaller firms on the Executive Committee, and to meet some of the criticisms of the peer review process.

The Executive Committee has been hard at work. In frequent meetings, it has begun to address some of the hard issues, not the least being those having to do with scope of practice, peer review, and sanctions. While, as yet, not many conclusions have been reached, I believe that the Committee is committed to finding reasonable and effective solutions. It must be recognized, however, that these are difficult issues and that there are wide differences of opinion within the profession about what should be done about them. At least two of these issues have been posed to the Oversight Board for its views.

But let's face it—the real tests of the effectiveness of the Section, of its Executive Committee, and of the Public Oversight Board are yet to come. To date, it has been mostly a matter of laying the groundwork, of putting the structure in place, of identifying the issues, and of beginning to move toward their resolution. Everyone is waiting to see what will happen when the hard decisions have to be made, when a firm is found wanting or flaunts the requirements or rules of the Section. Only time will give us the answers.

There can be no guarantees of success—certainly not of a success sufficient to satisfy the whole range of critics. It is my conviction that what has been set in motion is a strong and positive program, one which can do much to enhance the quality of performance and the credibility of the profession. I believe, too, that the program is accompanied by a strong sense of commitment. While all substantive suggestions for change should be given proper consideration, the program deserves the opportunity to proceed and to show what it can do.

This is not the total answer to all problems and concerns, nor will this program bring us close to perfection. But I cannot accept that further governmental intervention and regulation is a better alternative.

The private sector does not have all the answers; it is not immune to excesses, to shortsightedness, to deficiencies, and to failures. We need surveillance and prodding and, at times, intervention by government. Left totally to our own devices, I am afraid we might destroy ourselves. On the other hand, government must exercise great restraint and not just because increasing governmental involvement is inconsistent with the concept of a free society, although that should be reason enough. There is a more pragmatic reason: Government (and particularly Congress) has not demonstrated any high degree of success in solving complex social and economic problems. Without questioning intent or good faith, I have to conclude, regretfully, that the record has, on the contrary, and particularly in recent times, been less than satisfactory.

It is all too easy to justify and accept any one act of intervention, particularly if this act seems to be directed at someone else. But one fact of life about this process we cannot ignore: There is seldom, if ever, any withdrawal or retreat. Each new piece of legislation, each new level of regulation becomes locked in stone, to serve as the foundation for the next layer in the process.

Inevitably, and perhaps rightly so, there is a state of tension, if not conflict, between the public sector (government) and the private sector. The challenge is to keep the relationship in some reasonable balance. This takes restraint, a tempering of zeal and of the bias of self-interest on both sides, and an effort to bring some reasonable degree of perspective and detachment to the issues. Certainly, we in the private sector must keep our materialism and our self-interest within some reasonable limits and do more than pay lip service to the broader needs of society. Government, on the other hand, must recognize that it does not possess a good legislative or regulative answer to every perceived imperfection.

We will never find a perfect balance, but let's do our best to ensure that the process never gets so skewed that it damages the system irreparably. Despite all its imperfections, we have the best that can be found anywhere.

IV

Establishing Accounting and Auditing Standards

To a large degree, our view of how accounting and auditing standards should be established depends upon our preference for either the competency of the private sector or the legitimacy of the public sector. According to these three chapters there is little question that private firms can call upon better talent and resources. Thus, on the face of it, the private sector provides better resources for the FASB to use in determining standards, particularly since, by comparison, those formulating public policy do not have to bear the long-term costs incurred by imposition of the standards. Following this reasoning, Watts states in Chapter 9 that it simply does not pay investors to be completely informed because of the cost of the information itself. In other words, public policy may set standards which are too high.

With public scrutiny having increased, however, the question of appearances must at least be considered. Can the investing public have confidence in self-regulating agencies such as the FASB without SEC disclosure requirements? In Chapter 11, Kaplan says no, that governmental intrusion is the price to pay to ensure legitimacy. How should these checks and balances work in setting standards?

Watts concedes that regulation can produce optimal accounting information, but only for those with the best explanatory power. The basis for this conclusion stems from his belief that the public interest is best served through economic efficiency, since everyone acts only out of self-interest. Because of the self-interest of politicians and the media, the SEC focus becomes perceived abuse rather than some altruistic and benevolent purpose.

Magee attempts in Chapter 10 to explore the effect of regulation on auditor and management costs through use of a model incorporating behavior patterns. According to the model, regulation of the auditor is not the only way to influence the effectiveness of an audit. Magee calls for using methods that only slightly reduce economies, such as rotation of auditors by clients and review of Management Advisory Services agreements by the Practice Section's Public Oversight Board. Further models to evaluate other issues, Magee indicates, may help the profession respond to the demand for more regulation.

Kaplan examines the strengths and weaknesses of various forms of regulation. The private sector, he says, has the virtue of flexibility, in that it does not create rules following market failures based on aberrations; the private sector, however, lacks both legitimacy and power in this area. The best control of the profession, he believes, still comes from simple knowledge of auditors' reputations, but even so the current situation calls for SEC disclosure rules. Further government regulations would be set according to their perceived effect on the economy. Auditors, Kaplan predicts, might eventually become policemen for society. Disclosure standards might be bettered, he concludes, by the competition that would result if each of the fifty states were allowed to set its own standards.

9

Can Optimal Accounting Information Be Determined by Regulation?

Ross L. Watts

Graduate School of Management
University of Rochester

At least from the days of the earliest railroads, and perhaps even before, the rationale for government regulation of business has been the "public interest." This was the reasoning used for the 1933 and 1934 securities legislation which established the Securities and Exchange Commission (SEC) and provided for the regulation of corporate disclosure of financial information (Benston, 1969). Hence, it is not surprising that we have seen much debate over what financial and accounting disclosure is optimal for the public interest. In recent years, however, this debate and the actions of regulators have led people to question whether regulators can determine optimal disclosure—and, indeed, whether regulation itself is in the public interest. Can optimal accounting information, in fact, be determined by regulation?

Answering this question requires a criterion by which to assess accounting information. I shall begin by adopting the traditional criterion, the "public interest." Because the term is nebulous, my first task is one of definition. I shall define public interest in the manner long used by economists and some politicians, namely, as Pareto optimality or economic efficiency.

First, to answer the question of whether regulation *can* determine optimal accounting information, we have to know where things stand currently. Do the politicians writing the laws and the regulators making and enforcing the regulations in fact pursue the assumed objective for regulation? If they do, the question is: Are they successful or not? If they do not, the question is: Why not?

153

An examination of the actions of politicians and regulators suggests that the hypothesis that politicians and regulators act in the public interest is not consistent with the evidence. When I investigate the actions of politicians and regulators, I find that the hypothesis that politicians and regulators tend to act in their own self-interest is more consistent with the evidence.

Politicians and regulators, acting in their own self-interest, could produce the same set of optimal accounting information as would be obtained if all politicians and regulators diligently pursued the "public interest." However, a necessary condition for this result is that the costs of information and transactions in the political process be zero. Obviously, those costs are not zero, as we shall see.

The Criterion for Optimality

Most legislation and regulation is justified as being in the "public interest." For example, the Metcalf Subcommittee *Staff Study* (1977: 21–22) suggests that amendments to the securities laws should be made to protect the "public interest." Those who argue for legislation or regulation on "public interest" grounds, however, rarely define explicitly what they mean by this term. It is not apparent what actions (other than those specifically wanted or not wanted) would or would not be in the "public interest" from the arguments used to support or oppose legislation and regulation. Hence, the politicians' concept of the public interest is of no use in assessing whether optimal accounting information can be determined by regulation.

One measure of the "public interest," however, is well defined and widely used in the academic literature, and that is the economist's concept of Pareto optimality. Under the Pareto concept, a regulation would be in the public interest if it improved at least one person's condition without worsening any other person's condition. Obviously, many Pareto optima are possible. There is no way of ranking those optima that would be acceptable to everyone, because each individual will rank the option depending on his own costs and benefits; those costs and benefits differ across individuals for any given Pareto optimum outcome.

Let us use the Pareto optimality criterion to assess whether regulation and the actions of regulators are in the public interest. This assessment may demonstrate whether regulation can lead to a Pareto optimal level of accounting information; it may also demonstrate what politicians and regulators mean by the "public interest."

Are Legislation and Regulation Designed to Provide the Optimal Accounting Information?

In recent years, academics have questioned whether the general assumption that legislation and the actions of regulators are in the "public interest" is consistent with observed phenomena (Posner, 1974), public interest being defined in terms of Pareto optimality. This section will examine the arguments and evidence used to support regulation of corporate disclosure and accounting information for evidence that the original securities legislation and the disclosure regulation thereafter are designed to further the "public interest."

The Securities Acts

An important rationale for the securities acts, at the time of their passage, was that investors in general had been misled by inadequate corporate disclosure and that this lack of disclosure was responsible for the 1929 stock market crash (Benston, 1969: 23). It was argued that with adequate disclosure investors would have made realistic assessments of the value of securities and those securities would not have been "overvalued" prior to the crash. Thus, there would not have been any crash. By passing the securities acts and making the data available for investor decisions, Congress would reduce the tendency of the capital market to "overvalue" securities. In other words, Congress would make the market more efficient in the sense that prices would be better estimates of values.

This justification for the securities acts is incomplete. Increasing the amount of information available to investors or even decreasing the number of frauds are not necessarily Pareto optimal acts. Information is costly to produce; frauds are costly to prevent. Consequently, it does not pay investors to be completely informed or for all frauds to be prevented. Investors tend to invest in information up to the point where the private marginal cost of information equals the private marginal benefit. Similarly, the cost and benefits of investment in fraud prevention would be equated at the margin. To argue that provision of more information by government regulation of accounting information is Pareto optimal, it is necessary to argue that the regulation reduces the costs of providing information. That argument was not explicitly made at the time of passage of the securities act.

Academic accountants have seized upon an economic argument to fill the gap in the logic of the rationale for regulation of disclosure. They argue that information is a public good because one person's consumption of the information does not reduce another person's consumption. Further, presumably because of the costs of contracting, corporate managers are not able to stop nonpurchasers from using the information in annual reports (Gonedes and Dopuch, 1974). Because they are not paid for the use of the information by nonpurchasers (e.g., nonshareholders), corporate managers do not take the value of the information to those nonpurchasers into account when determining the quantity of information to produce. Hence, the conclusion is sometimes reached that corporate managers may "underproduce" information in the absence of regulation (Beaver, 1976: 66).

The "public good" rationale for disclosure regulation involves a relative cost argument which is ignored by most of its advocates. They forget that some users of corporate information are not charged for information because it is too costly for managers to establish the means for contracting with those users. Only if this cost of contracting is greater than the cost of government regulation is the regulation of the disclosure of information optimal. That point, however, is not recognized by many of those advancing the "public interest" argument.

The preceding analysis suggests that it is not obvious (*a priori*) that government regulation of disclosure is optimal. Rather, it is an empirical question. In such a situation, we would expect rational legislators motivated in the public interest to analyze the alternatives and seek evidence as to the costs and benefits of disclosure regulation. Is this what we observed in 1933 and 1934? The answer is a clear no!

There was no systematic consideration of costs and benefits in the hearings which preceded the securities acts. Further, there was little consideration of evidence. For example, the politicians provided very little evidence to support their contention that corporate financial statements systematically misled investors. Benston (1969: 53) reports that "a careful examination of the Senate hearings that preceded the passage of the Securities Act of 1933 and the voluminous Pecora Hearings that preceded the Securities Exchange Act of 1934 fails to turn up more than one citation of fraudulently prepared financial statements." As noted earlier, elimination of all fraud is not optimal, so the observation of one fraud is hardly justification for regulating all firms' disclosures.

The lack of concern with costs and benefits by those who pass the legislation suggests the purpose of the Securities Acts was not economic efficiency—that is, it was *not* to determine the optimal level of accounting information.

The SEC

Until recently, economists usually assumed that regulators acted in the "public interest."[1] It was assumed that employees of agencies such as the SEC would automatically determine policy on the Pareto optimality criterion. The officials of the SEC would objectively consider the economic effects of alternative rules and regulations and only implement those which increased economic efficiency. The evidence suggests that the SEC does not follow such a practice. A very small proportion of the SEC's budget is spent on cost-benefit analysis; a great deal more is spent on the drafting and enforcement of rules and regulations. The emphasis appears to be on the production and enforcement of rules rather than on their economic impact.

If the SEC were attempting to assess the costs and benefits of rules to various parties, we would expect it to identify the affected parties and objectively assess their costs and benefits. Instead, the SEC gathers evidence of costs and benefits in a manner which is necessarily going to cause that evidence to be biased. Former SEC chief accountant John Burton (1979: 7–8) describes the evidence gathering process as follows:

> In reaching such judgments [about the needs and interests of investors], the Commission has relied on the representations of analysts and investor organizations expressed in letters of comment, appearances at hearings and informal contacts, plus a continuing survey of the literature of security analysis such as the *Financial Analysts Journal*.

It is unlikely that analyst and investor organizations which make representations or appearances at hearings represent all investors. For example, I would not expect security analysts to represent the demands of investors. Security analysts typically want more information rather than less. This is not surprising since they probably do not bear the cost of the information (the shareholders and/or the customers of the regulated corporations probably do). Further, more information reduces the cost of security analysis and therefore increases the quantity of security analysis produced. Investors (or shareholders), however, bear part of the cost of the information and hence would not want as much information as security analysts.

Making a representation to the SEC is an economic decision, one in which the costs of the representation are matched against the expected benefits. Consequently, groups that make representations to the SEC represent only those individuals whose costs of coalescing and lobbying on rules and regulations are relatively low, or who will bear large costs or receive large benefits as a consequence of a proposed rule. Those whom it did not pay to contract to receive information without regulation are likely to be those whom it does not pay to coalesce and lobby with the SEC. Groups which have relatively low costs of coalescing and lobbying are likely also to have relatively low costs of contracting for an unregulated market. In other words, they are likely to be those who would receive information in the absence of regulation anyway.

Inspection of the representations and submissions made at SEC or Financial Accounting Standards Board (FASB) hearings will undoubtedly confirm the charge that the SEC only hears from those whose lobbying costs are low and those who have a lot to gain or lose from proposed rules.[2] For example, in the recent SEC hearings on oil and gas accounting we observe a study (Collins and Dent, in press) showing that banning the full cost method of accounting (as in FASB Statement Number 19) imposed significant costs on corporations which used that full-cost method.

In general, the way in which the SEC determines costs and benefits and collects evidence strongly suggests that it is not acting as if it were attempting to use its rules and regulations to achieve the optimum accounting information or disclosure in the Pareto sense. What we observe looks more like competition among interest groups than objective determination of optimal information. This impression is strengthened when we observe the SEC responding to political pressure in its rule making. For example, the SEC's nonendorsement of the Accounting Principles Board's (APB) Opinion No. 2 was undoubtedly in response to the strong reaction of corporate managers to that opinion and their threat of political action.[3] Furthermore, since almost every action of the SEC imposes costs on someone who does not get compensated and whose condition is therefore worsened, the SEC is not using the Pareto criterion.

In light of these observations, I have to conclude that neither the securities acts nor the SEC's actions in determining rules and regulations are motivated by a desire to determine the optimal accounting information in the Pareto efficiency sense.

An Explanation of Legislation and Regulation

If the assumption that politicians and regulators act in the "public interest" does not provide a good explanation for the actions of politicians and regulators, what does? One assumption suggested and used by economists and political scientists modeling the political process is that politicians and regulators, like other individuals, act in their own self-interest. Analyses of the political process based on this assumption have shown promise of substantial ability to explain the observed behavior of politicians and regulators.[4]

The costs of lobbying, forming coalitions, and information are central to the self-interest model of the political process. Downs (1957) argued that the probability of an individual's vote affecting the outcome of an election is almost zero. Hence, he has little incentive to incur the costs of being informed on the issues in the election. However, when members of votes have similar interests (e.g., members of the Sierra Club), they can form a group to share the fixed cost of being informed and increase the probability of affecting the outcome of elections. The outcome of the political process (i.e., the nature of legislation and regulation) depends on the relative costs to the various groups of coalescing and influencing the legislation. Those costs are affected by such variables as the size of the groups and the similarity of interests as well as the existing institutional arrangements (e.g., whether decisions are made by a referendum or a vote of elected officials; see Geisel et al., 1978).

The self-interest model of the political process, I suspect, has a great deal of ability to explain both the existence of regulation of disclosure and the nature of the rules and regulations made by the SEC and by the FASB. For example, the cost of information in the political process can explain the passage of the securities acts.

Legislation frequently follows crises such as the 1929 stock market crash.[5] Individual voters are aware of losses caused by the crash and would like to avoid future losses. It does not pay most voters, however, to be informed about the cause of the crash. Understanding macroeconomics requires an investment in some training in economics. Consequently, politicians are not motivated to provide the actual cause of the crash and a real remedy to the electorate. Instead, they are motivated only to provide a cause which will be accepted as correct by a (rationally) uninformed electorate and to supply a remedy which will appear to eliminate the cause. Given the attacks by Ripley on corporate disclosure[6] in the press, it was convenient for Congress to blame corporate disclosures and accountants for the crash and offer the securities acts as a remedy. It was too costly to determine and explain the real causes.[7]

Newspapers and the media, it is important to note, do not have incentives to seek out and determine the reason for a crisis. If because of the lack of benefits to being informed, voters (newspaper readers) do not demand information, newspapers will not supply information. They, like the politicians, have incentives to identify only apparent causes and remedies.[8]

Even regulators, interestingly enough, accept the notion that perceived and not necessarily actual problems cause legislation and regulation. In a recent speech, John Burton (1979: 3) states that "the structure of securities regulation in the United States has been legislatively designed to protect against *perceived* [emphasis added] abuse."

The cost of information can also explain why the SEC gathers evidence only from those who are prepared to bear the costs of coalescing the representing of their interests to the SEC. The others, including the small investor, will not be aware that their interests are being harmed by a proposed rule and therefore will not take political action which could affect the regulators at the SEC. Only those whom it pays to collect information will be aware of the effects of the SEC's actions and therefore will be able to take political action (such as lobbying with Congress) that affects the SEC regulator's self-interest.

The lack of concern with estimating the costs and benefits of proposed rules is also consistent with substantial costs of information in the political process. The regulator has no incentive to calculate the costs and benefits to those of the electorate who will not affect his (the regulator's) self-interest. Further, emphasis on perception rather than fact explains the emphasis on rule making and enforcement rather than cost/benefit analysis. Rule making and prosecutions are more cost effective in attracting the press's attention.

Implications

The conclusion that politicians and regulators act in their own self-interest does not necessarily lead to the conclusion that their products (legislation and regulation) will not be in the "public interest." For example, given perfect competition in politics, possibilities for side payments and zero transactions costs, individuals acting in their own self-interest in the political process might result in a Pareto optimum. But it is clear that a well-functioning political market does not exist. Further, there are substantial penalties for making side payments, or "bribing." Nor are transaction costs zero in the political process. Thus, if we follow those who conclude that there is a "market failure," that competition in markets will not lead to a Pareto optimum because of incomplete markets, positive transactions costs, and so on, we would have to conclude that the political process will not produce a Pareto optimum. Thus, we would also have to conclude that the political process does not lead to the optimal accounting information.

Those who are concerned with the "public interest" would probably respond to the preceding conclusion by arguing that regulation can lead to the optimal information. All we have to do is change politicians' and regulators' behavior or reduce information and transactions costs in the political process. The response to that argument is, how? Not only is it difficult to change people's behavior, how would these changes be achieved? Via the very political process which already produced the "wrong" result? Those who would solve "problems" in the market with government intervention in a "Nirvana"[9] world of "public interest"-oriented bureaucrats face a serious obstacle when confronted with the problems with government. Thus, if I take the same approach as that taken by many critics of the private market, I am forced to conclude, as an empiricist, that government regulation *cannot* determine the optimum accounting information. As we shall see, however, such a conclusion is premature.

As I noted earlier, the justification for government regulation of disclosure tends to ignore certain costs. For example, the "public good" rationalization often tends to ignore the reason why "free riders" on information exist—the cost of contracting.[10] Also, those who argue that the free market solution fails because some markets do not exist ignore the reasons—the costs of operating them. Consequently, as an empiricist, I do not regard the observation that certain users of information do not pay for it or the nonexistence of certain markets as evidence of market failure.

Likewise, when I observe certain investors not trying to influence SEC decisions, I conclude as an empiricist that the costs of those investors coalescing, being informed on the SEC's proposals, and lobbying for or against them exceeds the benefits. Hence, I cannot regard such inaction by investors as a failure of the political process but merely as evidence of relative costs and benefits. Thus, I must conclude that given the information and transactions costs in the political process, regulation is currently determining the optimal accounting information.

On the other hand, I abhor as an individual, some of the results of government regulation of accounting information. Rule making in accounting, because it is rationalized in public interest terms, creates a demand for accounting theories which imply a given accounting procedure (e.g., successful efforts or full cost) is optimal from a public interest standpoint. Corporate managers, public accountants, consumer advocates, and others who want to use accounting prodecures to achieve or prevent a wealth transfer for self-interest reasons demand public interest theories as excuses for their positions.[11]

This demand for excuses leads to the production of normative accounting research (i.e., to research which prescribes a particular accounting procedure) instead of to the production of research which enhances our understanding of why, for example, different firms choose different procedures. As an individual concerned with understanding what I observe, I do not like that outcome. That, however, is *my taste*. Given my tastes, regulation cannot and does not determine optimal accounting information. But tastes are a personal matter. Others, I am sure, would completely disagree with my personal opinion of regulation of accounting information.

In summary, the answer to the question: "Can optimal accounting information be determined by regulation?" depends on the perspective the responder assumes in his answer. From the perspective of a researcher, I must answer yes. From my own perspective, with my own preferences, I must answer no.

Notes

This chapter draws heavily on my published and unpublished research with Jerold Zimmerman. That research was supported by the Center for Research in Government Policy and Business, University of Rochester. I am grateful to Richard Leftwich and Jerold Zimmerman for helpful comments on an earlier draft.

1. For a summary of the literature based on this assumption, see Posner (1974) and McCraw (1975).

2. See Watts and Zimmerman (1978) for a discussion of the incentive of corporations to lobby on accounting standards.

3. See Zeff (1972: 180). Zeff implies that the Commission's *Accounting Services Release No. 96* which undercut Opinion 2 was in part due to the Commission's awareness of industry opposition.

4. See Downs (1957); Jensen (1976); Meckling (1976a, 1976b); Mueller (1976); Niskanen (1971); Peltzman (1976); Stigler (1971); and Geisel, Leffler, and Zimmerman (1978).

5. See Jensen (1976) and Meckling (1976a) for more detailed analysis of the role of crises in justifying legislation.

6. See Benston (1969: 52–53).

7. Friedman and Schwartz (1963: 306) point out that production, wholesale prices, and personal income fell at annual rates of 20 percent, 7.5 percent, and 5 percent, respectively, in the two months prior to the crash. That suggests the crash was due to real economic forces instead of accounting reports. Friedman and Schwartz go on to indicate that the government worsened the recession by its monetary policy.

8. See Jensen (1976) for an analysis of the behavior of the press.

9. This term is Demsetz's (1969).

10. Barzel (1977) makes the same point on the arguments that speculative behavior or signaling leads to market failures.

11. See Watts and Zimmerman (1979) for an analysis of the effect of government regulation on accounting theory.

10

Regulation and the Cost Effectiveness of Independent Audits

Robert P. Magee

Graduate School of Management
Northwestern University

Regulation and audit effectiveness would seem at first glance to be a straightforward issue. On closer inspection, however, it quickly becomes apparent that the number of questions this topic encompasses is overwhelming. How much of what types of auditing activity is "best"? What do we mean by "best"? How can we measure the level of audit activity? Can we hope to measure audit effectiveness in the "real world"? Who should pay for an audit? How does the audit payment system affect reported demands for auditing? What competitive pressures influence the supply of and demand for auditing services? Where may these competitive pressures fail, and what types of regulations may alleviate these problems? Do these regulatory actions create other problems? Can regulations concerning individuals other than the auditor (for example, board members or management) affect the auditor's effectiveness? The answers to these questions (and many more that are left implicit) are not only interesting to academic accountants, they are also important to the accounting profession as it seeks to respond to regulatory proposals and to find effective means of self-regulation.

Moreover, a host of research methodologies could be used to address these questions. Theoretical research may help us to predict the effects of regulatory alternatives on the behavior of managers and auditors. Empirical research may estimate the costs of various alternatives and measure the impact of audits on managers' behavior. I believe that both types of research are necessary to deal effectively with the questions to be addressed. My objective in this chapter is a modest one: to examine a few of these audit regulation issues in the context of a simple model of auditor/manager behavior.

The Auditor's Role

The role of the auditor arises through a series of delegation/accountability relationships that characterize our economic system. These relationships are often referred to as "principal/agent" relationships, where the principal delegates decision-making authority and responsibility to an agent. This sort of relationship obtains between shareholders and the board of directors, between the board of directors and the chief executive officer, and so on, throughout the organization. The principal's problem is to choose a performance evaluation system, including the measures of performance, so that the agent is motivated to make decisions that are in the best interests of the organization. A potential conflict occurs when the agent also has some control over the information that will be used in measuring performance. For instance, the manager should be getting information on the organization's activities to facilitate the planning and control tasks which he or she was delegated. The board of directors may be reluctant to expend the resources to duplicate this information, but at the same time they may hesitate to use information provided by the manager to compensate the manager. The board is faced with a dilemma: It could make the manager's compensation independent of performance measures, but that could result in inappropriate motivation; or, if the compensation does depend on performance measures, the manager may have an incentive to overstate the results. At this point, the auditor may enter the system to provide some independent verification that the reported numbers were produced according to prescribed rules. Ideally, this outside information enables the board to motivate and evaluate the manager without incurring large information costs.

Who are the potential beneficiaries of an audit? Certainly the shareholders can benefit from a properly motivated management, and the increased reliability of financial reports can smooth the capital allocation process. We should also note that the manager may benefit from the audit. If the board knows that it will receive reliable performance measures, it should be able to increase the manager's compensation and/or the resources that are allocated to the manager's activity. As Jensen and Meckling (1976) point out, these effects could cause managers to submit voluntarily to audits, bond covenants, and so on. That is, the manager may voluntarily restrict the courses of action that are available to him. I shall return to this phenomenon later in the chapter.

What auditing "product" is valuable in this situation? We may be able to measure the inputs, but the output is essentially a conditional probability distribution—that is, the probability of audit results depending on management's reporting strategy.[1] If owners cannot discern the conditional probability distribution produced by the auditor, then there may be considerable difficulty in reaching an agreement based on the amount of auditing output. As Ng (1978) has pointed out, this characteristic of unobservability, along with the public good derived from auditing, may cause some difficulties in relying on a competitive solution to the supply and demand for audit services.What follows is a simple auditing/reporting relationship to use in evaluating various regulatory proposals aimed at affecting the equilibrium levels of auditing and reporting.

An Auditor/Manager Game

To assess the effects of various "regulatory" alternatives on the behavior of auditors and managers, I will use a game in which the auditor chooses an auditing strategy and the manager chooses a reporting strategy.[2] To be sure, the game is a simplified representation of the relationship between an auditor and a manager. By reflecting the public's perception of the situation, however, it may be of value in assessing the effects of regulation, or at least the perceived effects of regulation. Various modifications or extensions are possible, and these would bring our model closer to the "real world," but at the cost of additional complexity.

Let us suppose that the auditor has two choices, to *audit some* or to *audit more*, and the manager has two choices also, to report financial statements which fairly (*truthfully*) reflect the firm's financial condition or to *overstate* the firm's financial achievements. If the manager reports the truth, he gets a salary, and the auditor receives his fee minus additional auditing costs if he chooses to *audit more*. (Tables 10-1 and 10-2 describe the auditor and manager payoffs, respectively, for different auditing and reporting decisions.) If the manager overstates and the auditor doesn't catch the overstatement by *auditing some*, the manager gets a salary plus a bonus, while the auditor incurs a loss when the overstatement is discovered. If the auditor *audits more*, then the overstatement is discovered, and a penalty is deducted from the manager's salary, while the auditor must only incur the additional audit costs. Obviously, many assumptions go into these payoffs, and we will be exploring these in the context of some regulatory possibilities.

Now we might want to find out, in this simple game, how much audit-

Table 10-1

AUDITOR PAYOFFS

	Manager Actions	
	Truth	Overstate
Auditor Actions	*Audit some* fee	Fee − loss
	Audit more fee − cost	Fee − cost

Table 10-2

MANAGER PAYOFFS

	Manager Actions	
	Truth	Overstate
Auditor Actions	*Audit some* salary	Salary + bonus
	Audit more salary	Salary − penalty

ing and overstating will be done, and we can do that by looking for equilibrium points. That is, is there a combination of an auditor action and manager action from which neither can better himself?

To answer, let us first assume that the manager receives no bonus based on the firm's financial results (bonus = 0). Then the equilibrium point is for the manager to tell the truth and for the auditor only to *audit some*. This result is consistent with the conclusion of Ng and Stoeckenius (1978) that the only "truth-inducing" incentive is one which is essentially a constant for different financial results. Of course, this sort of nonincentive system would affect the manager's other decisions, so it is unlikely that the owners of the firm would be willing to accept such an alternative. On the other hand, suppose there is a managerial bonus based on financial results but no penalty for overstating results. In this case, there is also one equilibrium set of actions: The auditor will *audit more*, and the manager will attempt to *overstate*.

Before we turn to a discussion of various regulatory proposals, it is useful to see how the auditor's economic situation affects the game. If the auditor's *loss* is less than the *cost*, then there is only one equilibrium, and that is for the auditor to *audit some* and the manager to *overstate*. If *loss* is greater than *cost*, and if there are positive bonus and penalty values for the manager, then no equilibrium point exists. That is, there is no combination of actions where either party can improve its position unilaterally. This situation produces what game theorists call a "probabilistic equilibrium," where the amount of auditing and overstating is not a deterministic event. The equilibrium will look like this:

Auditor:

$$\text{Prob (audit some)} = \frac{\text{penalty}}{\text{bonus} + \text{penalty}}$$

$$\text{Prob (audit more)} = \frac{\text{bonus}}{\text{bonus} + \text{penalty}}$$

Manager:

$$\text{Prob (truth)} = \frac{\text{loss - cost}}{\text{loss}}$$

$$\text{Prob (overstate)} = \frac{\text{cost}}{\text{loss}}$$

It is obvious that the behavior of the manager and the auditor (or the public's perception of that behavior) depends upon the relative sizes of the costs, bonuses, and penalties of the parties involved. What is the probability that a managerial overstatement will not be found by the auditor?

Prob (undetected overstatement)

$$= \text{Prob (audit some)} \times \text{prob (overstate)}$$

$$= \left[\frac{\text{penalty}}{\text{bonus} + \text{penalty}}\right] \times \left[\frac{\text{cost}}{\text{loss}}\right]$$

What are some of the implications of these equilibrium values? The larger the manager's bonus relative to the penalty, the more likely it is that the auditor will *audit more*. The larger the auditor's cost relative to his potential loss, the greater the probability is that the manager will overstate the financial results. In other words, when the audit technology makes it difficult (costly) to verify a part of the financial reports, the manager may tend to take advantage of that situation.

Now that we have a simple model of the auditor/manager relationship and the factors which influence the behavior of both parties, we can examine a number of regulatory issues. To be sure, our examination will be limited by the simplicity of our model, but it can serve as a useful starting point, to be extended as we learn more about auditor/manager/owner relationships.

Regulatory Issues

To begin with, many types of "regulatory" actions exist. Governmental actions (laws) make certain activities illegal and subject to penalty. Judicial actions determine the magnitudes of liabilities in civil actions. Organizations such as the Securities and Exchange Commission may regulate the amount of auditing, for example, by requiring that filings not have the scope of audit opinions qualified. Or the SEC may require the auditor to be responsible to an audit committee comprised solely of nonmanagement directors. These and other governmental "interventions" are forms of regulation that can be discussed in the context of the audit game.

Managerial Penalty

As noted in the previous section, the effectiveness and amounts of auditing are not determined only by the auditor; the manager's incentives also play an important role. What makes up the penalty for the manager if he or she attempts to overstate the financial results of the firm and is "caught" by the auditor? If a discovered managerial overstatement were made known, it is possible that the manager could suffer a human capital loss, since potential future employers might consider him less favorably. But if the auditor is responsible to the manager and reports that he would be unable to give a clean opinion, then an adjustment to the financial statements may be made. The manager may not get the bonus, but the penalty imposed may be small or even nonexistent. If this is the case, then the auditing equilibrium involves *auditing more* always.

An alternative would be for the auditor to be responsible to an independent party—for example, an audit committee of the board of directors. In this situation, the information about the manager's behavior is relayed to those who are in a position to impose a penalty of some form on the manager. This penalty does not have to be a monetary fine but could involve a reduction in influence, a change in future bonus arrangements, and so on. (A clear parallel with internal auditing exists, since it is seldom the case that an internal auditor is responsible to the individual being audited.)

In addition, a law making it illegal to lie to an auditor might affect the size of the manager's penalty and thereby affect the auditing/reporting equilibrium. Of course, our simple model would be hard pressed to take all the appropriate considerations into account in this case. If such a law re-duces the cooperation between auditors and managers, then the costs of audits and the fees required by the auditors will increase. As a result, it is difficult to determine whether such regulation would benefit the firm's shareholders. Proposing this sort of action, however, is a clear recognition that regulation of the auditor is not the only way to influence the effective-ness of auditing activity. We might say that the auditor is responsible for "overstatement detection," but that "overstatement prevention" is jointly determined by auditors, boards of directors, and the legal system as it deter-mines the economic liabilities of managers. The auditing/reporting equi-librium is not under the complete control of the auditor. Factors such as board representation, the existence and makeup of audit committees, mana-gerial penalties, and so on are determined by others, and they should be taken into account when evaluating the effectiveness of auditing activity.

The Auditor's Cost

The next factor is the cost which the auditor incurs by *auditing more.* As noted, the size of this cost, relative to the auditor's loss variable, is an impor-tant determinant of the auditing/reporting equilibrium. In fact, if the cost is greater than the auditor's loss, then the equilibrium is *audit less/overstate,* which is probably not in the shareholders' best interests. On the other hand, if the auditor is compensated for the additional costs, then the equi-librium is *audit more/truth.*

One obvious determinant of these costs is the technology available to accountants for auditing a firm's financial reports. The use of statistical sam-pling techniques, computerized audit procedures, sophisticated models for analytical review, and other techniques may be seen as attempts to get more auditing output per dollar. But it is not just the audit technology which affects the cost variable, but also the characteristics of the firm and its re-porting system. As the volume and variety of transactions increase and as the accounting system moves from large, centralized electronic data pro-cessing facilities to smaller, distributed facilities, it will become more costly to audit enough to detect an overstatement. As a result, our equilibrium would predict that an overstatement was more likely to occur. On the other hand, one effect of the internal control requirement of the Foreign Corrupt Practices Act may be to reduce the cost variable for the external auditor to detect overstatements, and this would reduce the frequency of undetected overstatements (at the cost of the increased internal control).

Another factor which might affect auditor's cost is the degree of inde-pendence between auditor and manager. If the auditor chooses to *audit more* and detects an overstatement, what happens to the auditor? If he can be dismissed with no disclosures, then the auditor's cost may include the loss of future fees. To limit this type of pressure, regulations that require disclosure of the reasons for dismissal or that require an audit committee of outside board members reduce these factors in the auditor's cost variable. The result of these types of regulations in our model could be to increase the amount of auditing and to reduce the frequency of overstatement at the equilibrium.

This model of the auditor/manager relationship clearly demonstrates how certain types of regulatory actions could influence the amount of auditing and the reporting strategies. Increasing the penalties faced by management and decreasing the dependence of auditors on management both serve to decrease the likelihood of an undetected overstatement. But one important factor yet to be discussed is the loss suffered by the accountant if an overstatement is not discovered.

The Auditor's Loss

The size of the auditor's loss in the event of an undetected overstatement plays an important role in the auditor/manager equilibrium. If the loss is less than the cost, then the equilibrium is a somewhat disconcerting one (*audit some/overstate*). If we assume that this game reflects the way the public views the auditor/manager relationship, then the auditor's potential loss plays a key role in the public's perception of the auditing and reporting equilibrium.

The loss suffered by the auditor when an overstatement is undetected could be divided into two factors. First, if the undetected overstatement is made known to the public, what penalties are imposed? Second, these penalties must be multiplied by the probability that the undetected overstatement will be made known to the public. Since it is the product of these factors that determines the auditor's loss, we must examine the factors which influence both of them.

If it becomes known that the auditor failed to detect an overstatement of the firm's financial statements, what changes occur in the auditor's economic well-being? In a purely competitive setting, the demand for the auditor's services may decline, since the public may view the auditor as less capable of the job for which he was hired. As a result, the auditor's loss is the reduction in income from clients he would have had if the undetected overstatement had not occurred. The auditor's "product" depends on his perceived independence. If he loses that, he has little left to sell. But these losses depend on the efficiency of the labor market for auditors, and on the information available to that market. Further, if the demand for auditing is set by managers and/or audit committees, there is no guarantee that the tradeoffs made by these persons will match those desired by the public. Therefore, it may not be the case that these competitive losses are sufficient to create the auditing/reporting equilibrium desired. At any rate, the size of these losses and the changes in them represent some interesting empirical issues.

It has been pointed out that an individual may voluntarily submit to some restraints or monitoring in order to signal to others that he will not take certain actions. For example, employees may voluntarily submit to supervision or a manager may voluntarily submit to an audit of his financial reports. In a way, the creation of an SEC Practice Section by the AICPA may be seen as an effort to impose (or to facilitate the imposition of) penalties on auditors who do not meet a set of standards. If the SEC should choose to require that filings be audited by a firm in the SEC Practice Section, the loss from an undetected overstatement increases, and the auditing/reporting equilibrium will produce fewer undetected overstatements. Therefore, we could interpret the creation of the two practice sections as a voluntary attempt by the accounting profession to change the public's perception of the auditor/manager relationship.

Of course, other factors influence the accountant's potential loss, most notably, the exposure to shareholder lawsuits. The magnitude of this sort of liability is largely determined by the decisions and interpretations of the judicial system. I do not intend to go into a lengthy analysis of the impact of various court decisions on the auditor's potential liability, but many of these could be analyzed in our framework or extensions of our framework. For instance, the Supreme Court decision in *Ernst and Ernst* v. *Hochfelder* could be seen as limiting the auditor's liability when a management fraud involves an overstatement that is not discovered because the accountant only *audits some* instead of *auditing more*. If this sort of loss is eliminated, and if we were to have serious doubts about the competitive losses an accountant could suffer, then the auditing/reporting equilibrium is not a very appealing one. This sort of perspective may underlie some of the criticisms that have been made of public accounting (e.g., Briloff's [1976] address) and could explain the increase in the number of regulatory proposals that we have experienced.

The other factor which affects the auditor's loss variable is the probability that an undetected overstatement will become public knowledge. This factor is just as important as the size of the auditor's potential losses of future revenues, legal exposure, and so on, because if the probability that the accountant's error will become known is zero, then these potential losses carry no impact. Many factors will influence the size of this probability. First, there is the likelihood of the accountant's discovering the overstatement after the reports have been certified and distributed. If the overstatement continues or increases, the probability of not detecting it should decrease over time. It is inevitable that ever-growing overstatements will eventually be detected by the auditor, unless continuing "blind spots" exist in the audit procedure. If the overstatement allows the manager to "smooth" the financial results, however, that is, increase year 1's income by "borrowing" from year 2's income, then the probability of a subsequent detection may decline. For instance, a manager could attempt to underestimate bad debt expense in year 1, and then, at the end of year 2, attribute the additional bad debt expense to events and experiences in year 2. In this case, the auditor may not be sure whether year 1's results were overstated or not.

In the event that an overstatement is discovered in a subsequent audit, what is the probability that it will be made public? Clearly we are treading in sensitive areas at this point, for while it is not illegal for an auditor to make an error, it is illegal to try to cover up that error. Having discovered the error, the auditor can choose to disclose it and incur the costs discussed earlier or he can choose not to disclose it and run the additional risk of criminal charges. It is clear from this double level of penalties that the latter course of action should be discouraged, but it is also clear that such discouragement is not entirely successful. Therefore we might inquire whether some regulatory action might increase the likelihood of discovery of an auditor's error.

Certainly, a requirement that auditors be rotated on a regular basis could be regarded as a partial solution to this sort of problem. Rotation may be within one accounting firm or to another firm. The costs of the latter are likely to be greater, but although a new accountant may have no greater probability of discovering the previous accountant's error, the new accountant is provided with less potential conflict about whether to disclose the error. It is also possible that if the new auditor uses some other audit procedures, the probability of discovery may be even higher than if the auditor was unchanged. We could look at this situation in the schematic in Figure 10-1. If the original auditor always chooses to disclose his past errors, the probability of an error being disclosed is $r \times p + (1 - r) \times p = p$, the probability of an error discovery, since branches (D) and (E) will never occur. On the other hand, if it is a situation in which a discovered error will not be disclosed by an unchanged auditor, an error is disclosed only on branch (A), with probability $r \times p$, so that back in the original auditor/ manager game, the expected "loss" variable that influences the auditing/ reporting equilibrium may depend upon the rotation of auditors. On the other hand, if auditors always disclose their errors, then audit rotation would not influence the auditing/reporting equilibrium.

One interesting point in this analysis involves the interaction between the probability that an error will be disclosed and the size of the loss borne by an auditor in the event that an error is disclosed. A regulatory action increasing the auditor's potential loss would, all things being equal, increase the auditor's loss variable. But if the action also decreased the incentives for

Figure 10-1

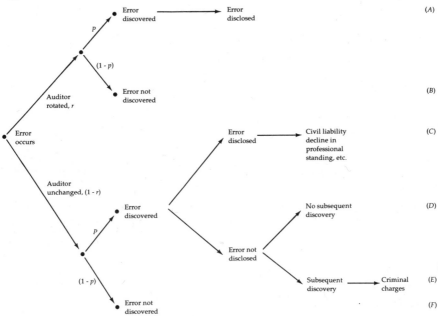

r represents the probability of rotation;
p represents the probability of discovering a previous error.

self-disclosure, the net effect could be to reduce the auditor's loss variable, and to result in an increased probability of an undetected overstatement. Only an increase in rotation will produce the desired effect, but rotation may bring additional costs to the system as well.

Other regulatory issues could influence the behavior of the auditor and manager in the game just described, but it is unnecessary to go into them here. The important point, rather, is to have a model of the environment in which the auditing profession operates and of the auditor's decision-making process. This model may be theoretically and/or empirically based, but if we are to project the effects of regulatory proposals, some form of model is necessary. Obviously the model presented here is too simplistic to be used in resolving regulatory issues, but it represents, I believe, a small step in the right direction. Some differences in opinion concerning regulatory issues could even possibly be resolved in this way by identifying differences that may be clarified by empirical research.

At the same time, some aspects of the situation are simply not observable, and that complicates matters considerably. For example, it might be rather difficult for one person to discern the risk aversion, ethical character, information-processing abilities, and other traits of another person. As a result, it is difficult to construct commercial relationships based on these characteristics. Auditors must certainly realize this difficulty because just this problem produces the demand for auditing services. Therefore, it may be necessary for auditors to submit to certain restrictions or penalties to maintain public confidence in auditing. Keeping these considerations in mind, we now turn to two regulatory issues.

Auditing and MAS

One simplification in the auditor/manager model is that the auditor only engages in auditing. But many accounting firms have found that their expertise is also applicable in such areas as taxes, the design of information systems and internal control systems, and so on. These tasks are different from auditing functions because their objective is not to verify but to improve the firm's financial results. So we might expect that the demand for an accounting firm's management advisory services (MAS) is, in part, dependent on their ability to help a firm meet its objectives, as measured in the financial reports. Of course, this situation presents a potential conflict of interest if an accounting firm is both a consultant and an auditor for a company. If an accountant, wearing a consultant's hat, makes a mistake, will the public believe that a member of the same firm will disclose the error while wearing an auditor's hat? Of course, this problem has become more serious with the requirement that firms maintain adequate, documented systems of internal control. Before this requirement, if an auditor found an inadequate internal control system, he could simply increase the intensity of other audit steps and still render an unqualified opinion. Now the auditor may have to provide some assurances that the system is adequate.

Does this mean that regulations should be imposed prohibiting one firm from providing both management advisory services and auditing services to a single client? While this question is different than those posed earlier in the chapter, it has many of the same characteristics. An accounting firm may argue that the costs borne by the investors will be higher under a forced separation of auditing and MAS, and that is most likely true if no auditors succumb to the potential conflicts of interest. But it is difficult to discuss regulation based on what auditors *ought* to do or on what auditors *say* they will do. Instead, we ought to consider what the public can *expect* an auditor (or various types of auditors) to do, and the model presented here may be helpful in this regard.

Under what conditions would we be willing to allow a company to be advised and audited by the same accounting firm? Clearly we would want the auditor to expect to be better off by "blowing the whistle" than by taking any other sort of action. As before, we would need a penalty level and a probability of detection that were large enough to discourage undesirable behavior. We already have the first one of these two factors, because covering up a previous error, say, in internal control system design, could lead to criminal charges, while disclosing the error might lead to reduced demand and a lower income level. What may need some consideration is the probability that a cover-up will be discovered. Rather than never allowing the same accounting firm to audit and advise or placing no restrictions on these arrangements, we might suggest that a probabilistic check be made in cases where one accounting firm audits and advises. For example, a party such as the Public Oversight Board could be given a list of situations where one accounting firm provides both services, and choose from that list cases to be verified by a second auditor. If the penalties are made large enough, the probability of verification can be made small and the expected cost of the second audit will decrease. This variant of peer review could be used to approach a "first best" situation in which the economies of one firm's auditing and advising are only slightly reduced, while avoiding the potential conflicts of interest.

Recent Self-Regulatory Actions

The accounting profession has recently taken steps to change the level of self-regulation, as in the AICPA's creation of the two practice sections and the Public Oversight Board. The role that the SEC Practice Section could play in the auditing/reporting scheme has been discussed earlier in this chapter, but a number of unanswered questions remain about the retention of firms in the division.

The Public Oversight Board may fulfill a variety of purposes for the accounting profession. As noted earlier, public perception of the auditor/manager relationship will influence the demand for regulation, and the Public Oversight Board may, in an advisory capacity, provide a source of information to the profession. That is, in evaluating alternative self-regulatory proposals, the Board may be in a better position to determine which are responsive to public perceptions. For example, in the case where a managerial overstatement is not detected in an audit, how should an accounting firm's membership in the SEC Practice Section be influenced? Are "due care" standards set up so that an auditor who meets them retains membership regardless of the quality of the financial reports? If so, then the Oversight Board may advise the profession on what levels and what types of "due care" or "professional" standards the public will perceive as leading to the desired auditing/reporting equilibrium.

In addition, one of the primary attributes of the Public Oversight Board is its lack of dependence upon the profitability of accounting firms or upon the voting behavior of some constituency. Therefore, when the Board takes a position, the public may have some confidence that no covert economic motive lurks behind it. Or, if there is an efficient labor market for members of public oversight boards, the Board's positions may attempt to preserve the long-run viability of the auditing/reporting system.

Other Issues

A number of regulatory issues were discussed in the context of the auditing/reporting model. For instance, the effects of auditor rotation on the auditor's loss variable and on the auditing/reporting equilibrium were examined. Proposals for the establishment of audit committees of non-management directors can be seen to increase the manager's penalty while decreasing the auditor's cost, leading to fewer undetected overstatements. I do not wish to belabor these points, but some additional issues can be discussed in the context of our model.

For instance, the membership of the SEC Practice Section has become more widespread than was perhaps originally envisioned by some. Whether this phenomenon is cause for concern depends on how the purpose of the section is perceived. If membership is supposed to denote some extra level of expertise or quality, then a large membership may defeat this purpose. If almost all CPAs are members, then membership may convey little information. On the other hand, in the context of the model, it is not necessary that beginning membership be exclusive to influence the loss variable faced by the auditor. That is, if the auditor still faces a penalty (such as loss of membership) due to undetected overstatements, the two sections still serve a useful function in influencing the auditing/reporting equilibrium. In fact, a larger SEC Practice Section may increase the competitive loss faced by the auditor and reduce the number of undetected overstatements.

Moreover, the competitiveness of the auditing profession may have a profound effect on the auditing/reporting equilibrium. If the market for auditing services is extremely competitive, then an auditing firm's "loss" due to an undetected overstatement will be sizable even without regulation. This occurs because the loss of competitive position will produce a greater loss in fees and because the competition may increase rotation of auditors and the probability that an undetected overstatement will be disclosed. These competitive pressures may cause the loss variable to be large enough that the auditing/reporting equilibrium is acceptable without regulation. On the other hand, certain types of regulation can decrease the level of competition. For instance, disclosure of auditing and MAS fees may reduce the chance of nonindependence within a firm, but it may also provide information that could be used to reduce the level of competition in the market for auditing services.

Conclusions

This chapter has evaluated some regulatory issues in the context of a simple model of the auditing/reporting equilibrium. There are still some important questions that are extremely difficult to answer. For example, how much auditing *should* be done? To answer this question properly, we would need a model that goes far beyond those now available. But more important, a definition of the word "should" is needed. To say that we want enough auditing to facilitate a smoothly operating capital market or to provide adequate control over management really provides us with little guidance. As academic accountants, we can project the *effects* of auditing alternatives, but to go beyond that usually puts us in the position of making arbitrary judgments. As we change the level of auditing, the benefits accruing to a diversified investor will differ from those accruing to an undiversified investor. Whose benefits *should* be maximized? Who should pay for the auditing services?

All these issues are important for auditors, investors, boards of directors, and others. Public perceptions of the auditing/reporting relationships will influence the demand for regulation, and auditors must respond to regulatory proposals based on what the public can expect them to do, rather than on what the auditors plan to do. As we have seen, the profession's self-regulatory actions can be viewed as responsive to these problems, but there may be limits to the profession's ability to affect the auditing/reporting equilibrium. Certainly, the most likely path to this end will be a cooperative effort between the accounting profession and the agencies responsible for investors' welfare.

Notes

1. Throughout this chapter, I assume that management chooses how it will report the firm's achievements and the auditor chooses "how much" to audit those reports.

2. The use of the word "game" is troublesome, since it is not meant to be pejorative. Here it will be used in the technical sense, where outcomes are determined by the actions of more than one decision maker.

11

Should Accounting Standards Be Set in the Public or Private Sector?

Robert S. Kaplan

Dean, Graduate School of Industrial Administration
Carnegie-Mellon University

Much academic scholarship, including other chapters in this book, considers whether accounting and accountants should be regulated at all. Little attention has been devoted to discussing the pros and cons of public or private regulation once it has been conceded that some amount of regulation is desirable or, more likely, inevitable.

Although extensive research has been done on public regulation, little is available to suggest a theory of private regulation. The limited amount of discussion that has occurred on the merits of public versus private regulation usually consists of vague and unsupported appeals either to the notion that a government agency better serves the "public interest" (public regulation advocates) or to the benefits of a private enterprise system (private regulation advocates). Even observation of the institutional arrangements in the United States for the last forty-five years does not yield direct evidence on the characteristics of solely private or solely public regulation of accounting standards. As Horngren (1973) points out, the existing system has a governmental agency (the Securities and Exchange Commission) overseeing the operations of a sequence of private standard-setting agencies. Therefore, it is difficult to generalize from past and current experience to predict the characteristics of a purely private standard-setting agency or those of a governmental standard-setting agency. Consequently, the following discussion does not have a strong research basis.

What follows will be a series of observations for which at least a shred of evidence should exist. But the arguments are anecdotal rather than scientific. Perhaps the greatly increased interest in regulation in general and the accounting profession in particular will enable future researchers to identify more carefully the unique characteristics of public and private regulation.

Theories of Regulation

To discuss the effect of regulation, one must necessarily assume a theory of regulation upon which to explain and predict behavior. My viewpoint will be consistent with the recently developed economic theory of regulation (Stigler, 1971; Posner, 1974) which attempts to explain the behavior and rule making of regulatory agencies as a process of maximizing behavior by legislators, bureaucrats, and regulators. Thus, I will attempt to analyze the behavior of a public or private standard-setting agency by identifying the constituencies of the agencies and the forces impinging on these agencies.

The theory of what constitutes maximizing behavior in an accounting regulatory agency is unfortunately still not completely developed. George Benston, who has studied this question more extensively than anyone else, has many interesting and provocative observations (Benston, 1975, 1976, 1977, 1979). Benston (1975: 255) explains the behavior of the Securities and Exchange Commission according to the economic theory's predictions of agency conservatism.

> An active regulatory agency has an incentive for insisting on conservative, explicit, even rigid accounting standards. Such standards reduce the risk to the agency that it will be criticized for "accepting" statements that, when viewed with the benefit of hindsight, appear misleading or fraudulent.
>
> It is not surprising that the SEC tends to want uniform, conservative reporting by corporations.

These observations were consistent with the SEC limitation on forecasts, revaluations, and the release of information about a company when it was in registration. They are also consistent with the generally observed behavior of governmental agencies to be careful about the information (or products) they approve without regard to the cost of not disclosing additional information (or approving new products) which have some risk or uncertainty associated with them. Thus, agencies are viewed as conservative and risk avoiding.

But these predictions are inconsistent with the behavior of the SEC since the early 1970s. *Accounting Series Release No. 190,* which requires large companies to disclose replacement cost information, produces subjective information that is difficult to verify. This requirement was particularly significant since it preempted a proposal by the Financial Accounting Standards Board (FASB) to adopt the more objective and verifiable General Price Level approach to inflation accounting. The SEC also became more permissive, if not encouraging, to the release of company forecasts. These actions could initially be explained by the activism of the Chief Accountant of the SEC at the time, John Burton. But this trend continued after Burton left the SEC. In 1978, the SEC overruled the conservative proposal of FAS 19 (requiring the exclusive use of the successful efforts method for oil and gas exploration) by allowing companies to continue to use nonuniform methods (successful efforts or full cost), and requiring the disclosure of an untested and highly subjective procedure (Reserve Recognition Accounting). These instances raise contradictions with the conventional wisdom of an agency as a conservative force stifling innovation in the industry it is regulating. Thus, there is still no satisfactory theory that explains these diverse phenomena for public agency regulation. The evidence on private agency regulation is even sparser. Further, while both public and private regulatory agencies may attempt to justify their actions by appeals to how they are serving the "public interest," neither the public (SEC) nor the private (FASB, since 1973) agency has the dispersed investing community as one of its direct constituents—as a source of power, legitimacy, or financing. Thus, neither type of agency has a comparative advantage in directly serving the public.

The second foundation for my discussion is a belief that accounting and disclosure do matter, that the form of presentation and amount of disclosure do affect resource allocation decisions throughout the economy. Therefore, the quantity and form of financial disclosure are important issues worthy of study and analysis.

Managers of companies may respond to mandated changes in accounting standards. Clearly, FAS 8 has led to different decisions within corporations on hedging exposure in foreign operations (Evans et al, 1978 and many articles in the popular financial press). FAS 13 probably affected companies' use of noncancelable leases. In addition, FAS 2, 5, and 12 could have led to changes in a company's decisions on research and development, self-insurance, and marketable securities, respectively, though there is little evidence yet that these three standards have led to many changes in companies' decisions (see, in particular, Goshay, 1978 on the lack of reaction of companies to FAS 5). None of these accounting standards affects the cash flows of a firm directly and we may not expect that a different but fully disclosed method of computing income or classifying liabilities would affect a manager's decision. But an accounting standard which changes net income or financial ratios can affect management compensation arrangements (Rappaport, 1978), political visibility, and regulatory commissions (Watts and Zimmerman, 1978). In addition, dividend, working capital, and debt-equity constraints arising from bond covenants and loan agreements are usually defined using generally accepted accounting principles (GAAP) so that changes in these principles could lead to tightening or even violations of these constraints (Holthausen, 1979; Leftwich, 1979). As a further example, if presently disclosed unfunded pension liabilities were required to be classified as part of the debt of a corporation (with, say, a corresponding charge to shareholders' equity), many companies would be thrown into default on loan agreements. As a final observation on the importance of accounting standards, there is evidence of at least a temporary decline in the price of the stocks of oil and gas exploration companies using the full-cost method when the FASB Exposure Draft, mandating the successful efforts method, was announced in July, 1977 (Collins and Dent, 1979; for a different view of this stock price reaction, see Dyckman and Smith, 1979).

Thus, measurement and disclosure affect the phenomenon being observed. But until recently, this principle was not widely accepted in accounting, where there continued to be a call for uniformity and truth in accounting measurement and reporting. Once we accept the fundamental notion that the act of measurement affects the activities being measured, we become less concerned with *a priori* notions of truth and more concerned with the consequences of our measurement (Ijiri, 1975; Prakash and Rappaport, 1976). Also, accountants and auditors, as monitors of the activities of human decision makers, must be concerned with the consequences of their measurements on the rights and incentives of these decision makers, not just the well-being of the recipients of the reported information. This is a major difference from measuring the characteristics of inanimate objects (Ijiri, 1976). Therefore, agencies promulgating accounting standards need to recognize the impact of the standards on the entity and managers being accounted for as well as the diverse set of users who gain access to the produced information.

With this background, let us examine the strengths and weaknesses of setting standards for accounting, first in the private sector, and then in the public sector.

Private Regulation of Accounting Standards

Standard setting in the private sector has evolved from AICPA-sponsored organizations, the Committee on Accounting Procedures (CAP; 1939–1959) and the Accounting Principles Board (APB; 1959–1973), to the present independent organization, the Financial Accounting Standards Board (FASB; 1973–?). Rather than discussing the characteristics of a private regulatory agency in the abstract, let us take the FASB as the prototype of standard setting in the private sector. The FASB differs significantly from its predecessors by drawing representation and financial support from a community much broader than the public accounting profession. Besides the academic and public accounting representatives who populated the CAP and APB, the FASB has obtained members who were formerly financial executives and financial analysts. Also unlike the CAP and the APB, the FASB obtains financial support from voluntary contributions of corporations as well as from public accounting firms. Some financing also is contributed by professional associations representing individuals involved in the production and interpretation of financial information. The Financial Accounting Foundation (FAF) and the Financial Accounting Standards Advisory Council (FASAC), which serve as supervisory agencies of the FASB, also consist of members from diverse professions, including accountants from the federal government. While representatives of the SEC have no formal role in the activities of the FASB, they attend many of the hearings and deliberations of the FASB and its task forces and seem to have good communication channels with the FASB. Thus, the FASB must be responsive to a broad constituency in its deliberations.

Recognizing its diverse constituency and the consequences of its actions on groups in this constituency, the FASB has adopted procedures that encourage comments and criticisms of proposed standards at many stages during the standard-setting process. Task forces are organized, drawing upon experts outside the FASB staff. Discussion Memoranda are distributed, raising the relevant issues on a subject, in an attempt to solicit specific suggestions or consequences of various alternatives. Following the comments on a Discussion Memorandum, the FASB proposes a specific approach in an Exposure Draft which becomes the subject for further comments and suggestions. Public hearings may be held at the Discussion Memorandum and Exposure Draft stages. Meetings of the FASB are open to the public. Thus, the FASB attempts to be responsive to its many interest groups and to follow procedures of due process and open debate. Naturally, it will be difficult if not impossible for any particular standard to satisfy all the groups interested in the format of financial statements. But at least the outcome comes after a process of open and extensive discussion, and is voted on by Board members with previous expertise in the production, interpretation, or verification of financial information in the private sector. It is worth noting that votes on FASB pronouncements are made public, and dissenting members are permitted to indicate their reservations about a standard receiving less than a unanimous vote.

Because the FASB draws voluntary financial support from diverse groups in the private sector and because these groups are represented on the Board, on the supervising FAF and FASAC, and on task forces, the FASB must be sensitive to the consequences of its promulgated standards. That is why the FASB reconsiders its previously issued standards, with particular attention to controversial standards such as FAS 5 and FAS 8. The FASB also sponsors research studies by independent experts to evaluate the consequences of various standards and to determine how newly proposed ideas on financial reporting could be implemented in practice.

Obviously, CPA firms have been a major constituency for all the private standard-setting bodies (CAP, APB, and FASB). The financial and personnel support from CPA firms have been essential for the operation of these agencies. Such support has enabled the private agencies to benefit from the considerable expertise in accounting and industry practices of the senior partners of major public accounting firms. There are a number of consequences that arise from the centrality of public accounting practitioners in a private standard-setting agency. The agency will be more receptive to non-uniform practices because of the diversity of clients and industries that are audited. Experienced auditors, with a wide-ranging background of clients, will be less willing to impose a uniform standard which does not provide some flexibility for companies in differing circumstances.

Because practitioners from CPA firms are primarily auditors, the auditing implications of any standard will receive a great deal of attention from a private standard-setting agency. There will be strong pressure for rules that can be implemented without requiring subjective estimates that are difficult to audit and even more difficult to defend should the financial statements be subject to question in a judicial proceeding. Given the present litigious climate, auditors wish to avoid having to certify figures for which objective verifiable evidence is unavailable. These feelings are reinforced by corporate executives, another principal constituency of the private standard-setting agency, who may also fear the legal repercussions from issuing "soft" data. In addition, the production of subjective data is expensive and introduces a degree of uncontrolled volatility to a company's financial statements. Thus, there will be pressure on a private standard-setting agency to avoid standards which involve subjective estimates, especially those that would require use of current market prices.

A third consequence of the influence of CPA practitioners on a private standard-setting agency could be standards which require increased disclosure and auditing. Complicated measurement or disclosure will increase the amount of required auditing and therefore the audit fees per engagement. Offsetting this tendency in a private agency is the representation from the corporate sector, which will resist attempts at costly new disclosure (costly in production, in verification, and in disclosing inside information to competitors). An indication of the paucity of research in this area is just how little we know about whether representatives from the public accounting profession tend to encourage the adoption of complex new standards (see Watts and Zimmerman [1979] for some preliminary evidence on this question). It would be possible to find anecdotal evidence on both sides of this issue with many practitioners, perhaps reflecting their own corporate constituency, resisting attempts to expand measurement and disclosure. At this time, there is a balance of power in the FASB (and previously in the APB) that serves to limit the expansion of accounting and auditing standards. Much of the recent expansion of auditing work has come from public agency (SEC) initiatives rather than from the private agency.

The private standard-setting agency will have a much greater representation of individuals with significant experience in the private sector. In particular, it will have a much lower number of lawyers in policy-making positions than a public agency does. This fact has a number of consequences. First, there will be a greater tolerance for ambiguity. Representatives from the private sector will be more appreciative of the diverse and complex operations of entities under its jurisdiction and the impossibility of ever eliminating the need for expert judgment by management and auditors in particular circumstances. Therefore, there is less need to codify every existing permissible practice and the agency can rely on common usage to define acceptable procedures. Public agencies, in contrast, attempt to protect themselves by extensive, highly detailed, and frequently undecipherable rules and regulations in an attempt to handle every conceivable circumstance.

Private sector representatives are also more likely to appreciate that no system of standards and regulations will prevent occasional manipulation or extreme use of permissible accounting standards. Instances of such aberrant behavior, however, provide the basis for activism in the public sector. With a public agency, new regulations or expensive new disclosure requirements are likely outcomes from isolated instances of "market failure" in the private sector. Such new regulation or disclosure is typically implemented with little regard for the cost of these actions on the vast majority of companies who were not guilty of the alleged infraction.

Lawyers are especially likely to generate across-the-board regulation and legislation to correct the consequences of isolated aberrations. In part, their self-interest will be advanced by either passing laws, enforcing them, or defending against them when working in private practice after a brief internship in government. Thus, significant virtue exists in a privately supported standard-setting agency, staffed by experts in financial accounting, that is not encouraged or motivated to respond to isolated extreme cases. Also, the FASB's budget or the future wealth of its members will not be directly related to the number of standards it promulgates in a given period of time.

One oft-touted benefit of a private standard-setting agency is the great degree of cooperation and voluntary support that would be provided to it by corporations, public accounting firms, and other interest groups. I find this argument unpersuasive. Were standard setting to shift to a governmental agency, I am sure that corporations and CPA firms would continue to volunteer their members for task forces and advisory committees for this agency. There are already innumerable examples of representatives from private industry working *pro bono* for the government and attempting to influence the regulatory and legislative process. If the case for a private standard-setting agency is to be won, it will not be because of a concern that expertise from the private sector, now readily available to the FASB, will not be responsive to requests from a public agency. Perhaps the appropriate argument is that the salaries of the top executives of a government agency will be well below those that could be paid by a private agency. Thus, a government standard-setting agency may have difficulty attracting the same level of expert accounting talent that is available to a private agency.

A purely private agency (which the FASB is not) would be relatively insulated from political pressure from the legislative and executive branches of government. A private agency, with wide-ranging and extensive support from private sector groups, would provide a degree of independence from short-term political interests which a public agency, whose budget must receive annual approval from Congress, would be likely to find irresistible. As it is, the FASB probably does not receive pressure to respond to special requests from congressmen for particular constituents, but it is susceptible to governmental pressure because of SEC oversight. Some of the insulation between the FASB and the legislative or executive branches of government may arise because these branches know that ultimate authority in standard setting and disclosure is vested in the SEC, a public agency.

A serious weakness, therefore, of any private standard-setting agency is its lack of true statutory authority and enforcement power. Acceptance of FASB standards requires voluntary agreement from the AICPA and the benevolent delegation of authority from the SEC. Lacking true statutory authority, the private standard-setting agency is always susceptible to end runs by aggrieved constituents when they feel their particular ox is about to be gored. For example, when the Accounting Principles Board made noises about eliminating the flow-through method to account for the soon-to-be-reinstated Investment Tax Credit in 1971, corporate officials appealed to Congress for relief. The acceptability of the flow-through method was subsequently mandated in the tax legislation. Similarly, in 1977–1978 many oil and gas companies, using the full-cost method, enlisted political support and extensive lobbying to the public agency (SEC) in a successful effort to maintain the full-cost alternative as an acceptable procedure. The oil and gas accounting controversy also provided another interesting example of the vulnerability of the FASB when a number of governmental agencies, including the Department of Energy and the Department of Justice, petitioned the SEC to overturn FAS 19. The lack of statutory and binding authority is an inherent weakness to any private standard-setting agency. Ultimately, it could prove fatal.

The due processes and extensive deliberations of the FASB suggest another inherent weakness of a private standard-setting agency. The FASB may take a long time to reach a conclusion as it attempts to satisfy its diverse constituents. We still do not have a standard on accounting for the effects of changing prices; discussion on the conceptual framework project will extend into the next decade; and little action is noted on pension-cost accounting. None of these is a simple matter and reasonable people may feel that extensive delay, if not abstinence, is the appropriate action on each of these issues. But in dealing with complex matters, we should not expect a private standard-setting agency, responsive to diverse constituents, to have rapidity of action as one of its virtues. A mitigating benefit is that the extensive deliberations may help to reduce unintended side effects or consequences of FASB decisions. But this benefit is more to be hoped for in the future rather than to be realized from past decisions.

I have previously identified a major strength of the FASB as its dependence on voluntary financing and representation from private groups in its constituency. This dependency, however, leaves the FASB vulnerable to the accusation that it is captured by private interests and is therefore not being responsive to the "public interest." As noted, neither the private or the public agency can provide evidence that it is serving the "public interest." But the private agency, lacking statutory authority and not being directly accountable to elected representatives, apparently must bear a greater burden of proof to justify its ability to serve a diversified and dispersed public constituency. This is a difficult task for any private agency. It must therefore expect continuing attacks on its legitimacy.

In summary, the arguments for a private standard-setting agency center on its responsiveness to diverse constituents, on its concern for the consequences of its actions on these constituents, on its ability to attract members and staff with extensive private sector experience who will therefore have an appreciation for the complexities of modern enterprises, and on its tolerance for judgment and interpretation among practitioners under its jurisdiction. The principal weakness of a private agency is its lack of statutory authority and the constant threat of override from Congress or a governmental agency. The private agency is vulnerable to charges that it lacks independence from large corporations and public accounting firms, its principal constituents, and that it is not responsive to the public interest, since consumer representatives or elected officials are not explicitly among the agency's constituents. The private agency will also respond slowly to major initiatives which have significant consequences on important groups among its constituents.

Government Regulation of Accounting and Auditing Standards

In attempting to determine the characteristics of a governmental standard-setting agency, there are two models from which to generalize. The first model is the SEC, the governmental agency most closely associated with financial accounting standards for private corporations. Despite considerable debate over the merits of SEC disclosure and registration regulation, the SEC still enjoys a reputation as one of the most effective regulatory agencies in the federal government. Many observers would not view with dismay the transfer of increased responsibility for determining financial accounting standards to the SEC. But it is important to note that throughout its history, the SEC has delegated considerable authority to a private standard-setting agency. Therefore, unique among governmental agencies, the SEC has been able to play a less active role in the development of detailed rules and regulations, though it still has a significant number of these. It is possible, indeed likely, that this freedom from setting standards has enabled the SEC to play a more independent role and not be subject to the constituent pressures felt by other governmental agencies. Were standard setting to be shifted entirely to a governmental agency, an entirely different set of pressures from those now impinging on the SEC might be brought to bear on the public agency.

As a federal agency, the SEC has greater legitimacy because of its explicit statutory authority. Thus, its enforcement power is greater than a private agency and it does not need to depend on voluntary agreements or adherence to professional codes of ethics to obtain compliance. Second, because the SEC does not have an explicit constituency, it does not need to engage in lengthy hearings in an attempt to obtain a consensus before embarking on major new initiatives. For example, the replacement cost disclosure of *Accounting Series Release No. 190* and the recently announced Reserve Recognition Accounting for oil and gas companies were accomplished by the SEC with little prior discussion and with considerable speed. Neither of these initiatives, which represented major departures from the conventional historical cost-based system, could have been accomplished by the FASB nearly so quickly or with so little public debate. Because of the statutory authority of the SEC, it is able to grant "safe harbor" provisions for such new and untested disclosure. Thus, the government agency is better able to shelter companies from some of the effects of experiments in disclosure policy.

Governmental agencies are alleged to be guilty of conservatism, inflexibility, and lack of responsiveness. These charges, however, have not been borne out by recent experience with the SEC. On uniformity, the SEC has expanded possibilities, not contracted them. The SEC overruled the FASB attempt to obtain uniform treatment of oil and gas exploration costs. Even in the 1960s, the SEC resisted an APB attempt to obtain uniform accounting treatment for the investment tax credit. Agency conservatism or inflexibility has not been noticed in the SEC initiatives on replacement cost accounting and valuation of oil and gas reserves. Besides these incidents, the SEC has increased the flow of future-oriented information with its disclosure requirements on leases and pensions and has intervened with the IRS to enable companies to disclose FIFO valuation of LIFO inventories. On responsiveness, we have already noted that the SEC has shown itself more capable of innovation and rapid action than the FASB. Whether the benefits of these innovative initiatives justify the considerable costs incurred is quite another matter, but we can certainly not accuse the SEC, at least, of inflexibility or slowness to respond to changes in the environment. We would be more sanguine, though, about the responsiveness of the SEC if it occasionally eliminated a reporting requirement rather than always adding to the existing stock. I am unaware of any major reporting requirement for the SEC that, once initiated, has ever been retracted. Note also that the SEC may have been able to undertake its disclosure initiatives because a privately supported agency also existed which has responsibility for determining the basic form and composition of financial statements.

The second model for governmental accounting standard setting arises from observing how standards are set in governmental agencies other than the SEC. Accounting standard setting has occurred or been attempted in the Internal Revenue Service (IRS), the Cost Accounting Standards Board (CASB), the Department of Energy (DOE), the Department of Health, Education and Welfare (HEW), the Federal Trade Commission (FTC), the Interstate Commerce Commission (ICC), the Civil Aeronautics Board (CAB) and probably a few more not mentioned here. As we observe the circumstances in which governmental agencies regulate accounting standards, it becomes obvious that in each case the agency and its accounting standards have a narrow mission to serve a particular goal of government rather than to inform diverse and disparate user groups; namely:

1. The IRS sets standards that enable it to collect tax revenues.
2. The CASB sets standards to provide the basis for government reimbursement of private contractors and to enable the Renegotiation Board to collect "excess profits."
3. The DOE is attempting to develop a financial reporting system for energy companies to regulate their activities and perhaps provide the basis for further ventures into price controls and divestiture.
4. HEW is developing a Standardized Hospital Uniform Reporting (SHUR) system for hospitals that is likely to provide the basis for

hospital cost containment regulation and Medicare/Medicaid reimbursement. Despite the title and statutory purpose to develop a reporting system, SHUR has evolved into a highly detailed, complex, and somewhat arbitrary accounting system.

5. The FTC is attempting to force an arbitrary line-of-business reporting system on companies to foster its antitrust activities.
6. The ICC provides a detailed chart of accounts for railroads and the CAB for the airlines to promote their regulatory activities.

In each of these cases, the governmental agency produces highly detailed and frequently arbitrary regulations to facilitate the mission of the agency. I am concerned that, were accounting standard setting to be shifted entirely to a governmental agency, that agency would soon find itself subject to pressures from a variety of specialized interests within the government. These governmental special-interest groups would wish to use financial accounting standards to accomplish their specialized missions. As a specific example of how this pressure might develop, consider the testimony of a critic of the present private standard-setting process. Complaining how the present lack of uniformity in accounting standards hinders antitrust administration, Chatov (1977) claims that:

> The private sector controlling these rules is simply not cognizant of the needs of the Federal Government with respect to developing the corporate financial information that we use for policy analysis purposes.

Chatov is bothered by the lack of coordination between the segmented reporting mandated by the SEC and the line-of-business reporting the FTC desires. He holds, as an ideal to be achieved, the system he perceives to exist in Europe:

> a financial system that will tie the report of the individual corporations to the needs of the Federal Government in terms of its national accounts.

Thus, the federal regulation of accounting standards can easily serve those who wish to have further central government management and regulation of the economy.

In addition to increased pressure on accounting standards to serve various missions of government, federal regulation of accounting standards could also lead to increased federal regulation of auditing standards. At present, auditing standards and the scope of auditing effort are mostly determined by committees of the AICPA. Occasionally, Congress or the SEC will impose additional auditing requirements (such as review of interim statements and a more detailed review of a company's internal control system). But to a considerable extent, the auditing profession presently determines its own auditing standards. It seems unlikely that a federal agency with statutory authority over accounting standards would not also play an active role in determining the scope of auditing services. Again, the increased federal regulation of auditing could lead to the use of private auditors to serve various missions of government.

At this time, we can only speculate on the consequences of federal regulation of accounting and auditing standards. But based on the experience of present governmental standard-setting agencies and given the pressures that the public sector is increasingly placing on the private sector, the following outcomes could arise under a regime of purely governmental standard setting:

1. Accounting standards could be influenced by their perceived effect on government management of the economy. The accounting for tax issues such as the Investment Tax Credit or the foreign tax credit would be determined by what actions the government was trying to encourage in private corporations. If tax revenues were declining because many companies had switched to LIFO, the release of FIFO valuations might be proscribed. The government's periodic experiments with wage and price controls would be facilitated by requiring companies to report on compliance with the current standards or guidelines. If major antitrust or divestiture activities were being initiated, accounting standards such as line-of-business reporting would be modified to facilitate these programs. In general, accounting standards could be made to serve specific missions of federal agencies with little attention paid to the role of accounting information for the diverse community of investors and creditors and the impact on the companies themselves from the production and disclosure of this information.

2. Financial accounting standards could become as detailed and complex as the tax code. The present reliance on GAAP, with many understood but not explicitly stated conventions, would be difficult to sustain under the bureaucratic pressures inherent in federal standard setting. Inevitably, financial accounting standards would resemble, but greatly exceed in volume, the types of pronouncements now being produced by the Cost Accounting Standards Board: highly legalistic, complex, and detailed. In fact, given the use of all previous government-determined accounting standards (revenue raising or price containing), it could be increasingly difficult to maintain separate reporting and tax systems. Present differences between financial reporting and tax reporting could narrow. For example, companies wishing to use straight-line depreciation with normal rather than guideline lives for financial reporting may be required to follow this scheme for tax purposes, too.

3. Little consideration would be given to the costs of meeting federally mandated standards or disclosure. The costs of developing, producing, disclosing, and auditing the data are not internalized by the federal agency and hence would be a minor consideration in its deliberations. Disclosure standards, once promulgated, would be unlikely to be rescinded. There is no organized constituency to complain about receiving too much information. The risk to the agency of eliminating previously mandated disclosure is too high because some incident might occur in which it could be claimed that the eliminated information would have obviated an abuse or misinterpretation. As long as the agency is responsible for the amount of disclosure but does not bear the cost of increased disclosure, it will consistently err on the side of excess and nonreversible disclosure. An additional but not internalized cost of the increased disclosure will be the release of internal company information to competitors.

4. Special-interest groups with political sophistication and influence may be able to extract special concessions or mitigate particularly onerous disclosure requirements. The congressional subcommittee and its staff with oversight responsibility for the standard-setting agency will soon become populated by persons with interest and knowledge of accounting and auditing. These persons will be the recipients of lobbying and attention from groups with a great stake in the outcome of standard setting and disclosure policy. The standard-setting agency will not be unaware nor can it be unresponsive to the inclinations of these congressmen and their staffs. Thus, standard setting may become increasingly politicized. It is difficult to predict just how this will turn out because of the constant shifting in the balance of lobbying power among labor, business, and so-called public interest groups.

5. Accountants and auditors will become the policemen of society. The Foreign Corrupt Practices Act may be only a precursor of the use of auditors to enforce the laws, regulations, and interpretations issued by Congress and federal agencies. Materiality could be redefined so that virtually any instance of corporate misconduct will be considered "relevant" to investors because of the potential shutdown of a firm's operations, heavy fines, "consent" agreements, mandated divestiture, or liability for civil damage suits. Thus, auditors, before certifying to the fairness of a firm's financial statements, may be required to give assurance that the firm is in compliance with the Sherman Act, Robinson-Patman Act, DOE pricing rules, and all OSHA, EPA, EEOC, NHTSA, NRC, NLRB, FDA, FTC, ICC, CPSC, FHLBB, MSHA, NTSB . . . regulations. As independent outsiders with presumed investigative expertise, the auditors will find it impossible to avoid the pressures to be the investigative arm of the government. When the government

ventures periodically into wage and price controls, the independent auditors will be asked to report on the company's compliance with the guidelines.

6. Any major or highly publicized corporate scandal could lead to new standards or disclosure designed to prevent or disclose, at an earlier stage, the incident that has just occurred. It would be important for the standard-setting agency to protect itself by showing how it has acted to prevent a recurrence of the abuse. The cost of the new standard and increased disclosure would fall on the vast majority of corporations who had nothing to do with the incident.

7. There could be increased delay in the release of financial statements and financial information if the staff of the standard-setting agency decides to review releases to verify that they are in compliance with the agency regulations. The agency would not bear the cost of delay of information or the reduced flow of information to the investor and creditor community. It would reap the benefit of having the larger budget and staff that would be necessary to review financial statements.

8. Federal control of the accounting and auditing profession could make corporate dissent from government policies even riskier than it is today. Administrations, both Republican and Democrat, have already threatened and used the sanctions of increased IRS audits, violations of agency regulations, or selective governmental purchasing policies to obtain corporate acquiescence to new federal legislation. Were independent auditors to receive direction and supervision from a federal agency, the cost to corporations of vigorous dissent from governmental policies would increase further.

A case can be made for government oversight and review of auditing rather than accounting standards. A government agency should verify that a profession, especially one with a statutory mandate, does not develop monopolistic practices. It is important to ensure that a profession does not erect barriers to entry through constraints on price and advertising competition, difficult educational and certification requirements, and onerous continuing education demands which fall disproportionately on small firms or individuals. At present, monopolistic practices do not seem to be present. Accounting firms actively encourage the education of accountants in colleges and universities. There is a large flow of new entrants into the profession. The public accounting industry is less concentrated than many U.S. industries and considerable competition for clients apparently does exist even among the largest firms (Bernstein, 1978; Anreder, 1979).

Interestingly, the SEC has been encouraging peer and quality review of CPA firms and periodic rotation of auditing partners among clients. These types of activities are easier and cheaper to accommodate among larger firms. Thus, instead of being alert to the potential dangers of increasing concentration or the introduction of requirements that will limit the ability of smaller firms to compete with the larger firms, the SEC is actively promoting activities that may make competition from smaller firms more difficult.

Governmental oversight and review of auditing have been justified by the need to assure high-quality audits. Since public accounting firms are engaged in repetitive, nonlethal activities, there would appear to be even less justification than usual for the government to intervene in private capitalistic arrangements between consenting parties. These arrangements include quality standards as well as price and scope of effort. A CPA firm's greatest asset would appear to be its reputation for independent, high-quality work. Substandard, sloppy audits will severely damage a CPA firm's reputation among those clients who wish to be associated with a high-quality firm and who are willing to pay an increased price for this reputation. Therefore, unless a CPA firm wished to position itself in the cheap and sloppy segment of the market, there are strong private incentives for a CPA firm to discourage substandard work among its employees. But with the sanction of an overcautious government regulator, CPA firms may establish auditing standards that are higher, not lower, than would be demanded in a competitive environment. These higher standards would raise audit fees and not be subject to competitive pressures in the marketplace.

Conclusions

It should be clear that I would not view the transfer of all accounting standard setting to a public agency as an improvement over the current system. There is no organized constituency for the receipt of financial accounting information so that a public standard-setting agency would look to other agencies of government for a support base. In an earlier time, either the producers (corporations) or the auditors might have represented powerful interest groups for a public standard-setting agency. But except on particular issues which affected specific industries, the corporate sector is not likely to be a potent lobbying force. It will tend to focus its lobbying on those regulatory bodies which can directly affect or restrict its output (e.g., EPA, FDA, OSHA) rather than one which just forces different forms of disclosure. Public accounting firms would remain as highly interested parties in financial accounting regulation, but they would not be decisive influences on controversial issues, since they are neither the producers nor direct consumers of the regulating agency's output. Thus, were accounting standards setting to be transferred to a public agency, the most likely outcome would seem to be for the standards to be determined to advance government policy, along the lines described in the preceding section, rather than to serve consumers of financial information in the private sector.

Given that some regulation of standard setting is required, I would not recommend that a private agency, such as the FASB, be given an exclusive franchise. Some statutory or enforcement authority is necessary to give legitimacy and backbone to the private agency. Thus, the present system, which has the SEC using its statutory authority to delegate standard setting to the private agency, may be a good arrangement. The SEC is able, periodically, to overrule the FASB and develop its own initiatives to demonstrate that it is doing its job as a monitoring agency and is not the captive of private interests. But the FASB still has a prime responsibility to develop accounting standards acceptable to its different constituents.

The problem with the present scheme is that there is no mechanism for the SEC to internalize the costs of its separate disclosure requirements. There is no self-correcting mechanism that will cause the SEC to reduce disclosure requirements which have little benefit but significant cost associated with their production and dissemination. This seems to be an inherent flaw with the current system and, over time, the burden of SEC disclosure might overwhelm or make irrelevant what the private standard-setting agency is attempting to accomplish. But I do not expect that legislators would ever permit financial disclosure and measurement to be the exclusive franchise of a private agency with no federal oversight. The bias to excessive SEC-mandated disclosure seems a high but necessary price to pay for obtaining statutory sanction for a private standard-setting agency.

It is possible to contrive a novel scheme for increasing competition among SEC-like public standard-setting agencies. At present, the fifty states have different legal requirements for the chartering of corporations. The "public interest" advocates attack these differential chartering rules as promoting permissiveness and a "movement towards the least common denominator" in shareholder protection (Cary, 1974). Recent research, however (Winter, 1978; Dodd and Leftwich, 1978), presents the contrary case; that corporations choose to locate in states that provide an appropriate, if not optimal, set of institutional arrangements for shareholder protection and rights at minimal cost. With this view, the competition among the states is healthy in providing alternative possibilities for legal codes from which corporations and investors select by computing the relative benefits and costs. It would not be optimal for a state to provide a legal environment that inadequately protects shareholder rights or is overly permissive to the management of a corporation. Because of reduced protection, rational investors would pay lower prices for the shares of corporations that incorporate in such permissive states.

One can extend this notion to financial disclosure. Just as no single public agency is in a position to determine the optimal corporate charter, no single agency can determine the optimal amount of disclosure. Perhaps, along with establishing rules for chartering of corporations, each state could establish disclosure rules for companies incorporated in that state. A corporation would then be in a position to select a disclosure policy that it felt balanced the costs of disclosure with the benefits to existing and potential shareholders and creditors. Decentralized disclosure laws would also permit more experimentation or innovation in disclosure methods and the opportunity to evaluate the effects of different disclosure laws. States with excessive disclosure requirements would find fewer corporations wishing to incorporate there. Corporations that incorporate in states with virtually no disclosure requirements may find it difficult to attract a significant following in the investing community. Therefore, market mechanisms could work to determine an appropriate amount of disclosure.

I am not optimistic that this proposal will receive widespread acceptance. But it serves to highlight the weakness in the current system, where there is little incentive for the SEC to recognize the costs of its mandated disclosure policy. I suspect, however, that we will have to continue to live with the current system of SEC oversight and delegation to a private standard-setting agency. A private agency cannot survive without SEC backing, and there is no reason for legislators to eliminate existing governmental supervision of private activity.

Note

I have received ideas and suggestions from many people in preparing these remarks. Before writing a first draft, I benefited from conversations with my colleague, Yuji Ijiri, and from remarks and discussion with coparticipants at the Seminar on Law and Economics of Accounting Regulation at the University of Miami (March 9–11, 1979), especially George Benston, John Burton, Sidney Davidson, Nicholas Gonedes, Orace Johnson, and Ross Watts. I received comments on the first draft from many individuals including Stanley Baiman, Paul Griffin, Robert Hagerman, Orace Johnson, James Murdy, Prem Prakash, Howard Rosenthal, Katherine Schipper, Shyam Sunder, Roman Weil, and Jerold Zimmerman. I thank all these people for their interest since, even though many of them will still find much to disagree with in this version, it is a far better work because of the time they took to provide their comments to me.

V

Summary and Conclusions

The attention presently focused on the accounting profession does not appear to be a fleeting phenomenon. This statement is one of the few that produces consensus among experts in accounting. The issue of regulation is simply not going to disappear, say, because the profession has initiated some reforms. The complexity of regulation issues, ranging from concentration through the cost-benefits of intervention, produces arguments that are so far-ranging in their implications that even summing them up is a complex task and one that elicits even further evidence, as Chapter 12 shows.

Weston does not merely review the preceding chapters. His emphasis is rather on examining the oligopoly theory and its applicability, audit responsibilities and review, and the theories of production of information and standards. And a theme emerges—the attempt to delineate just what the role of the accounting profession should be in society.

Those calling for more regulation, he points out, should realize that uniformity is just not the nature of today's world. Yet government regulations, by attempting to impose uniformity, may cause audits to be performed too carefully, to the point where they may actually discourage higher standards or patterns of diversity which are descriptive of and essential to the economy's progress and viability. Public confidence is needed, but not at the cost of overdramatization, Weston says, citing the failure of Penn Central, in which investors and management simply ignored facts. The factors producing a bankruptcy are so widespread and complex that accounting's role should not include pronouncing judgment on how the free market will perform. Bankruptcies, he adds, are part of that free market performance.

Weston asserts finally that a difficulty in enacting such proposals as HR 13175 comes from their leading to more rather than less restrictions on competition. There are better ways, he states, to develop competition than imposing regulations. Weston's principal alternative is to expand the profession's capabilities to include relationships with a larger number of societal functions. The challenge is to communicate more information more effectively.

12

Regulation and the Accounting Profession: An Evaluation of the Issues

J. Fred Weston

Professor of Managerial Economics and Finance
Graduate School of Management
University of California, Los Angeles

Congressional staff studies and reports have taken, in my view, an essentially structural approach to the accounting profession. The theme sounded again and again has been that the performance of accounting services takes place in a concentrated industry. For example, the Metcalf Committee *Staff Study* (U.S. Senate, 1977: 25) opened as follows:

> The accounting profession is dominated by eight giant accounting firms, collectively known within the business and financial community as the "Big Eight." The "Big Eight" are so large and influential in relation to other CPA firms that they are able to control virtually all aspects of accounting and auditing in the United States. . . .
>
> The source of the tremendous influence wielded by the "Big Eight" accounting firms is related to the size and influence of their clients, rather than to the number of individual accountants associated with these firms. The vast majority of large corporations, which control the bulk of the Nation's business wealth, employ one of the "Big Eight" firms as their independent auditor. Fees for accounting services are related to the size of the business for which such services are performed. Thus, big clients provide the "Big Eight" with the opportunity to earn big accounting fees.

The *Staff Study* emphasizes that the percentage of New York Stock Exchange company assets, net income, or employees for which a Big Eight firm acts as auditor is over 90 percent. By this and other indicators the Metcalf Committee concluded that accounting is a concentrated industry.

The structural theory predicts that bad conduct and bad performance will follow from the oligopolistic structure of an industry. Recognized interdependence and awareness of rivals' actions and reactions result in coordinated policies, tacit collusion, and shared monopoly. Such behavior would also result in undesirable performance. According to this theory, the concentrated nature of the accounting industry leads to the prediction of excessive fees and profits, barriers to entry, and domination by a small segment of firms that do not fulfill the high responsibilities of the accounting profession because of lack of competitive pressure. This basic framework of reasoning led to the following main recommendations in the March, 1977 version of the *Staff Study*:

1. Congress should set accounting practices for the federal government.
2. Congress should overturn the Hochfelder decision.
3. There should be increased competition in selection of auditors.
4. The federal government should set financial accounting standards.
5. The federal government should periodically inspect auditors' work.
6. The nation's fifteen largest accounting firms should file public reports.
7. The federal government should act to reduce concentration in the auditing and accounting services industry.
8. Management advisory services should be limited to prevent conflict of interest.
9. The SEC should stop discriminating against small firms and protecting large accounting firms in enforcement.
10. Membership of the Cost Accounting Standard Board (CASB) should not be dominated by individual accounting firms.

After additional hearings, the final version of the Metcalf *Staff Study* was issued on November 4, 1977. Its main findings and recommendations included the following:

1. Improve accounting standards.
   a. Broaden constituency and support of FASB.
   b. Bring public into hearings more effectively.
   c. Financial reports of publicly owned corporations should be more understandable to unsophisticated users while still providing sophisticated users with sufficient detailed information.
   d. Simplify reporting for smaller, privately held companies and the accounting firms that serve them.
   e. SEC should vigorously oversee standards and the standard-setting system.
2. Organize accounting firms to establish and enforce minimum standards of an auditor's independent performance.

3. Organize accounting firms similar to the New York Stock Exchange or the National Association of Securities Dealers on a mandatory basis.
4. Quality reviews by broad-based teams appointed by the executive board of the accounting organization—reviewed by the SEC and made public.
5. Establish independent-audit committees on boards of all publicly owned corporations.
6. Enhance the professionalism of management accountants.
7. Executive perquisites should be compiled and reported by auditors.
8. Emphasis on increased revenues has caused some accounting firms to accept time constraints and fees which result in their cutting costs, to the point of impairing the integrity of an independent audit.
9. Disciplinary actions of the proposed organization of independent auditing firms should be based on failure to follow high professional standards rather than violation of legal standards.
10. Independent audits should be continual throughout the year rather than rushed toward the end of the year.
11. Management advisory services by auditing firms reflect adversely on professionalism and independence.
    a. Auditing firms may use their inside position unfairly to market nonaccounting services.
    b. Involves auditing the auditor's own work.
12. The high concentration of work performed by the Big Eight results in restraints on market entry by smaller accounting firms.
    a. Smaller accounting firms should be permitted to inform clients of their abilities.
    b. Eliminate the artificial professional restrictions against advertising, talking with another firm's clients, and talking with another firm's employees about possible employment without first informing that firm.
13. Discovery of illegal or questionable activities by corporate employees should be reported to the corporation's audit committee and government authorities irrespective of materiality; rotation of audit firms should be studied.
14. Research into improved auditing and detection of management fraud should be increased.
15. Independent auditors of publicly owned corporations should be liable for their negligence to private parties who suffer damages as a result—adoption of the private attorney general concept.
16. Auditing of multinational corporations needs to be improved, as evidenced by disclosures in recent years of extensive illegal and questionable activities by multinational corporations.

17. The SEC should utilize its sufficient authority to become an effective government regulator of the auditing industry.
18. In performing its enforcement functions, the SEC should not favor large accounting firms at the expense of smaller accounting firms.
19. The CASB should represent a fair balance of interests; its standards should not be excessively burdensome for smaller firms seeking to do defense business.
20. Federal policies on awarding contracts to accounting firms may be unfairly biased toward large national accounting firms.

The Securities and Exchange Commission's report on the accounting profession was issued July 5, 1978. Its views may be summarized as follows:

1. The SEC was not wholly satisfied with the profession's efforts at self-regulation; it is too early to assess whether those efforts will be effective in the long run.
2. The profession has made a good beginning, but much remains to be achieved over a very short future.
3. Developments toward reform in the past year show sufficient promise for the accounting organizations to be permitted to continue to evolve toward effective self-regulation.

In Chapter 5, Nelligan argues the need for increased activity by the SEC. Reporting the introduction of HR 13175 in June, 1978, providing for a bill to establish the National Organization of Securities and Exchange Commission Accountancy (NOSA), he states that the function of NOSA would be further regulation of the accounting profession, under SEC oversight, with a goal of stronger protection for the investor public. Important members of Congress, Nelligan also reports, are concerned with the issues that have been raised. Ignoring the issues, therefore, will not provide a solution.

At least four major issues appear to emerge from the literature on regulation and the accounting profession:

1. The oligopoly doctrine
2. The issue of oligopoly in accounting
3. The delineation of the range of audit responsibilities and review
4. Theories of the production of accounting information and setting accounting standards

This final chapter will attempt to focus these issues and to determine the extent to which we have a basis for some guidelines from underlying principles and evidence. First, let us turn to the oligopoly issue, which has two aspects: first, the degree of validity of the oligopoly doctrine or structural theory in general and second, its applicability to the accounting profession.

The Oligopoly Doctrine

The structural theory may be summarized in its major propositions: Most output in the American economy is accounted for by industries that are highly concentrated. A few firms account for a large percentage of the industries' output and sales. Thus, the major proportion of industrial output and sales is accounted for by industries that have been characterized in economic terms as oligopoly—a few sellers.

Concentration and oligopoly are widely held to stimulate awareness in one firm of the effects of its decisions and actions on other firms. This mutual awareness of actions and reactions produces a recognized interdependence among large corporations. Such interdependence is further said to lead to conscious parallelism of behavior and results in tacit, if not overt, collusion. Thus, oligopolies are said to develop a common set of interests and to act cooperatively against outsiders.

It has been argued that when the concentration ratio measured by the share of the top four firms of a given industry in shipments, value added, or employees exceeds 50 percent, the behavior of that industry is likely to be different than that of more competitive industries. This is essentially the structural theory of industrial organization, which argues that concentration can be equated with noncompetitive behavior.[1] The elements in the structural theory include the following propositions:

1. If an industry is not atomistic, administrative discretion over prices exists.
2. Concentration creates recognized interdependence; lack of price competition in concentrated industries results in higher prices and monopoly profits.
3. Concentration is unnatural; for the "most efficient scale," no more than 3 to 5 percent of industry is required.
4. A positive correlation between concentration and profitability is evidence of monopoly power in concentrated industries—the ability to elevate prices and persistence of high profits; entry does not take place to eliminate excessive profits.

The structural theory in its clearest form was set forth by Ralph Nader and Mark Green in their presentation to the Kennedy Senate Subcommittee on Antitrust and Monopoly on May 11, 1977. They stated:

In our view, however, vigorous federal antitrust enforcement can encourage lower prices, greater innovation, greater efficiency and help reduce corporate-political power .... of 45 studies collected by economist Leonard Weiss correlating economic concentration and high profits, thirty-eight showed a significant positive correlation. The best studies of size and innovation demonstrate that moderate sized firms are the most innovative—not our largest firms who like to coast with a comfortable status quo.

This theoretical position raises three issues: the relations between concentration and prices, concentration and profits, and concentration and innovation.

Concentration and Prices

Does industrial concentration have pricing and employment effects which weaken government efforts at stabilization? Let us first consider the facts on pricing. Researchers at UCLA have monitored the relation between concentration and price change for a number of time periods. The results are consistent in showing that price increases have been lower in the more concentrated industries and higher in the less concentrated industries. For example, in the decade of inflation between 1967 and 1977, the Wholesale Price Index rose by 80 percent. When industries are divided into concentration quartiles, we find that the *least* concentrated industries had price increases ten percentage points *higher* than the industries of *highest* concentration. When concentration categories are divided into thirds, the least concentrated third showed price increases twelve percentage points higher than the industries with greatest concentration.

Much more sophisticated statistical analyses of the relationship between concentration and price change have also been made. In these studies, other factors such as output and wage and material price changes are held constant in a regression analysis. Again, the influence of concentration on price change is negative, sometimes statistically significant and sometimes not. The exception is the subperiod 1954–1958, which can be explained by the fact that the nation was coming out of the price controls of the Korean War period, controls that had borne more heavily on large firms and concentrated industries. The superior price performance of concentrated industries is not unique to the United States. Similar studies of concentration and price change for Western European countries (Phlips, 1969) have obtained comparable results.

Why the superior price performance of concentrated industries? Concentrated industries have substantially higher capital intensity ratios than less concentrated industries. The higher capital intensity of the concentrated industries is also associated with higher rates of labor productivity and higher rates of labor productivity growth. Competition in concentrated industries transmits these advantages into superior price performance.

Concentration and Profit Relationships

When we turn to concentration and profit, the most recent studies that introduce variables beyond just the two factors, concentration and profit, have obtained different results. Ornstein (1975), for example, using Statistics of Income data along with the Census price-cost margins, has found many exceptions to the positive correlation between concentration and profit. In other studies, when a measure of capital intensity or economies of scale is introduced into the profit concentration equation, the influence of concentration on profit is usually not statistically significant (Comanor and Wilson, 1967).

Thus, the concentration-profit nexus is dubious at best. The sheer volume of such studies is not in itself definitive. Most of them use the same data with the same defects and analyze single relationships, where concentration in fact stands as a proxy for capital intensity or economies of scale.

Concentration and Innovation

Many studies have been made of influences on innovation; the best have found evidence on both sides of the issue. We should first note that most of the studies use research and development inputs, not outputs, in their analysis. Thus, if the ratio of research and development to sales drops for large firms, we could argue either that large firms are more efficient in utilizing research and development inputs or that they are less vigorous in making research and development outlays. A summary of the evidence (Markham, 1974) concludes:

> The measures are inputs which do not indicate performance or are highly ambiguous, or are subjective output indicators. With these limitations, the evidence suggests a positive but weak association between concentration and innovation by industry. With regard to firm size, the evidence is mixed. In general, the empirical studies indicate that the ratio of R&D inputs to sales does not increase—and may decrease—in relation to firm size. But these are inputs; the negative association between inputs and size could indicate either efficiency in the use of R&D by larger firms or lack of incentives to make the effort. Studies that used "the most important innovations" in an industry as a measure of output were using subjective measures in which the results differed for individual industries. Of major influence on individual industries is the nature of the technological opportunities for innovation; firms in advanced electronics, chemicals, and metallurgical industries would be expected to be more technically dynamic than firms in the clothing industry.

In short, the evidence on the relation between concentration and pricing is that the greater productivity in concentrated industries results in a better price performance. The concentration-profit studies indicate that when account is taken of greater capital intensity or economies of scale or growth or measures of risk, that concentration is not correlated with higher profits. On concentration and innovation, most research and development expenditures take place in large firms in oligopolistic industries. But creative genius and the technological fertility of an industry appear to be more important than firm size or industrial concentration as an influence on the rate of innovation.

But what of the theory that concentration leads to awareness of interdependence which limits competitive behavior? What of the argument that concentrated industries are free from the discipline of the marketplace and have discretion over whether and when and by what amounts to raise or lower prices? Solid evidence has not been assembled to support the latter assertions. Additional studies on the cyclical price patterns of firms and concentrated industries demonstrates responsiveness to demand as well as cost changes. To see why this is so, we need to understand the processes of competition in concentrated industries.

The standard textbook view of oligopoly pricing is that because firms are aware that their rivals will react to price changes, this awareness leads to a recognized interdependence that forestalls competition. But such a theory assumes that everything else is held constant while only output and pricing decisions remain to be made. Practically speaking, however, in the long term a dynamic industry does not hold the many other factors constant because of their interaction with pricing decisions.

Active and continuous competition exists among large firms in concentrated industries along a large number of dimensions. These dimensions of competition include quality of product; differences in product characteristics in response to the consumer's demand for variety; competition in sales or dealer organization systems in marketing and product; competition in the use of sales organizations, advertising, and discount margins as alternative methods of promoting the sale of products; the extent of service organizations to support product sales and use; competition in providing financing support at various stages of the distribution process; and so on. Changes in the economic environment take place and interact with the influences presented by changes in products and the movement of firms into and out of various market segments. In response to such changes, large firms in concentrated industries continuously adjust their policies on product, quality, prices, sales methods, promotion efforts, service organizations, and financing facilities.

Thus, the ways in which firms of all sizes compete are so numerous that the kind of recognized interdependence assumed when all decision variables other than output or pricing are frozen is actually impossible to have. Firms compete over such a wide range of decision areas that collusion of the type assumed when the analysis is limited to pricing and output would be difficult to reach and impossible to monitor. Furthermore, the advantages gained by an advance in research and development capability production methods, or marketing organization system, product quality, and product characteristics that are favorably accepted by users, cannot be readily matched by rivals. A firm which achieves such an advantage can profit greatly. This is the incentive to compete because advantageous profits can be achieved. In addition, a learning process is involved in developing an effective organization system in the firm and achieving advantages in any one of a large number of the dimensions on which firms compete. Once a firm achieves an efficient organization system or leadership in research and development, production, or marketing systems, its rivals may have a difficult time catching up.

Concentrated industries are characterized by higher degrees of capital intensity than less concentrated industries. This is a worldwide phenomenon not limited to the United States. Concentration does not mean the absence of competition; the varieties of competition are too numerous to achieve effective collusion.

This summary review of oligopoly doctrine versus the theory of dynamic competition in concentrated industries describes an ongoing dispute that continues to be waged in empirical studies. Ten years ago, structural theory reigned supreme. More recent research has focused predominantly on dynamic competition in concentrated industries.[2] In public policy, however, agencies such as the Department of Justice and the Federal Trade Commission as well as congressional staffs are heavily influenced by structural theory. A heavy structural influence is observed in the antitrust cases brought against IBM, AT&T, three of the ready-to-eat cereal manufacturers, and eight petroleum firms, and in the investigation of the automobile industry. Thus, any concentrated industry is vulnerable to public policies based on structural theory. A concentrated industry must therefore muster evidence and develop a countertheory to defend its structure, conduct, and performance. Hence, we will next consider the issue of oligopoly in accounting.

Oligopoly in Accounting

By most criteria, we would be obliged to conclude that the accounting industry is concentrated. We might argue about whether the industry is more or less concentrated than manufacturing industries generally or other service industries. We might also argue about whether it is appropriate to measure concentration in accounting (as is typically done) by reference to some subset of firms in the economy as a whole. In Chapter 3, Dopuch and Simunic present evidence showing that the share of the Big Eight as auditors for the Fortune 500 industrials increased from 88.4 percent in 1955 to 96.8 percent in 1977. They also present data which show that the market share of the Big Eight rises with the size of auditee sales. The Big Eight have less than 60 percent of the share of auditees with sales of $1–$25 million, but over 90 percent of firms whose sales are over $1 billion.

Rather than quibbling about the *extent* to which the accounting industry is concentrated, let's accept the fact that it is concentrated and analyze why. A number of hypotheses have been suggested: (1) economies of scale, (2) critical mass, (3) specialization, and (4) efficient organizations.

Dopuch and Simunic note in Chapter 3 that Benston (1979) suggests "that the utilization of large public accounting firms by large corporations is due to scale economies of multi-office operations, or alternatively, the diseconomies which would be faced by a consortium of small CPA firms trying to perform a large audit." This reasoning suggests that the source of economies of scale is having a critical mass of personnel and offices to handle both the magnitude and the geographic scope required in the audit of large multiproduct, multiplant, multilocation, and sometimes multinational corporations.

Another possibility is that large investments are required to develop specialized expertise to handle the complexities of modern industrial economies. Revolutionary developments in modern data storage and retrieval systems require large-scale investments in computer hardware as well as expertise in using computer systems. Another explosion has taken place in areas subject to government regulation and in requirements for government reporting. A major factor in the increased market share of the largest firms in recent years may very well be the increased need for specialized expertise for dealing with the government. If so, government is responsible to a considerable degree for big accounting firms and high concentration, against which it then takes further regulatory actions.

A fourth hypothesis to explain concentration in the accounting industry is that some public accounting firms, because of their greater efficiency, abilities, knowledge, and experience, have developed reputations and brand-name capital which causes them to obtain consistently a significant share of the market. The literature also suggests that the brand-name capital of the large firms causes them to be sought out, to the detriment of the smaller firms. It is also argued that, for example, it is difficult for a non-Big Eight firm to obtain acceptance in connection with work related to the operations of the Securities and Exchange Commission.

These alternative explanations of concentration in accounting have not been tested empirically, however. Much more research is required. Let us next turn to evidence on tests of performance by considering data on price and profits.

In Simunic's study, data were developed for a sample of 397 publicly held companies. Auditees were divided into two classes, companies with sales less than $125 million and companies with sales greater that $125 million. The submarket for the audits of the smaller companies was considered an area of competition between large and small firms. Simunic found, after using control variables for factors which might affect the difficulty or quantity of work performed on an audit, that the fees paid to seven of the eight largest firms were on average lower across the entire market than the fees of the non-Big Eight firms. These results are consistent with the hypothesis of price competition for audit services. Further evidence of price competition were the criticisms that fee cutting was so severe that it produced a lower quality of audit services performed.

Although we have begun to get data in recent years on earnings of the public accounting firms, we do not have careful studies of profitability. The usual profitability measures are not applicable. The substantial investment in human capital requires much more careful adjustments and detailed analysis to develop meaningful measures of the earning behavior of public accounting firms.

A review of the general evidence supporting structural theory raises many questions. Structural theory is no longer regarded as something established either by abstract reasoning or empirical evidence. In recent years particularly, research studies have produced findings that do not confirm its validity. For the accounting industry, we simply do not have evidence to determine whether concentration has resulted in undesirable performance by the usual industrial organization tests. It is argued, however, that concentration in accounting has resulted in a number of undesirable patterns of behavior and other deficiencies. Let us next consider some of the issues behind these charges.

The Range of Audit Responsibilities and Review of Auditing Firms

Earlier congressional staff reports on the accounting industry criticized the continued failures, frauds, and bribery that had not been flagged in advance in audit reports by public accounting firms. In endorsing the establishment of NOSA, Nelligan in Chapter 5 emphasizes the same points. The organization would develop a staff to review registered public accounting firms that would not only examine the firms' quality controls but would also examine whether generally accepted accounting principles were followed and auditing standards were applied. In addition, the reviews would help improve the quality of audits. Furthermore, the SEC would immediately be assigned a significant oversight function over the organization.

Predicting Failure

Some hold that failure of the SEC to perform a strong and active oversight role involves risks that audits will be deficient in divining or disclosing failure, fraud, and bribery. Since the Penn Central bankruptcy has been cited as dramatic evidence of the need for further government supervision of auditing activities, let us use it as a test of the general proposition set forth. In an analysis I made of the Penn Central bankruptcy, my evaluation (Weston, 1971: 311–324) identified the basic causes.

The Penn Central bankruptcy had its seeds in government policy before the turn of the century. The decline in wholesale prices from the end of the Civil War until 1896 increased the burden of the mortgage debts of farmers. The economic troubles of the farmers resulted in their organizing the "Granger movement" to work for legislation to improve their situation. The farmers felt that industrial products were favored by railroad rate structures. The Granger laws of the individual states and the Interstate Commerce Act of 1887 provided for maximum railroad rates and forbade rate discrimination. Railroad rate regulations were based on "value of service," so that the higher unit values of manufactured goods would bear higher rates than the bulky, relatively lower value agricultural products. When new forms of competition for transportation developed, they could underprice the railroads on the transportation of manufactured goods. The railroads' share of long-distance traffic volume declined from over 90 percent at the turn of the century to two-thirds by 1940 and to under 42 percent by 1968. This decline in business resulted in persistent losses for the railroads. By 1937, 109 railroads, operating one-third of railroad mileage, were bankrupt and in receivership.

Thus, the effects of government regulation had put in motion chronic problems that gave ample evidence of the vulnerability of the transportation industry to widespread financial distress in the late 1800s and from 1929 on. Investors were surely given ample warning. Almost one half the Class I railroads had working capital deficits during 1970, the year in which the Penn Central bankruptcy took place.

Another study (Murray, 1971: 327) raised the following questions about the Penn Central bankruptcy.

> In specific terms, were conventional methods of appraising the credit standing of a corporate borrower equal to the task of determining well in advance of June 1970 that the Penn Central was not entitled to a satisfactory credit rating? Could a financial analyst, with no access to internal records but simply using published information from the usual sources, be expected to have anticipated the debacle by at least a year or perhaps longer?

Murray (1971: 332) concludes:

> Meanwhile, a conventional approach to the analysis of earning power, liquidity, and capacity to pay debt gave the signal in 1968, confirmed as 1969

progressed, that the Penn Central had financial problems which were not about to be solved even by a reversal of the general economic contraction. In conclusion, a careful financial analyst might well have recommended in favor of the sale of marketable securities and against the purchase of Penn Central commercial paper a year or more before the events of May and June 1970. . . .

Otherwise, the Penn Central debacle is simply a lesson in the need for firm adherence to time-tested methods of financial analysis which demand careful scrutiny of stubborn facts. Even in the case of corporate giants, the financial analyst cannot permit himself to be distracted from basic fundamentals by the euphoria generated by an inflationary environment and a speculative urge for risk taking.

These appraisals make no mention that the accounting reports were inadequate or that the audits should have broached the subject of bankruptcy. The information was there. The accountants and auditors did their jobs. But some analysts and investors did not take a hard look at the facts made available to them. Furthermore, bankruptcy cannot be readily or objectively determined in the individual case. As a statistical probability, the financial data provide a basis for a judgment. But much depends on the economic outlook for the industry, competitive factors, and the kind of restructuring of relationships with supplies of funds that can be worked out. It is neither the prerogative nor the function of auditors to make prognostications or to pronounce judgments on such matters.

Business failure and bankruptcy are normal processes in a free market system. Ease of entry and exit are characteristics of competitive industries. Hot new-issue markets and speculative gains are excesses associated with entry. Failure and losses accompany bankruptcy. Efforts to eliminate these basic characteristics of a profit and loss economy will have the consequence of further restricting the effective functioning of a market system. Also, considerable evidence suggests that investors can absorb such random and unsystematic effects by appropriate diversification. Therefore, the evidence so far suggests that continued business failures do not establish a need to "audit the auditors."

An Equilibrium Quantity of Auditing Services

Magee develops a more general basis for this conclusion in Chapter 10. Using a very simple model, he projects a system of market forces that imposes substantial incentives and penalties to produce an equilibrium quantity of auditing services. Magee does not claim that the process guarantees an optimal auditing and reporting equilibrium. Much more empirical evidence is necessary to judge where the industry is in a relation to an optimum—assuming that one could be identified or command a consensus. But only then could the need for additional monitoring or restraints be assessed.

Magee notes that the creation of the two AICPA practice sections could be interpreted as a "voluntary attempt by the accounting profession to change the public's perception of the auditor/manager relationship." The principle is a sound one. Symbols and signals that provide covenants of expertise and care, along with formal processes that cause substantial loss of brand-name capital for an auditing firm whose underperformance has been detected, may increase the public's confidence in auditing. But whether this principle is equally sound in terms of an equilibrium supported by cost-benefit considerations or giving in to pressure groups and overdramatized Penn Central episodes (erroneously evaluated) needs seriously to be reassessed. In application, the covenants provided may be excessive and may involve an uneconomic allocation of resources to auditing activities.

I have not studied the materials on fraud and bribery in the same detail as business failure. My impression of bribery is that much of it falls into two categories. One is foreign operations, where it is considered a part of the normal mores of business-government relations in foreign countries. Although this problem needs correction, the fundamental cure lies outside the scope of auditors' powers. The second category, domestic varieties of illegal payments, appears to stem from the threat of exercise of government powers over firms. The bribery problem therefore seems to be more one of containing the powers of governments and political parties rather than a deficiency of auditing processes.

Cases of fraud are dramatic; in hindsight, they appear to have been discoverable earlier. Their total magnitude, however, appears to be a very small percentage of the economy's assets and revenues subject to audit. Certainly, the goal should not be a zero amount of missed fraud. It would be useful to quantify the relations with some formal estimates. In my judgment, the percentage of fraud that is detected late in relation to actual fraud or fraud that never occurs at all is so small that it suggests audits are too careful rather than too careless. Auditors probably devote more resources to a higher standard of auditing than an economic equilibrium, free of sensationalism, would call forth.

Regulation of Auditing Competition

As Nelligan describes in Chapter 5, the proposed NOSA would have another area of responsibility—regulation of competitive practices, with sanctions, for example, against practices the organization judges unfair. But as Kripke points out in Chapter 4, if accountants themselves seek to effectuate such restrictions, they will run afoul of the antitrust laws, which forbid such practices as solicitation of customers of another accountant, and so on. Kripke also counsels that it would be helpful if the accounting industry "found the shelter it deserves and needs in more active participation by the SEC."

These recommendations cause me great concern. I have been able to find few examples of persistent restrictive behavior and anticompetitive practices that were able to persist without government support and implementation. We have come full circle: Accounting is concentrated; the structural theory predicts that bad conduct and behavior will result. But with more government participation to prevent excessive competition, government regulations end up hurting smaller firms. Kaplan observes in Chapter 11 that the SEC has been encouraging the type of peer and quality reviews that are easy for large CPA firms to accomplish and costly for smaller firms. In this way government itself plays a hand in making competition harder for small CPA businesses.

The State of Competition in Accounting

My studies of a number of other industries as well as accounting lead me to the following synthesis. Competition is fierce and effective in the accounting industry. Although the market shares of the Big Eight firms are high by most criteria, the position of any one firm is not assured and is even precarious. To provide opportunities for growth and advancement, to attract the best talent to compete against the best talent in other large firms, places an emphasis on growth in the volume, variety, and complexity of accounting and information-processing activities performed by firms.

The emphasis on expansion and growth by the largest firms surely makes life difficult for medium-sized and smaller firms. The breadth of management skills visible in the larger firms, along with their expertise in a number of areas of an increasingly complex economy (including multiplying interactions with government regulations), represents a competitive response to their environment that is difficult to match.

The medium-sized and smaller firms can develop some pockets of expertise as well as general competence. Lacking the critical mass required for many potential market opportunities, however, they are likely to be receptive to merger offers from larger firms to be a part of an organization with broad strengths over a wider range of areas. Merger activity in accounting is evidence of intensifying, not reduced, competition. But the broader strengths of the larger firms make life especially difficult for the medium-sized and smaller firms. While the ability to perform selected types of tasks may be as great, the brand-name capital effect and certain customs may even exaggerate differences in the capabilities of accounting firms of different sizes.

A general characteristic of antitrust policies and other regulatory activities in the United States is to limit the extent to which the superiorities of the large, successful firms do not erode the position of the other firms in the industry. The problem is that in most major industries, the competition is increasingly international. Policies which constrain and handicap large domestic firms in order to protect their smaller rivals also handicap large domestic firms in their international competition with large foreign firms.

Therefore, proposals to regulate competition in accounting so that it is not "excessive" and not "unfair" represent a familiar pattern across American industry. If experience tells us anything, the pattern will be repeated in the accounting industry. Impassioned rhetoric, dramatic extreme cases, and lack of a rational cost-benefit analysis of alternative policies will be the basis. But by economic criteria, the NOSA proposals to regulate competition translate to efforts to protect competitors. Without government sponsorship, restrictions on competition cannot be effective and cannot persist. Government intervention in industry is necessary to emasculate competition. The NOSA proposals for regulation of competition in accounting fall into a general pattern that has already affected too much of American industry—protection of competitors and limitations of competition in the name of constraining the advantages (economic efficiencies) of more successful firms.

Similar principles apply to the issue of the range of economic functions performed by public accounting firms. The revolution in information technology has occurred in an area in which accounting firms have had major responsibilities. They would have been deficient in carrying out their general accounting and auditing responsibilities not to have developed sophisticated utilization of the advanced information technology. Effective use of information processing is not possible without relating information flows to the broader strategic planning and operating decisions of organizations. Indeed, auditing is most meaningful when related to the functions, activities, and processes of firms and other organizations. To be consistent and serious in our concern for the quality of auditing services, we should strongly support the development of the widest range of competencies in general business and other organization processes by public accounting firms. In addition, the specialized expertise that must be developed to comply with an ever-growing body of government regulatory requirements for business firms can be applied more generally, spreading the costs over more activities.

Thus, there are reasons of both auditing and economic efficiency for accounting firms to compete broadly in all areas in which their comparative advantages make them effective competitors. The activities may be outside their traditional business, narrowly defined, but they lie at the heart of the broader responsibilities increasingly assigned to them even by their critics. From a broader economic perspective, the expanded rather than narrow definition of information services to be performed by accounting firms represents a form of interindustry competition. The expanded ranges of variables characterizing decision processes in purposive organizations have broadened the determination of all industries' boundaries.

Instead of being defined merely by products or services performed, industries now comprise missions and capabilities as well. *Missions* are customer needs, warrants, or problems to be solved. *Capabilities* are important developments in managerial technologies, including planning, information sciences, computerization of information flows, formal decision models, problem-solving methodologies, and the behavioral sciences. The added emphasis industries now place on missions, capabilities, and organizational processes for adapting to environmental change has further blurred their boundaries. Increasingly, therefore, business managers from formerly distinct industries interact in new areas of competition across traditional industry lines. Continuing efforts by firms to achieve a broadening range of capabilities results in rivalrous reactions in any number of previously separate spheres.

Public accounting firms represent almost half the fifteen top management consultants in terms of 1978 U.S. billings ("New Shape," 1979: 99). Traditional management consulting firms might predictably be unhappy about this stiff competition, complaining of unfair competition and conflict of interest. There is substantial evidence for neither. Whatever the risks of unfair or excessive "competition" may be, they are more than offset by a highly desirable increase in breadth in the capabilities of public accounting firms. In addition, an invigorated interindustry competition of this sort can only be good from an economic standpoint. The potential for abuse is counteracted by the penalties that would fall on the public accounting firms if hard evidence of unethical practices in this area could be marshalled. The incentive and penalty systems involved here are consistent with increased competition of the appropriate kind, not abuses.

In fact, I predict that without government restrictions, a number of manifestations of expanded competition would be developing further. I see increased international competition, with more offices of foreign accounting firms performing public accounting and auditing work in the United States. I see an increase in the number of offices and activities abroad by U.S.-based public accounting firms. Thus, interregional competition will continue to grow along with interindustry competition.

One indication that profits in public accounting are not excessive by traditional tests of industrial organization performance is that we do not see substantial entry by traditional management consulting firms into the public accounting industry. These firms already possess many of the requirements for successful entry into the public accounting business. That substantial entry from this source has not taken place is evidence that prospective returns, in relation to the organization capabilities required and risks involved, has simply not stimulated the flow of resources and manpower from the management consulting industry to the public accounting industry. It appears manifestly clear that a considerable degree of overlap of activities could be described as management consulting or public accounting and auditing.

The Production of Accounting Information and Regulation

The fourth area is the issue of the production of accounting information and the role of private and public agencies in the formulation of accounting standards. Here we move onto difficult ground.

Role of Analytical Models

Gonedes and Dopuch (1974: 116) have reasoned that analytical models do not really settle the fundamental issues involved. They suggest a wide range of organization structures, since "a general resolution of this problem involves profound issues of social choice." Gonedes and Dopuch also observe (1974: 116–117) that:

> If we rule out dictatorial schemes or the (somewhat mysterious) "rule by convention" schemes then we are essentially left with the market mechanism or some type of political (voting) scheme; . . . In general, the market mechanism cannot be used by firms to optimally select accounting techniques, given the current institutional setting. . . .
>
> One example of such a political organization is the recently founded Financial Accounting Standards Board (FASB). To be sure, the decisions of this institution are partially influenced by (somebody's) accounting theory. But, in the end, it is a political institution (nominally under private-sector control). Consequently, the actions of this (and any similar) organization should be viewed as political outcomes, rather than as outcomes of a process that is supposed to operationalize and implement an accounting theory in a pure and pristine manner. . . .
>
> Observe that our theoretical framework merely identifies a political organization as one vehicle for making the social choices under examination. It does not identify the details of the organization's operating rules or its composition. Thus, it most certainly does not identify the FASB as the organization that is needed. Many alternative institutional forms should be viewed as competitors vis-a-vis the FASB.

Nils Hakansson (1978: 719) has questioned the need for attempts at grand statements of accounting principles. He observes:

> In any case, it is worth noting that a similar situation does not exist in other disciplines. The American Finance Association, the American Economic Association, the American Marketing Association, and the American

Psychological Association, to name a few, apparently do not feel the need to appoint committees to improve on, or add to, what individual scholars have to say about the state of knowledge in their respective fields. Recall that financial analysts, psychiatrists, and practicing psychologists are also, like CPAs, licensed practitioners.

Ng has formulated the compensation rules for managers and owners in a way that gives rise to an incentive problem and hence a need for general accounting standards. He observes (1978: 917):

> Specifically, the manager would select a reporting method which will overstate the performance of the firm and, at the same time, provide less information to the owner. In contrast, the owner would prefer a more informative reporting method which does not overstate the performance of the firm. . . .
>
> If the manager were free to select any reporting method he likes, he would select one which is as coarse and as positively biased as possible. Consequently, a role of GAAP is to limit the set of acceptable reporting functions from which the manager may choose. For example, GAAP provides a guideline as to what constitutes the minimum level of disclosure of a firm's financial position. This implies that GAAP imposes a lower bound on the fineness of a firm's financial reporting function.

But all this emanates from the formulation of a given set of compensation arrangements. These could readily be modified, and compensation arrangements could also be developed to avoid the incentive problems so formulated and perhaps the need for broad statements of standards. The range of problems posed in this area of standards and standard setting is complex indeed.

Economic Theory of Regulation

The chapters in this book have made some valuable contributions in this area. In Chapter 9, Watts discusses whether regulation can determine optimal accounting information. He adopts the Pareto concept as his criterion of optimality. According to his construct, a regulation would be in the public interest if it made at least one person "better off" without making any other person "worse off." He then cites inadequate corporate disclosure as a rationale for the securities acts, but (aside from the influence of the more general macroeconomic collapse) observes that increasing the amount of information and reducing the number of frauds is efficient only up to the point at which marginal benefits and marginal costs are equated. Hence, more information by government regulation requires a demonstration that regulation reduces the costs of providing information, an argument not explicitly considered when the legislation was passed.

Watts considers the public good rationale for regulation of accounting information, which argues that accounting information is a public good because one person's consumption of the information does not reduce another person's consumption. Furthermore, corporate managers are not able to stop nonpurchasers from using the information provided, so they may not take the value of their benefits from information into account. Hence, corporate managers may underproduce information in the absence of regulation. But, Watts emphasizes, the issue is contracting costs. Only if the cost of contracting with users is greater than the cost of regulation is regulation justifiable.

Watts adopts the economic theory of regulation, which posits that regulators act in their own self-interests of job security, increased authority and income, and subsequent advancement in or out of government. He notes that the costs of lobbying, for example, form part of the self-interest model of the political process. Because this market does not function well, he predicts that the political process, being greatly influenced by private interests and public pressures mounted on the basis of perceived rather than actual abuses, does not produce optimal accounting information. But effective markets to produce different results do not exist because relative costs and benefit considerations do not bring them into being.

Watts concludes that, practically speaking, regulation currently determines optimal accounting information. But as an individual (and scholar), he observes that regulation leads to the production of prescriptive accounting research instead of research that illuminates why different accounting firms choose different procedures, and I would add, the effects of alternative procedures under a range of different circumstances.

Private versus Public Regulation of Accounting Standards

In Chapter 11, Kaplan summarizes the major characteristics of private regulation of accounting standards as compared with public regulation. Using the FASB as the prototype of a private agency, he observes that its representation and support, as compared with its predecessors, includes more sectors than the public accounting profession. The FASB interacts with representatives of the SEC on an informal basis. It draws widely on the use of outside experts and has developed a process to encourage wide participation, comments, and suggestions. The agency, he indicates, will be more receptive to nonuniform practices because of the diversity of companies, interests, and circumstances represented. Auditing implications of any standard will limit the requirement of subjective judgments subject to litigation. Kaplan judges that sufficient balance of representation of public accounting firms and companies (auditees) exists to avoid excessive complexity in auditing procedures and requirements. As compared with that of a public agency, the FASB's smaller representation of lawyers produces less detailed rules and regulations that show a greater tolerance of ambiguity and of individual aberrant behavior. A private agency's chief weakness is its lack of statutory authority and enforcement power. This voluntarism leads to long delays in adopting major new initiatives.

The SEC, he continues, as a public agency with power to formulate accounting standards, possesses explicit statutory authority over accounting matters. The SEC has demonstrated that it is able to take more rapid action than the FASB on some individual matters. Kaplan notes that other individual government agencies view accounting standards from the standpoint of facilitating their specific line function rather than producing information for diverse user groups. Thus, governmental standard setting carries a number of risks. Accounting standards could be promulgated to facilitate government management of the economy and subdue corporate dissent. Standards could become as detailed and complex as the tax code. Costs of compliance could be excessive in relation to anyone's benefits. The stakes for special interest groups would be increased, and standard setting could become increasingly politicized. Any highly publicized scandal or incident could lead to new restrictions that are borne by a vast majority of corporations who show little probability of committing the indiscretion.

Kaplan notes the usual weaknesses of governmental agencies: conservatism, inflexibility, and lack of responsiveness. The SEC, he feels, has given contrary evidence. Other interpretations are possible, however.

My concern with the role of the SEC is the tenor of its official presentation to the Subcommittee on Reports, Accounting and Management of the Senate Committee on Governmental Affairs on June 13, 1977. Its spokesman emphasized that accountants were slow in making changes to meet the expectations expressed by various groups. He said (Williams, 1977: 1, 2, 16):

> The public debate and discussion generated by these hearings, and the staff study which preceded them, have highlighted the profession's failure to come to grips with the responsibilities which the Congress, the Commission, and the public expect it to shoulder in today's business climate. . . .
>
> In general terms, however, accountants have not gone far enough in insuring that they are meeting the public's legitimate expectations. . . .
>
> The profession, including the major national firms, has consistently been slow to recognize its problems and unable to reach agreement on approaches to those problems. Thus, their ability to work together toward a solution is open to question.
>
> The Commission intends to take several initiatives during the coming months which, it believes, will respond to the challenges outlined by this Subcommittee and other commentators.

Given its powers and responsibilities, one hopes the SEC would have a research base for evaluating expectations and even influencing them. In my judgment, it is a matter of concern that a governmental agency gives evidence of behaving in the way the economic theory of regulation predicts it will operate. So this brings us back to Ross Watts's conclusion in Chapter 9 that regulation does in fact currently determine optimal accounting information. As individuals, we want the process to yield better (or different) results. As researchers, we may take some comfort from the forecast by Nils Hakansson (1788: 724–725): ". . . advances in finance, economics, and behavioral science are in the nature of a precondition for substantial further progress in accounting. . . These developments are well on their way, and from this angle the next 10 years or so look exceedingly promising for accounting research."

It is wise to consider, however, that this statement may only reflect the predisposition of researchers that more and better research will move us toward the optimal in information, standards, and regulation. It also raises questions of the effects of researchers' special interest viewpoints. And even if we were the single exception to the economic theory of special interest behavior, how much impact do we have on the processes? We believe that impact is possible, and this book is a testimony to that belief. But this again may be more presumption than reality. We should see ourselves as impelled by our own motivations to advance our individual goals by participation in the markets of competing viewpoints, outputs, and interests.

A General Framework for Viewing Accounting Standards

David Mosso has given a good account in Chapter 7 of his involvement in the process of setting accounting standards and his work with the FASB. He suggests that there may be three ways of looking at accounting standards: (1) measuring instruments for economic activity, (2) rules of conduct to guide economic behavior, and (3) providers of desirable economic incentives to promote national economic goals. To illustrate these three aspects, he draws an analogy to advertising. Where advertising has substantial future consequences, advertising outlays would be capitalized. Because the judgment of the persistence of advertising effects is inherently variable and subjective, the second criterion provides for a mandatory expensing of advertising outlays. By the third criterion, if we wanted to discourage all or some kinds of advertising, advertising for children's television can be expensed when incurred whereas institutional advertising can be fully capitalized.

It makes sense to look at accounting standards from a number of dimensions. Let's go even further. One of the criticisms of setting accounting standards in the private sector is that the process is slow and tortuous. The SEC and various oversight committees of Congress have admonished the FASB on a number of occasions: "If you don't get the job done faster and meet the broad public expectations of getting accounting standards established, then the SEC or some other government agency will have to take over the job."

Why is the FASB so slow in getting new standards adopted? Mainly because we live in a world of highly complex and differing circumstances and rapidly changing economic environments. What makes sense for one firm in a given context of an economic environment may be completely inappropriate for another in different circumstances. This basic fact of life gives rise to a number of difficulties and complications. Because individual firms differ in their interrelationship with the economic environment, no one grand conceptual scheme fits all firms, industries, and circumstances. The impact of a general purchasing power method of adjusting for price level changes, for example, makes sense in varying degrees for different firms in different industries and for different business strategies. The feasibility of measuring the replacement costs of inventories and investments, and the economic relevance or meaningfulness of making such adjustments, also varies widely.

Thus, at a theoretical level, conceptualization doesn't fit well for all firms, for all seasons. To require uniformity where circumstances differ is to cause distortions by putting the same suit of clothes on all individuals— male or female, tall or short, fat or lean, young or old, growing or senescent. Yet if the suit (or dress) is altered to fit the individual, some self-serving will occur and each of us will want to "look as pretty as possible." This desire is regarded by some as manipulation.

I would argue for the application of a number of basic principles. Principle 1 is to keep a link with the past. Principle 2 is to provide more raw material information. Principle 3 is to recognize that multiple methods, multiple measures, and multiple purposes exist for the use of information. Thus, building from the past, let's continue to work along the lines of small and moderate increments of accounting standards. As for grand conceptualizations and adjusting for inflation, let us have many more raw material inputs that can be extensively analyzed, from a number of standpoints, with modern information processing technology. Then, as *supplementary* information in the financial reporting of business firms, a wide variety of additional measures can be provided. The use of Method X provides one kind of information; the use of Method Y provides a different kind. Let the reader then judge the significance of the alternative supplementary materials provided. Alternative measures are already developed to a substantial degree in managerial accounting information.

In this way many users of the raw material of accounting information might have their needs met, including top executives, other managers, owners, creditors, labor unions, and consumers as well as investors and security analysts. The major emphasis would be how different methods and approaches lead to different results, inherently requiring some further analysis and interpretation.

Complex issues are involved here. Some people would like to see accounting information reflect generally accepted accounting principles. It would be nice to have the results mean just one thing, providing full guidance to investors. That, however, is not the nature of the world. Indeed, we could argue that to provide meaningful information to investors, financial reports would include materials on such items as:

1. Outlook for world economy and individual economies
2. Outlook for U.S. economy and sectors
3. Monetary and fiscal framework
4. Demand sensitivity of each segment of firm to alternative future economic environments
5. Sensitivity of cost structures to alternative future economic environments
6. Likelihood of governmental regulatory changes
7. Critical economic developments in the industry
8. Competitive developments in the industry

Clearly, this framework would give dimensions to the role of accounting information much broader than generally conceived. But in terms of giving full guidance to investors and other users of information, a truly broad range of subjects would have to be treated in a highly sophisticated way. Hence, we will always have to be satisfied with a given set of trade-offs. Tradeoffs always involve the advantages and disadvantages of doing more or doing less. The situation will be subject to tensions. But there never ever will be an adequate substitute for informed, sophisticated use of any accounting information presented.

Indeed, there is another dimension to the formulation and development of accounting information. A results-oriented system of measurement is always misleading in some sense. The process and the development of an effective communication process and information feedback system are what really matter. In another connection, the problem was presented as follows (Adizes and Weston, 1973; Weston, 1972a, 1972b):

> Both the theory and practice of management in recent years have placed increased emphasis on two-way communication and the use of standards to

facilitate a participative, dynamic adjustment and learning process in the firm. Rewards have not been based on the attainment of absolute goals, but on the ability to participate in the formulation of realistic potentials for the firm, reformulating the firm's product-market opportunity sets, and effectiveness in managing processes to achieve the potentials identified. In large measure, dissatisfaction expressed toward the performance of business firms stems from lags in the adoption and implementation of important new elements of the technology of management among U.S. business firms.

Thus, efforts toward the formulation of grand statements of accounting principles represent but one of a number of useful objectives in developing accounting standards. The staffs of congressional committees in particular have argued for a set of common principles and standards that would be simple and easy to interpret. But it is not possible to reduce a complex world to unambiguous simplicity. It is a much more practical and useful goal to be provided with supplementary raw materials of information that could be further processed in a number of different ways. We can keep close to traditional measures to achieve continuity while providing this supplementary information for further analysis. In short, accounting information for external uses can also be viewed in a broader framework of an information flow feedback system that relates accounting procedures, the business economics of the firm, interactions with its broad environments, and managerial decision processes.

The proposals for more government intervention in the accounting industry would do more harm than good. On the theory that accounting is a concentrated industry, a lack of competition is presumed. Yet the proposals for government intervention are for the objective of preventing "excessive" competition. Similarly in the area of accounting standards. The government proposals are for rules that are simple and easily understood. But the financial and economic processes to be portrayed by accounting information are dynamic, complex, and changing. Inherently, accounting procedures must be complicated, and the nature of the world requires that they be flexible in application. Government formulation of accounting standards would be overly rigid and inflexible. In a complex world, alternative measurement bases and procedures are required to better understand the performance of firms. The rules will be complex, but also a source of increased information. A good example of progress by the accounting profession in developing standards is FASB No. 33, issued in September 1979, concerned with presenting the effects of inflation. It includes adjustments both for changes in general purchasing power and in the prices of specific assets. A basis is provided for increased information and better understanding of business performance under inflation and therefore will provide a better foundation for public policy.

Notes

1. For economists representing structuralist views, see, for example: National Resources Committee (1939); Adams (1969); Bain (1951, 1956, 1968); Blair (1972); Collins and Preston (1968); Kaysen and Turner (1959); Mann (1966, 1974); Mueller (1970), Chapters 2–4, 6, and 11, and also Mueller (1974); Scherer (1970), Chapters 8, 12, 17, and 20, and also Scherer (1974); and Shepherd (1970), Chapters 2–4, 11–13, 15, and 16.

2. For economists representing nonstructuralist views, see, for example: Brozen (1969, 1974); McGee (1971), Chapter 6 and associated bibliographical material, and also McGee (1974); Neal (1942); Peltzman (1969); Stigler (1963), pp. 61–71; Weston (1960); and Weston and Lustgarten (1974).

Evidence consistent with dynamic competition in concentrated industries is found in Brozen.

Bibliography

Chapter 1

Abraham, Stanley Charles *The Public Accounting Profession*. Lexington, Mass.: Lexington Books, 1978.

"Accountants Adopt Self-Regulation in Revamping Plan." *New York Times*, September 19, 1977, p. 57.

"Accountants Join Growing List of Professionals Volunteering Services to Public-Interest Groups." *Wall Street Journal*, January 28, 1974, p. 24.

"Accounting Profession Is Termed Oligopoly by Chairman of Panel." *Wall Street Journal*, January 31, 1978, p. 33.

American Accounting Association. *Report of the Committee on the Social Consequences of Accounting Information*. Sarasota, Fla.: August, 1977.

American Institute of Certified Public Accountants. Report of the Study on Establishment of Accounting Principles. *Establishing Financial Accounting Standards*. New York: AICPA, March, 1972.

"Arthur Young & Co. Is Cleared by Judge over GeoTek Case." *Wall Street Journal*, April 9, 1976, p. 16.

Barber, Bernard. "Control and Responsibilities in the Powerful Professions." *Political Science Quarterly* 93 (4): Winter, 1978.

Bedingfield, J. P., and S. E. Loeb. "Auditor Changes—An Examination." *Journal of Accountancy* (March, 1974): pp. 66–69.

Benston, G. J. "Required Disclosure and the Stock Market: An Evaluation of the Securities Exchange Act of 1934." *American Economic Review* (March, 1973): pp. 132–155.

———. "Public (U.S.) Compared to Private (U.K.) Regulation of Corporate Financial Disclosure." *Accounting Review* (July, 1976): pp. 483–498.

Bentley, A. F. *The Process of Government*. Chicago: University of Chicago Press, 1908.

Berstein, M. *Regulating Business by Independent Commission*. Princeton, N.J.: Princeton University Press, 1955.

Biegler, John C. Statement before the Subcommittee on Reports, Accounting and Management of the Committee on Governmental Affairs. U.S. Senate, May 10, 1977.

Bonbright, J. C. *Principles of Public Utility Rates*. New York: Columbia University Press, 1961.

Briloff, Abraham. *More Debits than Credit*. New York: Harper & Row, 1976.

———. *Unaccountable Accounting* New York: Harper & Row, 1972.

Buckley, John W., and Marlene H. Buckley. *The Accounting Profession*. Los Angeles: Melville, 1974.

Carey, John L. *The Rise of the Accounting Profession*. New York: American Institute of Certified Public Accountants. Vol. 1, 1969: Vol 2, 1970.

Cates, David C. "SEC Regulatory Style and the Banks." *The Bankers Magazine*, Spring, 1975.

Caves, Richard. *American Industry: Structure, Conduct, Performance*. 4th ed. Englewood Cliffs, N.J.: Prentice-Hall, 1977.

Commission on Auditors' Responsibilities. *Report of Tentative Conclusions*. New York: 1977.

"Competition Comes to Accounting." *Fortune*, July 17, 1978, p. 70.

Dahl, R. A., and C. E. Lindblom. *Politics, Economics and Welfare*. New York: Harper & Row, 1953.

Davis, K. C. *Administrative Law Treatise*. St. Paul, Minn.: West, 1958. Supplement, 1970.

Dopuch, Nicholas. "Public and Private Regulation of Accounting." Paper presented at School of Business Administration, Washington University, St. Louis, Missouri, Fall, 1978.

Dun & Bradstreet, Inc. *Cost of Doing Business, Partnerships and Proprietorships*. New York: 1975, 1976, 1978.

Eckert, R. D. "Spectrum Allocation and Regulatory Incentives." In *Conference on Communications Policy Research: Papers and Proceedings*. Washington, D.C.: Office of Telecommunications Policy, 1972.

Fay, J. R., "Development of General Criteria Applicable for the Establishment of a New Accounting Practice," unpublished doctoral dissertation, University of Arkansas, 1976.

"FEI Studies Companies' Relationships with Auditors." *Journal of Accountancy* (May, 1978): 10–12.

Financial Accounting Standards Board. "Conceptual Framework for Financial Accounting and Reporting: Elements of Financial Statements and Their Measurement." FASB Discussion Memorandum, December 2, 1976.

Fiorina, Morris P., and Roger G. Noll. "Voters, Bureaucrats and Legislators: A Rational Choice Perspective on the Growth of Bureaucracy." *Journal of Public Economics* 9 (1978): 239–254.

Friedman, Morton. "Fair Versus Free." *Newsweek*, July 4, 1977, p. 70.

Friendly, H. J. *The Federal Administrative Agencies: The Need for Better Definition of Standards*. Cambridge, Mass.: Harvard University Press, 1962.

Goldberg, V. P. "Regulation and Administered Contracts." *Bell Journal of Economics* (Autumn, 1976).

Gonedes, N. J., and N. Dopuch. "Capital Market Equilibrium, Information Production, and Selecting Accounting Techniques: Theoretical Framework and Review of Empirical Work." *Studies on Financial Accounting Objectives: 1974.* University of Chicago.

Hanson, E. W. Statement before the Subcommittee on Reports, Accounting and Management of the Committee on Governmental Affairs. U.S. Senate, 1977.

Haskins & Sells. *The Week in Review.* February 28, 1975.

Hicks, J. O., Jr. "An Examination of Accounting Interest Groups Differential Perceptions of Innovations." *Accounting Review* (April, 1978). pp. 371–388.

Hunt, B. C. "Auditor Independence." *Journal of Accountancy* 59 (1935): 453–459.

Huntington, S. P. "The Marasmus of the ICC: The Commission, The Railroads, and the Public Interest." In P. Woll, ed., *Public Administration and Policy: Selected Essays.* New York: Harper & Row, 1966.

Joskow, Paul L. "Inflation and Environmental Concern: Structural Change in the Process of Public Utility Regulation." *Journal of Law and Economics* (October, 1974). pp. 291–327.

———. "Regulatory Activities by Government Agencies." Cambridge: Massachusetts Institute of Technology, Department of Economics Working Paper No. 171, December, 1975.

Leiserson, A. "Interest Groups in Administration." In F. Morstein Marx, ed., *Elements of Public Administration.* Englewood Cliffs, N.J.: Prentice-Hall, 1946.

Kreiser, Larry. "Maintaining and Improving the Audit Competence of CPAs: CPA and Selected User Reaction." *Accounting Review* (April, 1977). pp. 427–437.

Lavin, D. "Perceptions of the Independence of the Auditor." *Accounting Review* (January, 1976).

Lilley, W., and J. C. Miller. "The New 'Social' Regulation." *The Public Interest* (Spring, 1977): pp. 49–61.

Loebbecke, James K. "Priorities in Accounting and Auditing Research." AIS Working Paper No. 73-20, 1972, UCLA.

MacAvoy, P. *The Economic Effects of Regulation: The Trunk Line Railroad Cartels and the Interstate Commerce Commission Before 1900.* Cambridge, Mass.: The M.I.T. Press, 1965.

Manne, H. G. "Economic Aspects of Required Disclosure under Federal Securities Laws." In *Wall Street Transition: The Emerging System and Its Impact on the Economy.* The Charles C. Moskowitz Lectures, No. 15. New York: New York University Press, 1974.

Newton, L. K. "A Sociological Study of the U.S. Mandate for Replacment Cost Disclosures." AISRP No. 11, UCLA (1978).

Ng, David S. "Supply and Demand of Auditing Services and the Nature of Regulations in Auditing." Paper presented at the Arthur Young Professors' Roundtable, April 7, 1978, University of Chicago.

———. "An Information Economics Analysis of Financial Reporting and External Auditing." *The Accounting Review* (October 1978): 910–920.

Niskanen, W. *Bureaucracy and Representative Government.* Chicago: Aldine-Atherton, 1971.

Noll, Roger G. "Government Administrative Behavior and Private Sector Response: A Multidisciplinary Survey." Social Science Working Paper No. 62, California Institute of Technology, 1976.

Ostlund, A. C. "Advertising—in the Public Interest?" *Journal of Accountancy* (January, 1978): pp. 59–63.

Owen, Bruce M., and Ronald Braetigam. *The Regulation Game: Strategic Use of the Administrative Process.* Cambridge, Mass.: Ballinger, 1978.

Porter, M., and J. Sagansky. "Information, Politics and Economic Analysis: The Regulatory Decision Process in the Air Freight Case." *Public Policy* (Spring, 1976): pp. 263–307.

Posner, Richard A. "Theories of Economic Regulation." *The Bell Journal of Economics and Management Science* 5, 2 (Autumn, 1974): 335–358.

Reece, J. S., and S.R. Kinkade. "Demographics of Large Public Accounting Firms." Graduate School of Business Administration, Harvard University, Working Paper No. 75-19, 1975.

"Report of the Trustee of Equity Funding Corporation of America." 1974. " 'Sample' of Banks to File Loan Data, House Panel Decides." *Wall Street Journal,* May 14, 1975, p. 13.

Schieff, Allen, and H. Dov Fried. "Large Companies and the Big Eight: An Overview." *Abacus* (December, 1976): 116–124.

Schlosser, R. E. "Lifelong Learning Demands Supportive Structures and Attitudes." In *Accounting Education: New Horizons for the Profession.* Proceedings of the Arthur Young Professors' Roundtable, University of Michigan, 1977.

"SEC Seeks More Disclosure on Holdings: Ruling Delayed on New York City Debt." *Wall Street Journal,* January 8, 1976, p. 5.

Securities and Exchange Commission. *Report of the Special Study of the Securities Markets of the Securities and Exchange Commission.* Part I. Washington, D.C.: U.S. Government Printing Office, 1963.

———. *Accounting Series Release No. 126.* 1972.

———. *Accounting Series Release No. 190.* 1976.

———. "Inquiry into Certain Auditing Failures by Peat, Marwick, Mitchell & Co." *Accounting Series Release No. 173.* July, 1975.

"To Merge or Not to Merge, That Is the Question." *Forbes,* December 1, 1977, p. 58.

"Touche Ross Openly Strives for Growth as Accounting Firms Turn Competitive." *Wall Street Journal,* October 5, 1976, p. 20.

Sharp, D. "Constituency Based Accounting Policy: A Multidimensional Perspective." Unpublished Ph.D. dissertation, Graduate School of Management, University of California, Los Angeles, 1978.

Solomons, D. "The Politicization of Accounting." *The Journal of Accountancy* (November, 1978): 65–72.

Sprouse, Robert T. "The Role of the FASB." *The Journal of Commercial Bank Lending* (January, 1976): pp. 26–34.

Stanton, P. J., and D. M. Gilling. "Studies in the Structure of the Auditing Profession." Discussion Paper No. 7, Department of Accounting and Finance, Monash University (Australia), July, 1977.

Stigler, G. J. "Free Riders and Collective Action,: An Appendix to Theories of Economic Regulation." *The Bell Journal of Economics and Management Science* 5, 2 (Autumn, 1974): 359–365.

———. *The Citizen and the State: Essays on Regulation.* Chicago: University of Chicago Press, 1975.

———. "The Theory of Economic Regulation." *The Bell Journal of Economics and Management Science* 2, 1 (Spring, 1971): 3–12.

Truman, D. B. *The Government Process: Political Interests and Public Opinion.* New York: Knopf, 1951.

U.S. Department of Commerce. Bureau of the Census. *1972 Census of Selected Service Industries, Vol. 1, Summary and Subject Statistics.* Washington, D.C.: U.S. Government Printing Office, 1976.

U.S. Department of Commerce. Bureau of the Census. *County Business Patterns 1976—United States.* Washington, D.C.: U.S. Government Printing Office, 1978.

U.S. Congress. *Reform and Self-Regulation Efforts of the Accounting Profession.* Hearings before the Subcommittee on Oversight and Investigation of the Committee on Interstate and Foreign Commerce, House of Representatives, Ninety-fifth Congress, Second Session, January 30–31, February 1, March 3, and July 28, 1978. Washington, D.C.: U.S. Government Printing Office, Serial No. 95–131, 1978.

U.S. Congress. *Federal Regulation and Regulatory Reform.* Report by the Subcommittee on Oversight and Investigations of the Committee on Interstate and Foreign Commerce. Ninety-fourth Congress, Second Session. Washington, D.C.: U.S. Government Printing Office, 1976.

U.S. Senate. *The Accounting Establishment—A Staff Study.* Subcommittee on Reports, Accounting, and Management of the Committee on Government Operations. Washington, D.C.: U.S. Government Printing Office, 1977.

Watts, Ross L., and Jerold L. Zimmerman. "Auditors and the Determination of Accounting Standards, An Analysis of the Lack of 'Independence.'" Working Paper No. GPB78-06, Graduate School of Management, University of Rochester, 1979.

"When the Auditor Gets Audited," *New York Times,* November 23, 1975, S3, p. 1.

"The White House Likes Its Accounting Freebie." *Business Week,* August 15, 1977, p. 36.

Wilson, James Q. "The Politics of Regulation." In James W. McKie, ed., *Social Responsibility and the Business Predicament.* Washington, D.C.: The Brookings Institution, 1974.

Ziegler, H. *Interest Groups in American Society.* Englewood Cliffs, N.J.: Prentice-Hall, 1964.

Chapter 2

Armentano, D. T. *Myths of Antitrust.* New Rochelle, N.Y.: Arlington House, 1972.

Asch, Peter, and J. J. Seneca. "Is Collusion Profitable?" *Review of Economics and Statistics* 58 (1976): 1–10.

Bain, Joe. *Barriers to New Competition.* Cambridge, Mass.: Harvard University Press, 1965.

Benston, George. *Corporate Financial Disclosure in the U.K. and the U.S.A.* Lexington, Mass.: Saxon House, 1976.

Berle, Adolph, and Gardiner Means. *The Modern Corporation and Private Property*. New York: Macmillan, 1933.

Brozen, Yale. "The Antitrust Task Force Deconcentration Recommendation." *Journal of Law and Economics* 13 (1970): 229–292.

———. "Concentration and Structural and Market Disequilibria." *Antitrust Bulletin* 248 (Summer, 1971): 241–248.

———. "Entry Barriers: Advertising and Product Differentiation." In Harvey J. Goldschmid; Mann, H. Michael; and J. Fred Weston, eds., *Industrial Concentration: The New Learning*. Boston: Little Brown, 1974.

Burns, Joseph. *Accounting Standards and International Finance*. Washington, D.C.: American Enterprise Institute, 1976.

Caves, Richard. *American Industry: Structure, Conduct, Performance*. 4th ed. Englewood Cliffs, N.J.: Prentice-Hall, 1977.

Carter, John R. "Collusion, Efficiency and Antitrust." *Journal of Law and Economics* 21 (1978): 435–444.

Clark, J. B., and J. M. Clark. *The Control of Trusts*. New York: Macmillan, 1901.

"Collusion among Electrical Equipment Manufacturers," *Wall Street Journal*, January 10–12, 1962.

Demsetz, Harold. "Industry, Structure, Market Rivalry, and Public Policy." *Journal of Law and Economics* 16 (1973): 1–10.

Friedman, Milton, and Anna Schwartz. *A Monetary History of the United States, 1867–1960*. Princeton, N.J.: Princeton University Press, 1964.

Granfield, Michael. "A Further Look at Concentration and Profits." Hearings before the Subcommittee on Antitrust and Monopoly, 94th Congress, 1st session, U.S. Senate, July, 1974: 1025–1040.

Hay, George, and Daniel Kelley. "An Empirical Survey of Price Fixing Conspiracies." *Journal of Law and Economics* 17 (1974): 1–30.

"Inflation Hits a New High for 1979." AP, *Los Angeles Times*, May 15, 1979.

"Inflation Remains a Problem for Budget Forces," AP, *Los Angeles Times*, June 21, 1979.

Kirkland, Edward Chase. *The Economic History of the United States*. New York: Holt, Rinehart and Winston, 1961.

Kwoka, John. "The Effect of Market Share Distribution on Industry Performance." *Review of Economics and Statistics* 61 (1979): 101–109.

Liebler, Wesley. "Market Power and Competitive Superiority in Concentrated Industries." *UCLA Law Review* 55 (August, 1978): 1231–1300.

Neal, Philip, et al. *Report of the White House Task Force on Antitrust Policy*. Trade Regulation Report No. 1. Washington, D.C.: Government Printing Office, 1968.

Ornstein, Stanley. "Concentration and Profits." *Journal of Business* 45 (1972): 514–541.

———. *Industrial Concentration and Advertising Intensity*. Washington, D.C.: American Enterprise Institute, 1977.

———. "The Rise of Barriers-to-Entry." Working Paper No. 89, UCLA Program in Competition and Business Policy, Spring, 1977.

Reid, Joseph. "Regulatory Reform and the Securities and Exchange Commission." Paper presented at the Conference on Regulatory Change, Washington State University School of Business, April, 1978.

Steiner, Peter. *Mergers*. Ann Arbor: University of Michigan Press, 1975.

Stelzer, Irwin. *Antitrust Cases: Landmark Decisions*. Homewood, Ill.: Irwin, 1974.

Stigler, George. "The Case against Big Business." *Fortune* (May, 1952): 37–45.

U.S. Congress. Industrial Reorganization Act. Hearings before U.S. Senate Subcommittee on Antitrust and Monopoly, 1st session, 94th Congress, April, 1974.

U.S. Senate. *The Accounting Establishment—A Staff Study*. Subcommittee on Reports, Accounting, and Manangement of the Committee on Government Operations, Washington, D.C.: U.S. Government Printing Office, 1977.

Chapter 3

AICPA. The Commission on Auditor's Responsibilities [Cohen Commission]. *Report, Conclusions, and Recommendations*. 1978.

Asch, Peter. *Economic Theory and the Antitrust Dilemma*. New York: John Wiley & Sons, 1970.

Benston, George. "The Market for Public Accounting Services: Demand, Supply and Regulation." Unpublished manuscript, University of Rochester, 1979.

Chatfield, M. *A History of Accounting Thought*. New York: Dryden Press, 1974.

Clarkson, K. U. "Intangible Capital and Rates of Return." Washington, D.C.: American Enterprise Institute, 1977.

The CPA Examination. Gainesville, Fla.: Professional Publications, Inc., 1978.

Demsetz, H. "The Market Concentration Doctrine." Stanford, Ca.: American Enterprise Institute / Hoover Institute on War, Revolution and Peace, 1973.

Dow Jones & Co. *The Balance Sheet: Top Executives Speak out about CPA Firms*. 1978.

Elliott, R. K. and Korpi, A. "Factors Affecting Audit Fees." In M. Shakun, ed., *Cost-Benefit Analysis of Auditing*. AICPA, 1978.

Financial Executives Institute. "Big 8 to Big 20?" *Financial Executive*, June, 1973.

———. "The Annual Audit Revisited." *Financial Executive*. March, 1978.

Goldschmid, H.; Mann, H.; and J. F. Weston, *Industrial Concentration: The New Learning*. New York: Columbia University Center for Law and Economic Studies, 1974.

Gonedes, N., and N. Dopuch. "Economic Analysis and Accounting Techniques: Perspectives and Proposals." *Journal of Accounting Research*, Autumn, 1979.

Harris, Spencer P. *Who Audits America?* Menlo Park, Ca.: Data Financial Press, 1976.

Harris, M. and A. Raviv. "Optimal Incentive Contracts with Imperfect Information." *American Economic Review*, March, 1978.

Lev, Baruch. "Economic Determinants of Some Time Series Properties of Earnings." University of Chicago Center for Mathematical Studies in Business and Economics No. 7705, 1979.

Pashigian, B. Peter. "Occupational Licensing and the Interstate Mobility of Professionals." *Journal of Law and Economics* 20, 1 (April, 1977): 5385.

Pichler, Joseph A. "An Economic Analysis of Accounting Power." In R. Sterling, ed., *Institutional Issues in Public Accounting*. Houston: Scholars Book Company, 1974.

Rayback, E. "The Physician's Service Industry." In W. Adams, ed., *The Structure of American Industry*. New York: Macmillan, 1977.

Simunic, Dan A. "Determinants of Prices of Financial Audit Services." Ph.D. dissertation, University of Chicago, 1979.

Stigler, George. *The Organization of Industry*. Homewood, Ill.: Irwin, 1968.

Texas CPA Society. *Texas CPA News*. February, 1978.

U.S. Senate. Subcommittee on Reports, Accounting and Management of the Senate Committee on Government Operations. *The Accounting Establishment—A Staff Study*. Washington, D.C.: U.S. Government Printing Office, 1977.

Weiss, Leonard. "Quantitative Studies in Industrial Organization." in M.D. Intriligator, ed., *Frontiers of Quantitative Economics*. New York: North-Holland, 1971.

Chapter 4

Legal Cases

Arthur Andersen & Company v. *SEC*. N.D. Ill.

Appalachian Power Company v. *AICPA*. 268 F. 2d844 (2d Cir.).

Bates v. *State Bar of Arizona*. 433 U.S. 350 (1975).

Broadcast Music, Inc. v. *Columbia Broadcasting System, Inc.* 1979.

Goldfarb v. *Virginia State Bar*. 421 U.S. 773 (1975).

Gordon v. *New York Stock Exchange*. 422 U.S. 659 (1975).

National Society of Professional Engineers v. *United States*. 435 U.S. 679 (1978).

Ohralik v. *Ohio State Bar Association*. 436 U.S. 447 (1978).

Silver v. *New York Stock Exchange*. 373 U.S. 341 (1963).

Articles, Reports, and Books

AICPA. "Tentative Conclusions and Recommendations of the Reports by Management Special Advisory Committee." December 8, 1978.

———. Commission on Auditors' Responsibilities [Cohen Commission]. *Report, Conclusions, and Recommendations*. 1978.

American Law Institute. "Federal Securities Code, Tentative Draft No. 3." 1974.

Beaver, William H. "What Should the FASB's Objectives Be?" *Journal of Accountancy* 49 (August, 1973).

Chatov, R. *Corporate Financial Reporting—Public or Private Control?* The Free Press: New York, 1975.

"F.T.C. to Hear Appeal on A.M.A. Ad Restraints." *American Bar Association Journal* 65, 171 (February, 1979).

Federal Trade Commission. "Competition in the Accounting Industry." Press release. March 24, 1977.

Gaines. "Professional Engineers: Implications for Enforcement Strategy." Mimeographed address by the Assistant Director, Bureau of Competition, FTC, December 15, 1978.

Handler, Milton. "Antitrust—1978." *Record of the Association of the Bar of the City of New York* 33, 557 (December, 1978).

Chapter 9

Barzel, Y. "Some Fallacies in the Interpretation of Information Costs." *Journal of Law and Economics* 20 (October, 1977): 291–307.

Beaver, W. H. "The Implications of Security Price Research for Disclosure Policy and the Analyst Community." Unpublished paper, Graduate School of Business, Stanford University, November, 1976.

Benston, G. J. "The Effectiveness and Effects of the SEC's Accounting Disclosure Requirements." In H. G. Manne, ed., *Economic Policy and the Regulation of Corporate Securities*. Washington, D.C.: American Enterprise Institute, 1969.

Burton, J. C. "The SEC and Financial Reporting: The Sand in the Oyster." Unpublished paper, Columbia University, March, 1979.

Collins, D. W., and W. T. Dent. "The Proposed Elimination of Full Cost Accounting in the Extractive Oil and Gas Industry: An Empirical Assessment of the Market Consequences." *Journal of Accounting and Economics*, in press.

Demsetz, H. "Information and Efficiency: Another Viewpoint." *Journal of Law and Economics* 12 (April, 1969): 1–22.

Downs, A. *An Economic Theory of Democracy*. Harper & Row: New York, 1957.

Friedman, M., and A. H. Schwartz. *A Monetary History of the United States 1867–1960*. Princeton, N.J.: Princeton University Press, 1963.

Geisel, M.; Leffler, K.; and J. Zimmerman. "Equilibrium Organizational Structure in Local Government: Theory and Evidence." April, 1978.

Gonedes, N., and N. Dopuch. "Capital Market Equilibrium, Information and Production, and Selecting Accounting Techniques: Theoretical Framework and Review of Empirical Work." *Studies on Financial Objectives: 1974, Journal of Accounting Research* 12 (supplement): 48–129.

Jensen, M. "Towards a Theory of the Press." Unpublished paper, Graduate School of Management, University of Rochester, June, 1976.

Meckling, W. H. "Towards a Theory of Representative Government." Paper presented at the Third Annual Conference on Analysis and Ideology, Interlaken, Switzerland, June 4, 1976. (1976a)

———. "Values and the Choice of the Model of the Individual in Social Sciences." *Revue Suisse d'Economic Politique et de Statistique* (December, 1976): 545–560. (1976b)

Mueller, D. C. "Public Choice: A Survey." *The Journal of Economic Literature* (June, 1976): 295–433.

Niskanen, W. A. *Bureaucracy and Representative Government*. Chicago: Aldine-Atherton, 1971.

Peltzman, S. "Towards a More General Theory of Regulation." *Journal of Law and Economics* (August, 1971): 211–240.

Posner, R. A. "Theories of Economic Regulation." *Bell Journal of Economics and Management Science* (Autumn, 1974): 335–358.

Stigler, G. J. "The Theory of Economic 'Regulation.'" *Bell Journal of Economics and Management Science* (Spring, 1971): 3–21.

U.S. Senate. Subcommittee on Reports, Accounting and Management of the Committee on Government Operations. *The Accounting Establishment—A Staff Study*. 94th Congress, 2nd Session, 1976.

Watts, R. L., and J. L. Zimmerman. "Towards a Positive Theory of the Determination of Accounting Standards." *The Accounting Review* (January, 1978): 112–134.

———. "The Demand for and Supply of Accounting Theory: The Market for Excuses." *The Accounting Review* (April, 1979): 273–305.

Zeff, S. A. *Forging Accounting Principles in Five Countries: A History and an Analysis of Trends.* Arthur Andersen Lecture Series. Stipes Publishing Co., 1972.

Chapter 10

Legal Cases

Ernst and Ernst v. *Hochfelder.* 503 F. 2d 1100 CCA 7 (1974).

Articles and Addresses

Briloff, A. J. "The Accountant's Responsibility to Society." Beta Alpha Psi Distinguished Lecture at Hofstra University, May, 1976.

Jensen, M. C. and W. H. Meckling. "Theory of the Firm: Managerial Behavior, Agency Costs and Ownership Structure." *Journal of Financial Economics* (October, 1976): 305–360.

Ng, D. S. "Supply and Demand of Auditing Services and the Nature of Regulations in Accounting." *Arthur Young Professors' Roundtable Conference Proceedings,* 1978.

Ng, D. S. and J. Stoeckenius. "Auditing, Incentives and Truthful Reporting." Paper presented at the University of Chicago's Conference on Accounting Research, May, 1979.

Chapter 11

Anreder, Steven S. "Profit or Loss?" *Barrons,* March 12, 1979, pp. 9, 18, 20, 31.

Benston, George. "Accounting Standards in the U.S. and the U.K.: Their Nature, Causes, and Consequences." *Vanderbilt Law Review* 28 (January, 1975): 235–268.

———. "Public (U.S.) Compared to Private (U.K.) Regulation of Corporate Financial Disclosure." *Accounting Review* 51 (July, 1976): 483–498.

———. "An Appraisal of the Costs and Benefits of Government Required Disclosure." *Law and Contemporary Problems* 41 (Summer, 1977): 30–62.

———. "The Market for Public Accounting Services: Demand, Supply, and Regulation," Liberty Fund Seminar, Law & Economics Center, University of Miami, (March, 1979).

Bernstein, Peter W. "Competition Comes to Accounting." *Fortune* (July 17, 1978): 87–96.

Cary, W. L. "Federalism and Corporate Law: Reflections Upon Delaware." *Yale Law Journal* 83 (March, 1974): 663–707.

Chatov, Robert. Statement. U.S. Senate. Hearings on Accounting and Auditing Practices and Procedures. Before the Subcommittee on Reports, Accounting, and Management of the Committee on Governmental Affairs. 95th Congress, 1st Session. Washington, D.C. U.S. Government Printing Office, 1977. pp. 75–96.

Collins, Daniel W., and Warren T. Dent. "The Proposed Elimination of Full Cost Accounting in the Extractive Petroleum Industry: An Empirical Assessment of the Market Consequences," *Journal of Accounting and Economics* 1 (March, 1979): 3–44.

Dodd, Peter, and Richard Leftwich. "The Market for Corporate Charters: Unhealthy Competition vs. Federal Regulation." University of Rochester Working Paper, October, 1978.

Dyckman, Thomas R. and Abbie J. Smith. "Financial Accounting and Reporting by Oil and Gas Producing Companies: A Study of Information Effects." *Journal of Accounting and Economics* 1 (March 1979): 45–75.

Evans, Thomas; Folks, William; and Michael Jilling. "The Impact of Statement of Financial Accounting Standards No. 8 on Foreign Exchange Risk Management Practices of American Multinationals: An Economic Impact Study." FASB Research Report, November, 1978.

Goshay, Robert C. "Statement of Financial Accounting Standards No. 5: Impact on Corporate Risk and Insurance Management." FASB Research Report, October, 1978.

Holthausen, Robert W. "Bond Covenants and the Choice of Accounting Techniques: The Case of Alternative Depreciation Methods." University of Rochester Working Paper, February, 1979.

Horngren, Charles. "The Marketing of Accounting Standards." *Journal of Accountancy* (October, 1973): 61–66.

Ijiri, Yuji. *Theory of Accounting Measurement.* Studies in Accounting Research No. 10. Sarasota: American Accounting Association, 1975.

––––––. "The Accountant: Destined to Be Free." *Tempo* (Touche Ross & Co.) 21 (Spring, 1976): 38–39.

Leftwich, Richard. "The Impact of Mandatory Changes in Accounting Principles on Corporate Loan Agreements." University of Rochester Working Paper, February, 1979.

Posner, Richard A. "Theories of Economic Regulation." *Bell Journal of Economics and Management Science* 5 (Autumn, 1974): 335–358.

Prakash, Prem, and Alfred Rappaport. "Information Inductance and Its Significance for Accounting." *Accounting, Organizations and Society* 2 (1976).

Rappaport, Alfred. "Executive Incentives vs. Corporate Growth." *Harvard Business Review* 56 (July-August, 1978).

Stigler, George J. "The Theory of Economic Regulation." *Bell Journal of Economics and Management Science* 2 (Spring, 1971): 3–21.

U.S. Senate. Hearings on Accounting and Auditing Practices and Procedures. Before the Subcommittee on Reports, Accounting, and Management of the Committee on Governmental Affairs. 95th Congress, 1st Session. April 19, 21; May 10, 12, 24, 26; June 9 and 13, 1977. Washington, D.C.: U.S. Government Printing Office.

Watts, Ross L., and Jerold L. Zimmerman. "Towards a Positive Theory of the Determination of Accounting Standards." *Accounting Review* 52 (January, 1978): 112–124.

———. "Auditors and the Determination of Accounting Standards." University of Rochester Working Paper no. GPB 78-06, March, 1979.

Winter, Ralph K. *Government and the Corporation.* Washington, D.C.: American Enterprise Institute, 1978.

Chapter 12

Adams, Walter. "The Case for Structural Tests." In J. Fred Weston and Sam Peltzman, eds., *Public Policy towards Mergers.* Pacific Palisades, Ca.: Goodyear, 1969.

Adizes, Ichak, and J. Fred Weston. "Comparative Models of Social Responsibility." *Academy of Management Journal* 16 (March, 1973): 112–128.

Bain, Joe S. "The Relation of Profit Rate to Industry Concentration: American Manufacturing, 1936–1940." *Quarterly Journal of Economics* (August, 1951): 293–324.

———. *Barriers to New Competition.* Cambridge, Mass.: Harvard University Press, 1956.

———. *Industrial Organization.* Rev. ed. New York: John Wiley & Sons, 1968.

Benston, G. J. "The Effectiveness and Effects of the SEC's Accounting Disclosure Requirements." In H. G. Manne, ed., *Economic Policy and the Regulation of Corporate Securities.* Washington, D.C.: American Enterprise Institute, 1977.

John M. Blair. *Economic Concentration: Structure, Behavior, and Public Policy.* New York: Harcourt Brace Jovanovich, 1972.

Brozen, Yale. "Significance of Profit Data for Antitrust Policy." In J. Fred Weston and Sam Peltzman, eds., *Public Policy toward Mergers.* Pacific Palisades, Ca.: Goodyear, 1969.

———. "Entry Barriers: Advertising and Product Differentiation." In Harvey J. Goldschmid, H. Michael Mann, and J. Fred Weston, eds., *Industrial Concentration: The New Learning.* Boston: Little, Brown, 1974.

Caves, R. E., and M. E. Porter. "From Entry Barriers to Mobility Barriers," *The Quarterly Journal of Economics* 111 (May, 1977): 241–261.

Collins, Norman R., and Lee E. Preston. *Concentration and Price-Cost Margins in Manufacturing Industries.* Berkeley: University of California Press, 1968.

Comanor, W. S., and T. A. Wilson. "Advertising, Market Structure and Performance." *Review of Economics and Statistics* 49 (November, 1967): 423–440.

Demsetz, H. "Industry Structure, Market Rivalry, and Public Policy." *The Journal of Law and Economics* 16 (April, 1973a): 1–9.

———. *The Market Concentration Doctrine.* Washington, D.C.: American Enterprise Institute, 1973b.

Goldschmid, Harvey J.; Mann, H. Michael; and J. Fred Weston, eds., *Industrial Concentration: The New Learning.* Boston: Little, Brown, 1974.

Gonedes, N., and N. Dopuch. "Capital Market Equilibrium, Information and Production, and Selecting Accounting Techniques: Theoretical Framework and Review of Empirical Work." *Studies on Financial Objectives: 1974, Journal of Accounting Research* 12 (supplement): 48–129.

Gonedes, N.; Dopuch, N.; and Stephen H. Penman, "Disclosure Rules, Information-Production, and Capital Market Equilibrium: The Case of Forecast Disclosure Rules." *Journal of Accounting Research* 14 (Spring, 1976): 89–137.

Hakansson, Niles H. "Where We Are in Accounting: A Review of 'Statement on Accounting Theory and Theory Acceptance.'" *The Accounting Review* 53 (July, 1978): 717–725.

Kaysen, Carl and Donald F. Turner. *Antitrust Policy: An Economic and Legal Analysis.* Cambridge, Mass.: Harvard University Press, 1959.

Mann, H. Michael. "Seller Concentration, Barriers to Entry, and Rates of Return in Thirty Industries, 1950–1960." *Review of Economics and Statistics* (August, 1966): 296–307.

———. "Advertising, Concentration and Profitability: The State of Knowledge and Directions for Public Policy." In Harvey J. Goldschmid, H. Michael Mann, and J. Fred Weston, eds., *Industrial Concentration: The New Learning.* Boston: Little, Brown, 1974.

Markham, Jesse W. "Concentration: A Stimulus or Retardant to Innovation?" Chapter 5 in *Industrial Concentration: The New Learning,* H. J. Goldschmid, H. M. Mann and J. F. Weston, eds. Boston: Little, Brown and Company, 1974.

McGee, John S. *In Defense of Industrial Concentration.* New York: Praeger, 1971.

———. "Efficiency and Economies of Size." In Harvey J. Goldschmid, H. Michael Mann, and J. Fred Weston, eds., *Industrial Concentration: The New Learning.* Boston: Little, Brown, 1974.

Mueller, Willard F. *A Primer on Monopoly and Competition.* New York: Random House, 1970.

———. "Industrial Concentration: An Important Inflationary Force?" In Harvey J. Goldschmid, H. Michael Mann, and J. Fred Weston, *Industrial Concentration: The New Learning.* Boston: Little, Brown, 1974. pp. 280–306.

Murray, Roger F. "Lessons for Financial Analysis," *Journal of Finance* 26 (May, 1971). 327–332.

National Resources Committee. "The Structure of the American Economy." Part I. Washington, D.C.: U.S. Government Printing Office, June, 1939. pp. 138–145.

Neal, Alfred C. *Industrial Concentration and Price Inflexibility.* Washington, D.C.: American Council of Public Affairs, 1942.

"The New Shape of Management Consulting." *Business Week,* May 21, 1979, p. 99.

Ng, David S. "An Information Economics Analysis of Financial Reporting and External Auditing." *The Accounting Review* 53 (October, 1978): 910–920.

Ornstein, S. I. "Empirical Uses of the Price-Cost Margin." *Journal of Industrial Economics* 24 (December, 1975): 105–117.

Peltzman, Sam. "Profit Data and Public Policy." In J. Fred Weston and Sam Peltzman, eds., *Public Policy toward Mergers.* Pacific Palisades, Ca.: Goodyear, 1969.

Phlips, L. "Business Pricing Policies and Inflation—Some Evidence from EEC Countries." *Journal of Industrial Economics* 18 (November, 1969): 1–14.

Scherer, F. M. *Industrial Market Structure and Economic Performance.* Skokie, Ill.: Rand McNally, 1970.

———. "Economies of Scale and Industrial Concentration." In Harvey J. Goldschmid, H. Michael Mann, and J. Fred Weston, *Industrial Concentration: The New Learning.* Boston: Little, Brown, 1974. pp. 16–54.

Securities and Exchange Commission. "Report on the Accounting Profession."
July 5, 1978.

Shepherd, William G. *Market Power and Economic Welfare*. New York: Random
House, 1970.

Stigler, George. *Capital and Rates of Return in Manufacturing Industries*. Princeton,
N.J.: Princeton University Press, 1963.

Strickland, Allyn D., and Leonard W. Weiss. "Advertising, Concentration, and
Price-Cost Margins." *Journal of Political Economy* 84 (October, 1976): 1109–
1121.

Thomadakis, Stavros B. "A Value-Based Test of Profitability and Market Structure." *The Review of Economics and Statistics* 59 (May, 1977): 179–185.

Thomadakis, Stavros B., and Jerold L. Zimmerman. "Towards a Positive Theory of
the Determination of Accounting Standards." *The Accounting Review* 52 (January, 1978): 112–133.

U.S. Senate. *The Accounting Establishment—A Staff Study*. Subcommittee on Reports,
Accounting, and Management of the Committee on Government Operations. Washington, D.C.: U.S. Government Printing Office, 1977.

Weston, J. Fred. "Structure, Performance, and Behavior." In J. Fred Weston and
Sam Peltzman, eds., *Public Policy toward Mergers*. Boston: Little, Brown, 1969.

———. "The Industrial Economics Background of the Penn Central Bankruptcy,"
Journal of Finance 26 (May, 1971): 311–326.

———. "ROI Planning and Control." *Business Horizons* 15 (August, 1972): 35–42.
(1972a)

———. "Pricing Behavior of Large Firms." *Western Economic Journal* 10 (March,
1972): 1–18. (1972b)

Weston, J. Fred, and Stephen Lustgarten. "Concentration and Wage-Price
Change." In Harvey J. Goldschmid, H. Michael Mann, and J. Fred Weston,
eds., *Industrial Concentration: The New Learning*. Boston: Little, Brown, 1974.

Weston, J. Fred, and Sam Peltzman, eds. *Public Policy toward Mergers*. Pacific Palisades, Ca.: Goodyear, 1969.

Williams, Harold M. Statement. U.S. Senate. Hearings on Accounting and Auditing Practices and Procedures. Before the Subcommittee on Reports, Accounting, and Management of the Committee on Governmental Affairs. 95th
Congress, 1st Session. June 13, 1977. Washington, D.C.: U.S. Government
Printing Office, 1977.

Index

Abraham, Stanley 50
Academic accountants, criticism of 124–125
Accounting
 art v. science 131–132
 v. other professions 99
Accounting firms
 large v. small 13, 25
 market shares 80, 81
Accounting principles, establishing 6
Accounting Principles Board 6, 103, 105,
  158, 181–183, 185
Accounting Series
 Release No. 4 102
 Release No. 126 43
 Release No. 150 102
 Release No. 173 33
 Release No. 177 105
 Release No. 190 18, 179–180, 187
Accounting standards
 designed to restrain behavior 130–131
 geared to economic–national goals 130–
  131
 measuring economic activity 130–131
 private v. public 181–193
 private regulation 181–186
 setting, public v. private 218–220
 should be private sector function 128–
  129
 views of 129–131
Accreditation of accounting programs 5
Action 41
Adizes, Ichak 222
"Administered prices" 58, 203
Administrative Procedure Act 103, 104
Advertising
 by CPAs 37, 67
 prohibition of 37
 restrictions on 8
Air Quality Act of 1967 19
Alan, Joseph 13
Alan & Company 13
Albany 114
Alexander Grant & Co. 32
American Accounting Association 50
American Bar Association 9
American Dental Association 97
American Institute of Accountants 6
American Institute of Certified Public
  Accountants 6, 8, 10, 11, 12, 16, 31,
  34, 37, 38, 39, 43, 44, 95, 101, 102,
  107, 110, 113, 114, 115, 116, 117, 143,
  144, 145, 146, 171, 175, 181
American Stock Exchange 81
Anreder, Steven S. 192
Antitrust and accounting, legal cases 95 ff.
"A priori collusion" 59
Arizona State Society of CPAs 90

Armentano, D. T. 66
Armstrong, Marshall S. 31
Arthur Andersen & Co. 26–29, 35, 80, 81,
  82, 84–85, 105
Arthur Young & Co. 26–29, 80, 81, 82, 84–
  85
Asch, Peter 66, 79
Audit
 committees 8–9, 10
  required 8, 10
 failures 72–73
 fees
  range of 38
  relation to assets and sales 80
  relation to client size 89
 responsibilities 209–216
Auditing
 an equilibrium quantity 211–212
 more or less? 168–174
 Standards Executive Committee 9, 10, 34
 and MAS 174–175
 as a public good 44–46
Auditor changes 9, 10
 reasons for 36
Auditor-manager game 165–168
Auditor's role, defined 164–165
AuditSCOPE 35
Audits of large companies by firms 26–29
Australia 25

"Back scratching," in relation to peer
  reviews 115
Bain, Joe 58
Bank Merger Act 60
Barber, Bernard 6
Barr, Andrew 31
Barriers to entry 57, 66–67
 in accounting 82–89
 defined 82
Bates vs. State Bar of Arizona 95–97, 100,
  101
Beaver, William H. 155
Bedingfield, J. P. 36
Benston, George 47, 74, 81, 153, 155, 156,
  179, 208
Berle, Adolph 57
Bernstein, Peter W. 192
Biegler, John 23, 31–32
"Big Eight" firms 7, 8, 12–13, 16, 30–31, 45,
  59–60, 70–74, 75, 78–79, 80, 81, 82, 90,
  91, 109, 110, 113, 117, 144, 199, 208–
  209
 dominance of 114
 market shares 80, 81
 mergers 113
Blair, John 58